RECKONING WITH BARTH

RECKONING WITH BARTH

Essays in Commemoration of the
Centenary of Karl Barth's Birth

Edited by
NIGEL BIGGAR

MOWBRAY
LONDON & OXFORD

Copyright © The Contributors, 1988
First published 1988
by A. R. Mowbray & Co. Ltd,
Saint Thomas House, Becket Street,
Oxford OX1 1SJ

All rights reserved. No part of this publication
may be reproduced, stored in a retrieval system,
or transmitted, in any form or by any means,
electronic, mechanical, photocopying, recording,
or otherwise, without the prior permission in writing
from the publisher, A. R. Mowbray & Co. Ltd.

Photoset, printed and bound in Great Britain by
Redwood Burn Limited, Trowbridge, Wiltshire

British Library Cataloguing in Publication Data

Reckoning with Barth : essays in
commemoration of the centenary of Karl
Barth's birth
1. Theology. Barth, Karl 1886–1968
I. Biggar, Nigel
209'.2'4

ISBN 0–264–67173–2

Contents

Acknowledgements	*page*	vii
The Contributors		ix
Abbreviations		xi
Introduction	NIGEL BIGGAR	1

Part I: Historical Theology — 7

1. The Influence of Barth after World War II
   GEOFFREY BROMILEY — 9

Part II: Dogmatic Theology — 25

2. Barth on Jesus Christ, Theology and the Church
   ALISTER MCGRATH — 27

3. Karl Barth on 'The Work of Creation'. A Reading of *Church Dogmatics*, III/1   W. A. WHITEHOUSE — 43

Part III: Philosophical Theology — 59

4. No Other Foundation. One Englishman's Reading of *Church Dogmatics*, Chapter V   COLIN GUNTON — 61

5. Karl Barth's Hermeneutics   WERNER G. JEANROND — 80

Part IV: Ethics & Politics — 99

6. Hearing God's Command and Thinking about What's Right: with and beyond Barth   NIGEL BIGGAR — 101

7. The Christian in Revolt. Some Reflections on The Christian Life   J. B. WEBSTER   119

8. On Honour: By Way of a Comparison of Barth and Trollope   STANLEY HAUERWAS   145

9. Barth, War & the State   ROWAN WILLIAMS   170

Part V: Epilogue   191

10. The Christian in Society. A Commemorative Sermon.   W. A. WHITEHOUSE   193

Notes   199

Bibliographical Data for *Church Dogmatics* and *The Christian Life*.   215

Acknowledgements

Since this volume largely comprises the proceedings of the Oxford Conference in Commemoration of the Centenary of the Birth of Karl Barth, which was held at Wycliffe Hall, Oxford, 18–21 September 1986, it is fitting to offer thanks here to: the Revd Professor Oliver O'Donovan and the Rt Revd Richard Harries, Bishop of Oxford, for their encouragement of a nascent and delicate piece of imagination; the British Academy and the Board of the Faculty of Theology of the University of Oxford for their more than moral support; the Canons of Christ Church for inviting the conference to bring itself to a fitting conclusion with a commemorative service of worship in Oxford's cathedral; and the Council of Latimer House for its readiness to free its Librarian for unusual distraction from his normal duties.

The Contributors

NIGEL BIGGAR is Librarian at Latimer House, and Tutor in Ethics at Wycliffe Hall, Oxford. He is co-editor of *Cities of Gods. Faith, Politics and Pluralism in Judaism, Christianity and Islam* (Westport, Connecticut: Greenwood Press, 1986).

GEOFFREY BROMILEY is Professor of Church History and Historical Theology at Fuller Seminary, California. He was responsible for editing the English translation of Barth's *Church Dogmatics*, much of which he undertook himself. He has also written an invaluable synopsis of the *Dogmatics* under the title of *An Introduction to the Theology of Karl Barth* (Grand Rapids: Eerdmans, 1979).

COLIN GUNTON is Professor of Systematic Theology at King's College, London. He is the author of *Becoming and Being: the Doctrine of God in Charles Hartshorne and Karl Barth* (Oxford: OUP, 1978); and, most recently, of *Enlightenment and Alienation* (Basingstoke: Marshall, Morgan, Scott, 1985).

STANLEY HAUERWAS is Professor of Religious Ethics at the Divinity School of Duke University, North Carolina. His first of many books was *Character and the Christian Life* (San Antonio, Texas: Trinity University Press, 1975). This has been followed most recently by *Against the Nations* (New York: Seabury Press, 1986) and *Suffering Presence* (Edinburgh: T. & T. Clark, 1987).

WERNER JEANROND lectures in Systematic and Philosophical Theology at Trinity College, Dublin. His first book, *Text and Interpretation as Categories of Theological Thinking*, has been published in Germany, the British Isles and the United States (Tubingen: Mohr & Siebeck, 1986; Dublin: Gill & Macmillan, 1988; New York: Crossroads, 1988). He is currently writing an historical introduction to hermeneutics.

ALISTER MCGRATH lectures in Christian Doctrine at Wycliffe Hall, Oxford. In addition to books on Luther and the Reformation, his fields of special expertise, he has lately published a two-volume history of the doctrine of justification, *Iustitia Dei* (Cambridge: Cambridge University Press, 1986), and *The Making of Modern German Christology* (Oxford: Blackwell, 1986).

JOHN WEBSTER is Professor of Systematic Theology at Wycliffe College, Toronto, and is author of the first English introduction to *Eberhard Jüngel* (Cambridge: CUP, 1986).

W. A. WHITEHOUSE, Emeritus Professor of Theology at the University of Kent, is author of *The Authority of Grace: Essays in Response to Karl Barth* (Edinburgh: T. & T. Clark, 1981).

ROWAN WILLIAMS, Lady Margaret Professor of Divinity at the University of Oxford, contributed an essay on Barth's doctrine of the Trinity to S. W. Sykes, ed., *Karl Barth – Studies of his Theological Methods* (Oxford: OUP, 1979). More recently, he has written *The Truce of God* (London: Fount, 1983) and *Arius. Heresy and Tradition* (London: Darton, Longman and Todd, 1987).

Abbreviations

All references to the *Church Dogmatics* and to *The Christian Life. Church Dogmatics, IV/4; lecture fragments* are to be found in parentheses in the text.

Church Dogmatics is abbreviated to *CD*, with volume number in roman, and part number in arabic, numerals. Page numbers follow immediately after a colon. So, a reference to *Church Dogmatics*, volume three, part four, page ninety-nine will appear as: *CD* III/4:99.

The Christian Life is abbreviated to *ChrL*.

Bibliographical data for these volumes may be found below on p. 215.

Introduction

NIGEL BIGGAR

On the occasion of Karl Barth's only visit to the United States, Paul Tillich was reported by *Time* magazine to have hailed him as 'the most monumental appearance in our period'.[1] 'Monumental' is a supple word; and exactly which of its several connotations Tillich intended is not clear. Nevertheless, in its most formal sense, it is undoubtedly apposite to the author of 8,500 pages of *Church Dogmatics*.[2] The massive scale and architectonic nature of Barth's systematic work easily win it a place alongside those other grand edifices of Christian theology, Aquinas' *Summa Theologia* and Calvin's *Institutes of the Christian Religion*.

But Barth has also been regarded as 'monumental' in other, more evaluative respects. T. F. Torrance, for example, judges him to be exemplary in his ecumenical scope when he writes, with evident approval, that 'his comprehensive grasp and wrestling with the whole history of Christian thought makes him essentially a catholic theologian'.[3] And Hans Urs von Balthasar reckons that Barth comprises the Protestant acme, when he exclaims that 'in his work authentic Protestantism has found its full-blown image for the first time'.[4]

But there are others who would use 'monumental' in a critical fashion. We cannot be sure, but is there not a hint of irony in Tillich's remark? Barth's achievement may be massive in scale and impressive in architecture, catholic in scope and protestant in perfection, but is it not, in the end, simply a memorial to the past? There is a story that on one occasion Barth met Tillich with the words, 'Greetings to the twentieth century's greatest theological *journalist*!'; to which Tillich retorted, 'And greetings to the greatest dogmatician of the *seventeenth* century!' Whether or not this encounter ever took place, and regardless of how faithfully it represents Tillich's opinion of Barth, it certainly represents the judgement of some. To these, Barth represents a fundamentally regressive moment in recent Christian theology; his work stands as a monumental example of how *not* to proceed. *The New Dictionary of Christian Theology* (1983), for example, sees fit to devote a mere eight lines to 'Neo-Orthodoxy' – of which Barth is usually reckoned the foremost exponent – in order to dismiss it as 'the deplorable imposition of an out-dated synthesis of theology and secular thought in an altered contemporary situation'.[5]

There are, of course, others who regard Barth as 'monumental' in precisely the opposite sense: as indicating the only theologically viable way forward. Those who already claim him as *the* outstanding protestant theologian of the 20th century presumably tend toward this estimation.[6] As Geoffrey Bromiley mentions in the first essay of this collection, there may not be many Barthians pure and simple, but there are many who believe that, though the way forward must go *beyond* Barth, it must nevertheless go *through* him.[7] He may not have said everything, but there are some vital things that he did say, which the Christian Church at the end of the second millennium cannot afford not to hear.

It was out of this conviction that Latimer House, an Anglican research institute in Oxford devoted to the contemporary appropriation of biblical and reformed theology, took the opportunity presented by the 100th anniversary of Barth's birth to sponsor a commemorative conference in September 1986. With the support of the British Academy and the Board of the Faculty of Theology of the University of Oxford, it gathered together 120 academics, clergy, theological students and lay-people – mostly from within the British Isles, but also from South-East Asia, Zimbabwe, the United States, Canada, Iceland, Sweden and the Netherlands – to consider what helpful direction Barth's thought might give to the consideration of dogmatic, philosophical and ethical issues of current moment. All but one of the essays in this volume had their original form as addresses delivered before the Oxford conference.[8]

At the most general level, this collection draws its integrity from the common brief given to most of the conference lecturers. This was to select issues within a particular theological field and to ask at least the following questions: What of value does Barth have to offer? What are the shortcomings of his contribution? And where beyond Barth might we go to make up his deficiency? Geoffrey Bromiley alone was exempted from this directive, being asked instead to provide the conference with a sense of its historical location by describing the fortunes of Barth's influence from 1945 to the present.

On a purely formal level, the remaining essays cohere in two ways. First, it was planned that they should combine to cover a range of crucial fields within dogmatic, philosophical and moral theology – Christology (Alister McGrath), the doctrine of creation (W. A. Whitehouse), religious epistemology (Colin Gunton), hermeneutics (Werner Jeanrond), moral epistemology (Nigel Biggar), worship & ethics (John Webster), moral agency (Stanley Hauerwas), and politics (Rowan Williams). Second, many of the essays may be treated as critical readings of the *Römerbrief* (Williams), *Rechtfertigung und Recht* (Williams) or of particular parts of the *Church Dogmatics*: I/1,2 (Jeanrond); II/1 (Gunton); II/2, chapter VIII (Biggar); III/1 (Whitehouse); III/4 (Biggar, Williams), III 56.3 (Hauerwas); IV/4 (Webster); ChrL (Webster).

Furthermore, several recurrent themes conspire to provide this collection with a third, material level of coherence. The first of these is *the peculiar integrity of theology*. Bromiley suggests that one of Barth's more enduring achievements may prove to be his revolutionary re-focussing of Christian theology upon its own special and proper theme – the God who has made Himself known to us in Jesus Christ – and his subsequent re-establishment of theology as a discipline with its own methodological and structural integrity (pp. 18, 22); and Colin Gunton reckons it part of Barth's genius to have recognised that Christian theology is a function of the community of those who have faith in the God of Jesus Christ (pp. 73–4). Alister McGrath concurs (p. 33); and both he (pp. 37–41) and Nigel Biggar (p. 101) pay silent homage to this turn to the divine subject, when they write approvingly of Barth's conviction that, when the Church engages in social criticism, she must do so according to her own, special, *theological* criteria. Rowan Williams is of like mind when he commends Barth's discussion of the state as 'one of the most integrally theological . . . in this century' (p. 173). Both Gunton (pp. 77–8) and W. A. Whitehouse (*passim*), however, regret that Barth's affirmation of the integrity of theological science is marred by a methodical neglect of the non-theological sciences; while Williams registers some frustration at Barth's failure to advance very far from his theology of politics to political tactics (pp. 189–90).

A second recurrent theme is *the ecclesial and ecumenical matrix* of Christian theological and ethical reflection. Gunton welcomes this as an alternative to the individualism and naive objectivism of Enlightenment epistemology (pp. 67–8, 73–4). McGrath, too, endorses the conception of theology as the activity of the community of faith seeking understanding (p. 33); its correlate, the theological competence of all believers (pp. 36–7); and the consequent marginalization of professional, academic theology (pp. 35–6). In a similar vein, Biggar finds that Barth's insistence upon the Christian community as the place where one should expect to hear the divine command, militates against ethical solipsism and elitism (pp. 106, 108–9). He also notes that Barth's definition of the Church is sufficiently elastic to comprehend the world (pp. 109–11). Werner Jeanrond, on the other hand, calls into question the adequacy of an account of the hermeneutical role of the community that fails to deal with the possibility of a pluralism of legitimate interpretations or of sheer interpretative conflict (p. 92).

The third and fourth refrains are by far the loudest. The issue lying at the heart of the third, *the relation between divine and human reason*, may be stated in the form of a question: must divine reason transcend human reason *absolutely* in order to preserve its critical function? To Jeanrond, it seems that Barth's insistence upon the self-disclosure of the theme of the text, and the correlative subordination of the interpreter to its active objectivity, leaves the interpreter without any scope for assessing whether what claims to be the Word of God is indeed the Word of *God* (pp. 90–96). Stanley Hauerwas lodges a similar complaint when he protests against Barth's entertaining the possibility of an absolute qualitative distinction between God's concept of honour and human concepts (p. 168). On the other hand, Biggar (pp. 108–11) and Webster (p. 122) concur in arguing, with regard to Barth's concept of divine command, that divine moral reason is not a sheer heteronomy, and that it does not so much displace human reasoning as limit and qualify it.

Closely allied to the third, the fourth refrain is *the relation between divine and human agency*. Williams notes the categorical disjunction between salvation history and human history in the second edition of the *Römerbrief*, but holds that these categories are increasingly connected as Barth's christology matures (pp. 177–8). Others, however, object to the very nature of this connexion, in which – they claim – God's agency in effect swallows up man's. Jeanrond, for example, argues that this is so in the case of hermeneutical activity: the illuminating operation of the Holy Spirit displaces hermeneutical methodology (p. 192). And Hauerwas remains, in the end, unconvinced that real, faithful, responsive humanity retains, according to Barth's account, any substantial independence (pp. 147, 149, 165ff.). In contrast, Webster contends that Barth 'has a much fuller and rounder account of the human moral agent than we are often led by his critics to expect' (p. 120), and Gunton contradicts 'the frequent assertions or at least suggestions to the contrary in the secondary literature' when he asserts that, in Barth's account, 'human knowledge of God is not the conditioned reflex of the automaton' (p. 69). Biggar pursues a similar line of argument in connexion with human apprehension of God's command (*passim*).

There is, finally, a fifth, minor refrain that deserves mention: *Anglo-Saxon resistance to Barth's project*. Bromiley notes the general American distaste for Barth's dogmatic approach to theology (pp. 14–15); and he also alludes to a still-prevailing Anglican (and therefore English) reluctance to pay much sustained attention to him (pp. 21–2). McGrath remarks upon the derision that Barth is still prone to suffer in English theological circles (p. 42); while the English 'difficulty' with Barth is one of the themes of Gunton's essay, whose title alludes to the continuing eccentricity of both being English and taking Barth seriously (p. 61).

Twenty-five years ago, John Baillie (a Scot) wrote of Barth that, 'whatever the measure of our agreements and disagreements with him, we have all to reckon with him. . . [T]here can be no hopeful forward advance beyond his teaching, . . . if we attempt to go *round* it instead of *through* it.'[9] If Bromiley, Gunton and McGrath are correct, then much English and American theological thinking today remains pre-Barthian; it is still trying to go beyond Barth without going through him. In that case, we Anglo-Saxons have a lot of reckoning with Barth yet to do. Here follow ten contributions to that enterprise.

PART I
HISTORICAL THEOLOGY

1

The Influence of Barth after World War II

GEOFFREY BROMILEY

A listener once put to Barth the loaded question of who was the greatest 20th century theologian. Barth commented that 'great' and 'theologian' are a contradiction in terms. He then characteristically suggested that in God's judgement some unknown teacher of an obscure Bible class – a village Calvin as it were – might well emerge as the greatest theologian of the century.[1]

We begin with this sample from the store of Barthian anecdotes in order to introduce the needed note of modesty in trying to assess not merely the greatness but also the influence of any figure. Even at a purely historical level, a true appraisal is not really possible until we attain the proper distance, if then. From the divine standpoint we always do well to heed the advice of Paul – although we seldom do – and judge nothing before the time, not even, or least of all, ourselves, but also not even the work of those who might seem to our eyes to have had the most decisive impact (*cf.*1 Cor.4:1ff.).

With these reservations in view, however, we may surely attempt some provisional estimation in the case of so public a figure as Barth, who not only exercised an imposing ministry of teaching and writing but also stirred up such decided responses both positive and negative. What I should like to do, then, in this account of Barth's influence during the last forty years is first to engage in a very brief general survey, then to consider his influence in a little more detail under the four heads of direct impact, stimulation, assimilation, and diffusion, and finally state some pious wishes, *i.e.*, list some areas in which I myself would like to see a greater Barthian impact than seems thus far to have been achieved.

Beginning with the general survey, we note that the end of World War II saw Barth at the height of his power and prominence. He had found a secure theological base in his native Basel. He had launched the massive project of the *Church Dogmatics* and peppered the world with shorter but none the less impressive writings and speeches. He had emerged as a leading Christian champion in the opposition to Hitlerite Germany but was speaking no less vigorously as an advocate of German restoration and reconstruction. He would have an important say in the pivotal Ecumenical Council at Amsterdam which formed the World Council of Churches through the fusion of the Life & Work and Faith & Order branches of the ecumenical movement. If the war had reduced the student body at Basel, theological students from at home and abroad and from all churches were flocking back to the Swiss centre to attend Barth's lectures, seminars, and colloquiums, and to do doctoral work under his supervision.

Nevertheless, the theological leadership of Barth did not go unchallenged as the forties moved into the fifties and beyond. The rise of Bultmann's demythologizing and existentializing, followed or accompanied by new enthusiasms for Tillich, Bonhoeffer, and Robinson, by the Death of God movement, and by Liberation Theology, brought new life to Liberal Protestantism and the erosion of Barth's own support. Barth's advice to East Europeans like the Czech Hromadka, coinciding as it did with the violent anti-communist drives of the West, attracted charges of inconsistency as well as angry denunciations, not merely from reactionary conservatives, but even from highly regarded theologians like Emil Brunner and Reinhold Niebuhr, as Barth noted with some sadness in a letter to Hromadka in July 1963.[2] The demands of the *Church Dogmatics*, which Barth humorously accepted as his Moby Dick,[3] prevented him from playing the more active public role, *e.g.*, in the ecumenical movement or in conferences, which would perhaps have helped him to retain his earlier eminence. At home in Basel, and in Switzerland as a whole, he often had occasion to experience the truth of the biblical adage that a prophet is not without honour save in his own country.

The general picture, then, is the not atypical one of a period of leadership gradually giving way to a comparative neglect from which, in spite of the strenuous efforts of the Barth societies, the ongoing publication of the Collected Works, and such special celebrations as those of this centennial, there has not yet been any very substantial recovery. Barth himself, in the very last address that he was preparing, tells us how one young pastor put it to him, not very kindly, in his later years: 'Professor, you have made history, now you are history. We younger people are setting out for new shores.' (In a mildly ironic reply, Barth agreed that this was good, but then asked for information about these new shores, and there was nothing to tell.)[4]

With this general movement in view, we may now ask in more detail what seems to have been, in retrospect, the influence of Barth on the second part of the century.

We ask first about the direct impact. Has Barth left immediate disciples? Has he formed a specific Barthian group? Is there such a thing as Barthianism? Now undoubtedly there have been many pastors and teachers in such diverse lands as Switzerland, Germany, France, Holland, Hungary, and Scotland who have been strongly committed to Barth's theology and vehemently opposed to criticism or deviation. Nevertheless, their numbers have on the whole been relatively small and are rapidly dwindling, so that it is hard to speak of any large-scale impact in this sense. Nor perhaps, would Barth have desired it, for he often expressed his aversion to all 'isms'[5], refused to think even of himself as a Barthian,[6] and claimed that any who used that term did not really know what his theology was all about. In a statement about Calvin for the 1959 commemoration he praised the Genevan reformer for leading us to the essential theme but then letting us see and hear it with our own eyes and ears. This might or might not be true of Calvin, but it certainly corresponds to Barth's view of himself and his ministry.

Barth's main influence, then, is to be sought more in the stimulation of others than in the making of immediate disciples who might easily become boring.[7] We see such stimulation, for example, in the work of T. F. Torrance on theological science, the rationality of God, and the implications of incarnation and resurrection, in which Torrance does independent investigation on an obvious Barthian basis. Similarly, Ray Anderson shows stimulation by Barth in both his anthropology and his reconsideration of natural theology, in which he adapts and develops motifs from Barth himself. Did not Barth in an early letter to Thurneysen refer (beneath his breath) to the possible emergence of a new form of natural theology? – cut short in Barth's case by the rise of National Socialism and the German Christians. In the same general field one might also recall Vaaela Vassidy of Hungary, who tried to bring insights from Barth to bear on his concern for the psychology of faith. Along somewhat different lines Jacques de Senarclens and Pierre Maury in France found in Barth a foundation for their rethinking of the Reformed theology that they had inherited from Calvin. Eberhand Jüngel, of course, claims our attention too. So does Helmut Gollwitzer of Berlin, whom Barth would have preferred as his successor at Basel. Nor should we neglect to mention Otto Weber and Hendrikus Berkhof, who wrestled persistently with Barth in their own volumes of dogmatics. Berkhof, it is true, found serious weaknesses in Barth's teaching, but in his attempt at a fuller theology of the Holy Spirit he was making a contribution that Barth himself perceived the need for, and even in his critical discussions Berkhof was always conscious of the stimulus of Barth's prior work.

In other cases the stimulation might be less direct but by no means negligible. Jürgen Moltmann is a name that comes to mind. Barth had considered him as a possible theological successor, his so called 'child of promise'. He had found *The Theology of Hope* disappointing, but Moltmann responded positively to his reservations[8] and in his own distinctive way developed themes that Barth had focused on with such intensity. Helmut Thielicke, who briefly attended Barth's classes in the thirties, might also be mentioned in spite of his profound disagreements with Barth, *e.g.*, on law and gospel. His distinction between Cartesian and non-Cartesian theology, his stress on the ministry of the Spirit, and his general conception of a theological ethics all have a plain Barthian derivation. Another outstanding thinker who owes a great debt to Barth, as he himself acknowledges,[9] is the colourful lay theologian of France, Jacques Ellul. Ellul defies classification, and much of his voluminous output lies outside the range of Barth's influence on the more specifically theological and ethical writings. The choice of freedom as a basic ethical concept in *The Ethics of Freedom* offers an immediate example (*cf. CD* III/4). The christological typologising in the work on Jonah is obviously in the tradition of Vischer and Barth (cf. especially *CD* II/2). Ellul's *Theology of the City* and *Subversion of Christianity* are also cast in a Barthian mould. His stress on dialectic (*cf. Ce que je crois I*,4) also deserves mention, and as we learn from his *Politics of God and Politics of Man*, his general portrayal of the human situation, though done in darker apocalyptic hues than one finds in Barth, stands finally under a slogan very dear to Barth: In the confusion of man, the providence of God.

Along with the stimulation that Barth has given to independent constructive work, we have also to think of the process whereby his theology, or one or other part of it, has been assimilated into the thinking of those who by and large belong to very different traditions. In this regard we must refer first to the unexpected influence, surprising to himself at first, that Barth had on some Roman Catholic theology. This began at Münster, where Barth had more interesting contacts with the Roman Catholic faculty than its Evangelical counterpart. It progressed through fellowship with Hans Urs von Balthasar and then increased steadily up to and after Vatican II. In spite of his treatment of Roman Catholicism as a major dogmatic deviation, Barth felt that he received more serious and sympathetic consideration from Roman Catholics than he did from many Lutherans and Reformed. One might mention here a number of important figures. There was the younger Hans Küng, who wrote the challenging work on justification and shared confidences on Vatican II. Balthasar not only enhanced Barth's love of Mozart and sense of the beauty of theology but wrote an appreciative account of Barth's own theology, though Barth wondered if he did not have more interest in certain of its philosophical structures than in the theology itself.[10] Henri Bouillard wrote a massive dissertation on Barth – Barth attended a humorous *viva* as both subject and examiner! – and rather ironically chided Barth for indulging in allegorical exegesis. A. J. Maydieu deserves notice too. In a debate with Barth about the status of the papacy, he broke off with a sentiment that might have come from Barth himself: Let us talk about Jesus Christ and not about the pope. To some degree Karl Rahner also assimilated much from Barth, though so far outdoing Barth in obscurity of style that his brother is credited with the wish that someone would translate him into German. The formative function of Barth found recognition in the suggestion that he be invited to Vatican II as an observer. He was not well enough to go but kept himself informed through Cullman and Küng, and later he made a personal visit to Rome, had an audience with the pope, exchanged gifts, and entered into a brief, inconclusive, but illuminating discussion of natural law in relation to the rulings of *Humanae Vitae*.[11]

Barth's theology underwent a different kind of assimilation in North America, which at first had little first-hand material to work on and was more generally resistant to his attacks on the second great dogmatic deviation of Liberal Protestantism. Barth did, of course, find some enthusiastic supporters such as Arthur Cochrane and Paul Lehmann, along with a number of his former students. But the prevailing American temper and the dominance of Tillich and the Niebuhrs acted as a buffer against a more effective and widespread impact. To some extent the earlier dialectical emphases of Barth – the moment of crisis, the individual, the leap of faith, the ruthless analysis of the human situation and especially of religion – did allow of integration into the expositions of Reinhold Niebuhr, and many of Barth's theological insights, particularly in the form given to them by Emil Brunner, had no difficulty in finding a place in American Neo-Orthodoxy. But how could American theology assimilate the Barth who gave himself to what seemed to be a more traditional and scholastic theology, who described the *anhypostasia* as forceful teaching that ought to be put back on the lampstand,[12] and who increasingly differentiated himself from Bultmann's existentialism even to the point of discovering a new theological disease of Bultmannitis?[13] Very little. Indeed, Niebuhr could complain sadly about Barth's fundamentalism in his handling of scripture. Nor did Barth himself see any serious possibility of integration with the supporters of Bultmann. When Gregor Smith of Scotland once expressed the wish for a future reunion of Barth and Bultmann, Barth rejected this as a salvation history that needed the sharpest possible demythologizing.[14] He would certainly not want to regard as his disciples those who were impressed by Robinson's *Honest to God*, a work which Barth described as 'the abyss of banality', a mixture of the froth of Bonhoeffer, Bultmann and Tillich peddled as the latest theological cure-all, and shamefully published in German by his own former house, the Kaiser Verlag.[15]

Barth, of course, observed in *Church Dogmatics* III/3[16] that we cannot control what happens to our words once we have spoken or written them. We must leave them to the divine concursus. Hence many American theologians have been able to apply Barth's thoughts in ways that often enough must have astonished him. A few, like Martin Marty and Langdon Gilkey, have simply incorporated essential elements from Barth into their own thinking. Others, however, have seized on particular aspects and developed them in unexpected ways. Thus Robert McAfee Brown has found a path from Barth to Liberation Theology by way of Barth's protest against Hitlerism in the thirties and the American protest against the Vietnam war in the sixties, to which Barth gave some endorsement with his indictment of pharaoh Johnson.[17] Similarly Harvey Cox, reaching even further back to the red parson of Safenwil, has used the precarious thesis of F. W. Marquardt, namely, that socialism is basic to Barth and that his theology is ultimately a political theology, to work out a combination of Barth and Bonhoeffer, with Liberation Theology again included. At the furthest extreme some scholars, like John Cobb, have even argued that Barth himself was negatively responsible for the quickly deceased Death of God theology, though Barth himself, who regarded the authors of this movement as 'theological fools',[18] saw no reason to think that this aberration was the result of his own theological effort or vision, even if he had said as vigorously as any Death of God theologian that the supposed God of human religion is not God: 'He is an idol. He is dead' (in an address at Aarau in 1916).[19]

An interesting measure of assimilation has taken place in some American Evangelical circles. Here at first Barth met with the same implacable hostility as in the Liberal world; necessity makes strange bed-fellows. Van Til of Westminster echoed a familiar Dutch reaction in his *New Modernism* and the philosopher Gordon Clark followed this up with his *Barth's Theological Method*. Carl Henry has maintained the attack, and heavily influenced by such leaders Evangelicals have been mostly unreceptive and suspicious. Nevertheless, there are significant exceptions. The Dutch theologian G. C. Berkouwer set a trend with his sympathetically critical study *The Triumph of Grace*, and he increasingly brought insights from Barth into his own haphazard but not unimportant dogmatic series. In America itself Donald Bloesch, a United Church of Christ theologian, has not only wrestled critically with Barth and incorporated many of his positive contributions, but could hardly have done his work at all without Barth's prior achievements. The Baptist Bernard Ramm, who has attracted a large following with his teaching and writing, has also moved gradually to a more positive appreciation of Barth, and has caused some stir with his latest work in which he argues that Evangelicals have never really faced the challenge of the Enlightenment, to which, perhaps, Barth suggests the only effective response. Even the Canadian Clark Pinnock, an unabashed Arminian and tenacious apologist, who previously complained of Barth's subjectivist fideism, has begun to see that what Barth proposes, far from being subjective or fideist, in reality offers a new and legitimate apologetics. Two recent works from a Reformed context give additional testimony to a process of tacit assimilation in spite of vocal dissent. Paul Jewett in his *Election and Predestination* formally rejects Barth but still writes at many points in a way that would not have been possible prior to Barth, and Anthony Hoekema in his anthropology, *Created in God's Image*, plainly adapts to his own purposes many of the emphases of Barth. More openly indebted to Barth is J. Daane's interesting work *The Freedom of God*, which along with a Barthian theme also takes up a Barthian concern, namely, the preaching of election. From a very different setting comes the attempt of John H. Yoder to make a Free Churchman out of Barth, with a stress on his opposition to infant baptism, his developing pacifism face to face with atomic weapons, his emphasis on following Jesus, and his attraction to a gathered church. Apart from these more obvious instances of assimilation, attentive readers of a wider range of writings will quickly catch Barthian echoes that show how willy-nilly his thinking has invaded this supposedly more isolated and insulated sphere.

This reminds us, of course, of what I have called the diffusion of Barth's influence. We have here a large field and therefore can give only a sketch of some of the main features. Negatively, Barth made a massive and not unsuccessful protest against the forms of Liberal Protestant theology which had dominated much of the thinking of the later 19th and early 20th centuries: against the fixation on historico-critical exegesis of scripture; the absorption of theology into religion and religious psychology or sociology; the subjectivizing grounding of faith upon this or that religious or moral *a priori*; the secularizing of eschatology; the reversal of the *imago Dei*; and the christological reductionism which meant a virtual rejection of the Nicene *homoousion* on the one side and of the vicarious humanity of Christ on the other. To appreciate the effectiveness of Barth's protest one need only make a general comparison of theological productions at the beginning of the century with those of more recent decades.

Barth never believed, however, that a 'No' can be the last word. He had not only to show the inadequacy of what was passing for theology but also to indicate some possible lines of reconstruction and renewal. Academically, this involved a crucial shift of interest that has had momentous consequences and may well rank among Barth's more enduring achievements. Briefly, it meant a new concern for theological and not just historical exegesis, a development of such special fields as hermeneutics and biblical theology, a sense of the relevance of the past which refashioned the history of doctrine as historical theology, a resolute commitment to the special task of theology which restored to dogmatic theology its proper place, and an insistence on the close relation between theology and practice which resulted in theological ethics on the one side, and on the other side in an authentic homiletical or practical theology as distinct from a mere study of pastoral and preaching techniques. Nor was this merely an academic restructuring, for plainly underlying it was the determinative conviction that theology is a discipline in its own right, that it is so because, as a ministry of the church, it has its own special theme and therefore its own methodology and structure, and that this theme, unlike all other themes of human investigation, is not a creature, whether organic or inorganic, whether vegetable, animal, mineral, or human, but the God of all creatures, although God, of course, in relation to the creature. The restructuring of the theological agenda is thus the necessary consequence of a recalling of theology to its proper subject-matter and therefore to a more faithful discharge of its proper task.

Yet the theological concentration did not prevent Barth from contributing to the larger life and ministry of the church both inwardly and outwardly. Inwardly, Barth brought insistently before the church, whether by teaching or by practice, the relevance of theology to proclamation as a critical and constructive norm. He also restored to the church a much needed emphasis on confession. From one standpoint the Declaration of Barmen might also prove to be one of Barth's most lasting accomplishments; in some listings it has already moved into the august company of the early creeds and the reformation confessions. This example of a confession ties in with Barth's lectures on the confessions, his teaching on confessions as secondary authorities in *Church Dogmatics* I/2,[20] and the model he offered to the World Council when he contrasted basic Christian confession in the singular with detailed historical confessions in the plural. Speaking of the ecumenical impact of Barth, which he made both by personal appearances and by his influence on Visser't Hooft, we must also remember that his interrelating of the church with Christ, the Spirit, and the world lies behind some of the most constructive work of Faith and Order in the post-war world, and that his influence on Roman Catholicism has helped to open the door to more cordial and fruitful relations between it and other communions.

Outwardly, Barth made his supreme mark in the Hitler period with a powerful plea for the church's freedom from ideological control. Even in less critical situations he stressed the ongoing need to avoid the secularizing and contextualizing which would attenuate Christianity as a civil religion or a cultural adaptation. Barth's thinking in this whole area led him to the challenging concept of the political service of God which might take such varying forms as cooperation, non-cooperation, and resistance. In the case of Christians under hostile regimes in East Europe, he argued for flexibility rather than intransigence, not in the sense of acquiescence in the state's agenda, but in that of securing for the church its specific ministry and witness. Barth's position on this issue led both to angry criticism on the one side and at times to overenthusiastic collaboration on the other, as we see from Barth's friendly warnings to Hromadka in Prague.[21] Nevertheless, many churches and organizations have come to appreciate its wisdom, as, for example, the Bible Societies, which have found that working through official channels to print or import Bibles provides a better supply than the cloak-and-dagger Bible smuggling that often claims attention.

Apart from politics, Barth's influence has also been felt in the area of mission; indeed, the common use of the singular rather than the plural owes not a little to Barth's example. Now it is true that Barth personally had no great experience of work outside Europe. He had foreign students, including those especially from Japan, where he made an impact that we cannot go into here. But the complaint has sometimes been made, *e.g.*, by Dietrich Ritschl, that there is finally something parochial about his ministry, that he never entered into living dialogue with Buddhists or Mohammedans or Hindus. Nevertheless, in various ways – some of them conflicting perhaps – Barth did contribute strongly to missionary thinking and effort. To some, his clear-cut distinction between divine revelation and human religion seemed, rightly or wrongly, to nullify all points of contact. To others, his stress on the relative nature, not of the dogmatic theme, but of our statements about it, seemed to suggest that very different forms of statement are possible in different ages and cultures so long as there is faithfulness to the theme and to the normative prophetic and apostolic witness. For Barth the Jews, as the ongoing people of God, came into a different category from pagans, and he thus helped to set a trend whereby Jewish mission comes into a different category, preferably entrusted, as Barth once suggested,[22] to Jews themselves rather than to Gentiles who are newcomers to the people of God.

Not all Barth's practical suggestions enjoyed equal success. His focus on expository preaching seems not to have revived this form to any great extent, nor, indeed, to have revitalized preaching in any form, though he noted some encouraging improvement among Roman Catholics.[23] His liturgical suggestions attracted little attention – a friend at a service he conducted once gave him an A for preaching and a D for worship. His cautious approach to abortion in *Church Dogmatics* III/4[24] did little to check the flood of abortions that has engulfed much of the West. His plea for women has run into difficulties among modern feminists who are not impressed by his trinitarian analogy. Nevertheless, with his larger emphasis on the implications of the gospel, and his warning against the twin dangers of secularization and sacralization, Barth has undoubtedly helped the church to a better understanding of its ministry and of the call to relate this ministry, not merely to the needs of the hour, but primarily and radically to the revelation of God in Christ according to the biblical testimony and the supporting wisdom of councils, confessions, and fathers.

By way of conclusion I follow the example of Spener and express a few pious wishes regarding Barth's present and future influence. The first and more parochial of these wishes – I speak here as an Anglican in England in spite of years of exile in California – is that Barth might ultimately have a greater impact on English and more specifically Anglican theology. A fruitful interchange is now too late to do Barth any good, as it might have done even though he had once dismissed all Britons as Pelagians, but it is not too late to do Anglican theology a great deal of good. We have, of course, many Anglicans who have worked on Barth, but by and large the Anglican world has not given itself to the study of Barth that his work deserves. Though it is many years ago now, I remember talking with a learned bishop who on no less authority than that of William Temple suggested that Barth's view of revelation undercut the incarnation. I could not resist replying with one of Barth's shorter statements: 'To say revelation is to say "the Word became flesh"' (*CD* I/2:119). At that time, of course, most of Barth's work was not readily available, but over the wider field of clergy and people there is not much evidence of greater knowledge or concern today when all the main works may be read in English. My wish is not that Anglicans adopt Barth's theology wholesale but that beyond the diffuse influence that they cannot escape, they derive profit, as they surely would, from a more energetic and constructive interaction with Barth's theses and insights.

My second and central wish is that the theological world as a whole learn to take the Copernican turn that Barth himself made and find the theological centre once again in God and not in us. Elsewhere I have described this contribution by Barth as a recalling of theology to its proper theme. To an extent Barth has indeed succeeded already in breaking the preoccupation of many circles with the religious subject and focusing attention on him who is at once both primary subject and object. To a large extent he has already shown the implications of this orientation more forcefully to those who had never yielded to the modern aberration. Nevertheless, the issue is by no means decided. Pre-Copernican thinking in this theological sense dies hard, the more so since the human self is the substituted centre, and the conviction is deeply rooted that the proper study of mankind is man. If the Barthian reorientation should indeed prevail, with all that it implies, this might well be the supreme service by which Barth is permanently remembered.

My third wish is that there be a better appreciation of Barth's effort to establish theology as the critical norm of preaching. This need not entail either specific agreement with Barth's theology or acceptance of his detailed view of preaching. Its advantages would be twofold. It would enrich theology by making it less of an abstruse intellectual game for initiates, and integrating it more fully into the servant ministry and mission of the church. It would enrich preaching by removing it from the arbitrary realm of individual opinion or the purely technical sphere of communication, and giving it the tested evangelical content and authority whereby it may go forth and be heard and received as an authentic Word from God.

My fourth and final wish is that we learn from Barth to do theology in a spirit of humility, prayer, and praise. Now it is true that Barth himself was sometimes a better teacher in this regard than he was an example. In his earlier years especially he could be belligerent and almost bad-tempered, as in his famous *No* to Brunner. His brother Heinrich complained once that it was difficult to discuss things with Karl, since he would brook no opposition. Even in his mellower years he did not take too kindly to opposing theologies. Yet even at his least attractive Barth had the saving grace of humour. He could laugh at himself, and even laugh with others as they laughed at him. Furthermore, he always insisted that, since theology has to do with God, to be worth anything it must begin with prayer and end with praise. This does not mean that we must always put prayers and doxologies in theological discussions. But it does mean – and this is what I wish that all of us may see and appropriate – that if we are really dealing with the true theme of theology, then we must always ask God to tell us about himself (humility comes in here); for when we have done so, we will realize that this theme – the one God who is Creator, Reconciler, and Redeemer – is greater than can be thought, so that our thinking (humility comes in again here) will necessarily issue in thanksgiving, wonder and praise.

A graphic incident from the Hitler period acts as a parable in this regard. An edict went forth from the Führer that teachers should open every class with the Hitler greeting and the Hitler salute. Barth's reply in Bonn was simple. He always opened the study of theology with a prayer and hymn to God. Did the government really expect him to replace these with a greeting and salute to Hitler? Barth and his classes never gave the Hitler salute. His theology could control his practice because it had God as its theme, and therefore it learned from God and gave God the glory.

PART II
DOGMATIC THEOLOGY

2

Barth on Jesus Christ, Theology and the Church

ALISTER McGRATH

It is becoming increasingly common to designate Barth's *Church Dogmatics* a 'classic', in that the work transcends the horizons of any one reader – and possibly, as the revival in interest in Barth suggests, any one *generation* of readers. As Kermode perceptively points out,[1] a classic allows us to think of its age and our own together, so that the former may inform and stimulate the latter. It has a 'surplus of meaning' after meeting any one particular situation, allowing it to be drawn upon by others in a different, if not totally unrelated, historical context. For this reason, a new generation of theologians may look to Barth as a fruitful resource in a new era of the history of the western church. This essay will explore some aspects of the Barthian legacy, centering upon the relevance of Jesus Christ for the Christian church and Christian theology.

Barth is not the exclusive preserve of theology faculties or research students rummaging around for a suitable topic for doctoral research. It is perhaps inevitable that this unfortunate impression should have been gained, given Barth's prolific theological output and the intense interest in his ideas evident from the vast body of literature concerning him. This essay is written in the conviction that Barth's theology can provide a vital stimulus to and resource for the thinking of the Christian church as it attempts to reassert its identity and relevance within western culture in the aftermath of its culturally-enforced marginalization and the decline of liberal and neoliberal theology. It is a plea for theological seriousness as the church wrestles with social and political issues in a western cultural context. Part of the 'post-liberal theological construction' is the search for usable roots in the past, which may be appropriated. Barth's theological insights are increasingly being recognized as providing a resource upon which the western church may draw while preparing to face a new era in her existence, as the quest for a 'post-liberal' theology gains momentum. This essay explores some of these many insights.

I

> When Holy Scripture speaks of God, it concentrates our attention and thoughts upon one single point and what is to be known at that point . . . And if we look closer, and ask: who and what is at this point upon which our attention and thoughts are concentrated, which we are to recognize as God, . . . then from its beginning to its end, the Bible directs us to the name of Jesus Christ (*CD* II/2:52–3).

For Barth, 'God' is not a concept which may be derived from a free inquiry, but is given to us in the manner in which God 'posits and makes known Himself' (*CD*I/1:416) in Jesus Christ. It is Jesus Christ who is the centre of Christian theology, determining our understanding not merely of God, but also of humanity[2] and election,[3] to name but two of Barth's theological concerns. The present essay is not concerned with examining Barth's Christology,[4] but represents an attempt to evaluate Barth's emphasis upon Jesus Christ as the centrepoint of Christian theology, and to consider how his insights might act as a stimulus and a challenge to contemporary reflection upon the nature and task of Christian theology. Although the relevance and permanent value of Barth's insights appeared to have been denied by the rise of currents such as 'secular theology' in the United States and Europe in the 1960s, there has been a growing recognition that Barth may have laid a substantial theological foundation upon which contemporary theology may build.[5] We begin by considering how Barth's concept of 'Christological concentration'[6] developed.

Barth's early affinities lay with the liberal tradition, particularly the form associated with Wilhelm Herrmann.[7] The strong emphasis upon the religious personality – the 'inner life', as Herrmann preferred – of Jesus which is associated with this movement points to it being Jesus-centred. The historical actuality, the existence in human history, of Jesus Christ initiates an historical process which mediates the experience of God to us. Faith is 'awakened by God's historical revelation' in Jesus.[8] Like Ritschl, Herrmann treats Jesus as the historically contingent event through which our inner experience of God is mediated: it need not have been Jesus, but the historical (if contingent) fact is that it *was* Jesus who initiated this significant development.[9] Jesus is the occasion by which this essentially self-sufficient idea or experience was introduced into human history. In this sense, liberal theology may be said to be Jesus-centred, in that the 'religion of Jesus', his inner life, his religious personality, is treated as the point of departure for contemporary religious reflection.

It will therefore be clear that both the later Barth and the liberal school regarded Jesus as normative for Christian understanding and existence – but for very different reasons. For the liberals and the 1912 Barth,[10] Jesus was the historical realization of the full human spiritual and moral potential, whereas for the later Barth, he was the historical self-revelation of God. This point should be emphasized in contrasting the superficially similar attitudes towards Jesus adopted by the liberal school and the later Barth. For the liberal school (and the early Barth), Jesus was the historical manifestation of the human religious ideal; for the later Barth, he was the historical self-disclosure of God, a divine act in human history. Both the liberals and the later Barth centred upon the same historical figure – but with very different understandings of precisely what that historical figure represented and embodied.

In his later reflections upon his theological development, Barth frequently portrays his disenchantment with the liberal school as dating from August 1914, with the publication of the co-called 'manifesto of the intellectuals'.

> One day in early August 1914 stands out in my personal memory as a black day. Ninety-three German intellectuals

impressed public opinion by their proclamation in support of the war policy of Kaiser Wilhelm II and his counsellors. Among these intellectuals I discovered to my horror almost all of my theological teachers whom I had greatly venerated. In despair over what this indicated about the signs of the times, I suddenly realized that I could no longer follow either their ethics or dogmatics, or their understanding of the Bible and of history. For me at least, nineteenth century theology no longer held any future.[11]

Perhaps modelling his recollections upon those of Augustine or Luther,[12] who describe their sudden 'conversion' experiences in similar terms, Barth appears to indicate a sudden disenchantment with his earlier theological beliefs. This disenchantment does not appear to be reflected in his writings of the period, which indicate a progressive engagement with questions around which the 'dialectical theology' would eventually crystallize.[13] Furthermore, the historical reliability of Barth's statement has been called into question: the 'manifesto' seems to date from 4 October 1914, yet no reaction to it may be found in Barth's correspondence for this period.[14] It seems that in his later reflections upon his theological development, Barth may have unconsciously merged a number of his dissatisfactions with German liberal theology at the time, and concentrated them upon this single focus.

In its initial phase, Barth's 'dialectical' theology may be regarded as a passionate proclamation of the *otherness* of God, and the total inability of a theological or cultural system adequately to encompass him. Barth's frequently-repeated assertions of the 'infinite qualitative distinction' between God and humanity, between eternity and time, characterize both the first and the second editions of his *Romans* commentary. Theological iconoclasm has, however, but limited protest value. Barth appears to have realized that his insights, if they were to serve any long-term purpose, required consolidation. The lecture course 'Instruction in the Christian Religion', given at Göttingen in the summer term of 1924, represents a transitional point in Barth's thinking, in which the negative and critical aspects of his early dialectical theology are developed in a manner which would ultimately yield a positive Christocentric theology which retained a critical dimension.[15]

From 1932 onwards, Barth may be regarded as unfolding the theological ramifications of the fundamental insight that God reveals himself as Lord in Jesus Christ.

> We have to do with God himself as we have to do with this man. God himself speaks when this man speaks in human speech. God himself acts and suffers when this one triumphs as a man. The human speaking and acting and suffering and triumphing of this one man concerns us all, and his history is our history of salvation which changes the whole human situation (*CD* IV/2:51).

The full significance of Jesus Christ derives from the divine decision to reveal himself *through* himself, to abolish the 'otherness' of God. Revelation is the man-ward Christologically *determined* and Christologically *concentrated* movement of God, the fact that God 'turns to us, that indeed he comes to us, that he speaks with us, that he wills to be heard by us and to arouse our response' (*CD* I/1:407). Here is no 'God-conscious man' or 'religious genius' – here is *God* revealing *himself* through *himself* as Lord.[16]

For Barth, the recognition that God revealed himself as Lord in Jesus Christ was the means by which theology could be freed from the baleful influence of culture, anthropology and metaphysics, allowing it initially to become emancipated from its cultural matrix, and subsequently to develop and maintain its intellectual autonomy. No cultural, political, anthropological or epistemological insights or presuppositions may ever take precedence over the recognition of the lordship of Jesus Christ over the church, and over all its actions and thinking. The self-revelation of God as Lord in Jesus Christ is something which is 'given', which no amount of ideological protest can undo. Who God is, and what he is like; who we are, and what we are like – these are not disclosed by nature, philosophy or the social sciences, but are to be discovered on the basis of the historical form which the self-disclosure of God takes. Our preconceptions of divinity and humanity are shattered through God's self-revelation, which forces us to consider God as he wishes himself to be known, rather than as we have preconceived him. Thus – to give one of Barth's favourite examples – God's sovereignty is *demonstrated in*, and not *contradicted* by, his becoming an impotent human being.

It is on the basis of this insistence that Christian theology is centred upon Jesus Christ that Barth develops a theology of liberation – liberation of the life and thought of the Christian church from the prison of its social, cultural and intellectual matrix. Such a theology of liberation was precisely what the German church required as it found itself increasingly subjected to pressure by the social and cultural values of National Socialism – but Barth's insights are of continuing relevance to the life and thought of the church in our own day and age. In the remainder of this paper, we propose to consider two areas in which Barth's understanding of the relation of Jesus Christ to theology and the church has a direct bearing upon questions which impinge upon the life of the church today in a western cultural context.

II

There is in progress today – as there has been since the Enlightenment, and even before then – a debate concerning the nature and task of Christian theology. Is it a neutral, disinterested academic subject, completely free from any precommitment of any kind on the part of its practitioners, or is it a committed subject which operates within a framework which places certain restrictions upon them?[17] With the Enlightenment and its aftermath came the view that Christian theology, if not simply the republication of some form of natural religion, was certainly not to be credited with any insights which could not be obtained in other ways, particularly through the intelligent use of human reason and moral senses.[18] Theology is thus to be seen as an essentially academic exercise, concerned with generally-accessible truths or insights, and capable of being pursued by anyone, irrespective of their attitude, for example, to the Christian tradition.

For Barth, this attitude is nonsensical: theology is a discipline carried out within the community of faith as a response to the self-revelation of God in Christ, in an attempt to unfold the intricacies of the man-ward movement which is the ultimate basis and *explicandum* of faith.[19] Many, daunted by the sheer size of the *Church Dogmatics*, manage to penetrate no further than the first few pages. If they managed to get no further than the first few lines, they would find the following memorable phrases, enough food for thought for some considerable time: 'As a theological discipline, dogmatics is the scientific self-examination of the Christian church with respect to the content of its distinctive talk about God . . . Dogmatics is a theological discipline, but theology is a function of the church.' (*CD* I/1:3). In other words, theology is an attempt on the part of those within the community of faith to analyse, understand and explore something over which they do not have control.

In the self-revelation of God in Jesus Christ is something 'given', something which we cannot ignore or marginalize, the self-positing and self-authenticating word of God to which we must respond. Barth, with an at times irritating pedanticism, points out that God is not an object (German: *Gegenstand*) which we can seek and scrutinize in a manner and at a time of our own choosing, but is one who stands over and against us (German: *Gegen-Stand*). We cannot adopt a neutral and detached attitude to theology, precisely because the man-ward movement of God concentrated and focused in Jesus Christ has generated both the context within which responsible theological reflection must take place (the church), and also the substance of that faith. *Fides qua creditur* and *fides quae creditur* alike are generated by the word of God in its three-fold form.[20] Humanity is obliged to respond to, rather than attempt to dictate the preconditions of, God's self-disclosure. Time and time again, Barth emphasizes the fundamental *uncontrollability* of God, the simple *fact* of God's self-disclosure in Jesus Christ: it has happened, and no amount of ideological protest can undo it.

Barth, of course, was writing in the early 1930s, before the hermeneutical insights of Gadamer and Polanyi had been formulated and had gained such widespread recognition. It is clear that many at that time seriously believed that it was possible to adopt an utterly unprejudiced attitude to existence and experience, free of all overt precommitment. Now we are gradually coming to realize that our delusions of objectivity simply blind ourselves to our own prejudices, and that prejudice – or *precommitment*, to use a more neutral term – is actually important in our process of understanding.[21] As Gadamer emphasizes, to detach oneself from a tradition is to impede the process of understanding, which takes place within precisely such a tradition. The Christian tradition, which defines the arena within which the three-fold form of the word of God is encountered, establishes the sole 'given' and 'authorized' context for theological understanding. As the brilliant interpretation of Eberhard Jüngel has it:

> The mode of speaking of the Christian tradition insists that we must be told what we are to make of the word 'God', so that it is only God himself, by speaking to us, who can, in the end, tell us what we are to understand by the word 'God'.[22]

Matthias Grünewald's Isenheim altarpiece 'The Crucifixion' hung above Barth's desk from 1920 onwards, an eloquent testimony to Barth's own conviction that the only legitimate definition of 'God' was that indicated by the pointing hand of John the Baptist – the crucified Christ.[23] The 'two hands' motif is pivotal to Barth's anthropology and theology: the hand of John the Baptist points to the true God, and the hand of Pontius Pilate points to the true man.[24] We might prefer to base our thoughts of God upon Tuscan landscapes or Mozart flute concertos – but in the end, Barth insists, we are forced to recognize a normative and definitive, an *authorized* stimulus for such thoughts – not one of our own choosing, but one which is *given* to us.

Who, then, is authorized as a *practitioner* of this theological discipline? Whom are we to recognize as the true theologians? For Barth, theology is a matter for the church.

Theology is not a private subject for theologians only. Nor is it a private subject for professors. Fortunately, there have always been pastors who have understood more about theology than most professors. Nor is theology a private subject of study for pastors. Fortunately, there have repeatedly been congregation members, and often whole congregations, who have pursued theology energetically while their pastors were theological infants or barbarians. Theology is a matter for the Church.[25]

Barth's stress upon the importance of practical theology – especially preaching – derives from his conviction that it is here that God *acts*. Through the proclamation of the word of God, the church and the world are forced to hear that word and respond to it. The function of theology is *critical*, in that it is obliged to ensure that the church's proclamation remains faithful to the word to which it bears witness.[26] But it is also *positive*, in that theology is also written from the standpoint of faith as a function of the church – and hence is practised by all those who proclaim the gospel. In this way, Barth marginalizes, but does not eliminate, the role of academic theologians, whom he treats as good servants, but poor masters.

This essay has been written in the conviction that Barth has continuing relevance for the church – not just for university faculties of theology, nor as a quarry to be mined for the production of doctoral theses, but for the life and well-being of the Christian church in its totality. For Barth, the mission of the church, the basis of its proclamation, worship and adoration, is none other than the word of God in its three-fold form: in Jesus Christ, in scripture, and in the proclamation of the church. It is those entrusted with the exposition of scripture, with the proclamation of the word of God and with the criticism of the doctrine and practice of the Christian church upon their basis, who should be recognized as theologians: 'The task of theology consists in again and again reminding the people in the Church, both preachers and congregations, that the life and work of the Church are under the authority of the gospel and the law, that God should be heard.'[27] The recognition of the centrality of Jesus Christ to Christian theology involves the concomitant demand that the life and doctrine of the church should be critically evaluated on the basis of this sole authorized criterion – and the pastor's study and pulpit are essential elements within this process which cannot be dismissed or marginalized by those who regard themselves as 'theological professionals'. The epistemological prioritization of academic theology is to be rejected. To be a theologian is to be a preacher of the word of God, proclaiming and re-enacting that act of God which we know as Jesus Christ.

It is insights such as these which establish Barth's importance as a father of the church, rather than merely as an academic theologian. For Barth, theology is intimately concerned with preaching, with *proclamation*, with the well-being and life of the church. It is theology which undergirds the life and doctrine of the church, as a discipline which is exercised by that church as a totality. The 'papacy of the professors' (Martin Kähler) is to be rejected as implying a false understanding of the nature of theology itself, in that theology is an enterprise undertaken by the community of faith within that community of faith.

> The task which is laid upon theology, and which it can and should fulfil, is its service in the church, to the Lord of the church. It has its definite function in the church's liturgy, that is, in the various phases of the church's expression: in every reverent proclamation of the gospel, or in every proclaiming reverence, in which the church listens and attends to God. Theology does not exist in a vacuum, nor in any arbitrarily selected field, but in that province between baptism and communion, in the realm between the scriptures and their exposition and proclamation.[28]

Just as Luther proclaimed the 'priesthood of all believers', so Barth proclaims the theological competence of all believers. And just as Luther insisted that the 'priesthood of all believers' did not abolish the ordained ministry, but merely set it in its proper context, so Barth's stipulations serve to emphasize the necessity of maintaining a proper link between theology and faith, between the theologian and the believer. The theologian cannot be allowed to set his own agenda, following his own methods, in that these have already been selected, not *by* him, but *for* him.[29] It is the context of worship, adoration, preaching and proclamation which defines the parameters within which theology operates – all of which directly concern the life and doctrine of the church. Barth's views may appear as anti-intellectual, verging perhaps even on Pietism[30] – but it is evident that Barth's protests are directed entirely against a false concept of *theology* itself. Theology is a function of the church – it is a committed discipline, whose service is to the Lord of the church, and whose servants are those – *whoever they may be* – who are obedient hearers of the word of God.

III

One of the more important developments in recent Barth-interpretation has been the recognition that what is essentially a very conservative approach to theology should so consistently give rise to critical political thought and concrete political opposition to the *status quo*.[31] Particularly in the period 1933–45, Barth's life was marked by conscious engagement with social, political and moral issues, despite the fact that Barth was primarily concerned with dogmatic writing during this period. The full force of Barth's ethical pronouncements – which contrasted sharply with the insipid character of the ethics of Bultmann[32] and Tillich – was gradually recognized to derive from the power and consistency of his massive theological system.[33] The dialectic between God and his world, which Barth came to see as decisively and definitively disclosed in Jesus Christ, functioned as the basis of a socially relevant and potentially revolutionary ethics. This ethics did not derive from some contemporary pre-understanding of the human situation, scientifically ascertained, but on the basis of the Christologically disclosed understanding of that situation. A correct understanding of the human situation is the consequence, not the precondition, of an authentically Christian theology.

This point may be illustrated from a sermon preached by

Barth at Osnabrück in April 1934. Dealing with the subject of the reaction of the churches to the political situation of the day, with the situation of the German church under the Third Reich very much in mind, Barth pointed out how the church tended to endorse, rather than criticize, contemporary cultural, political and social presuppositions. While liberal Protestantism must not be dismissed out of hand, in that it fulfilled a useful function in the aftermath of the collapse of Hegelianism in the 1850s, it is impossible to overlook the tendencies within its general *Weltanschauung* which allowed the values of German society and civilization to be identified with those of Christianity. And so God is judged by culture, and God cannot judge culture.[34] Thus it was leading liberal theologians who endorsed the Kaiser's war policy in 1914, and – perhaps even more surprisingly for those who project the culturally-conditioned 'liberal' values of our own day onto the 1930s – it was chiefly liberal theologians who initially supported Hitler's programme, seeing in it a revival of German culture, and hence of religion.[35]

In a powerful attack on this tendency, Barth argued that the church tended to treat its own distinctive contribution to such debates – the recognition of Jesus Christ as Lord – as merely the *ornaments*, and not the *foundation*, of its social views. For Barth, the Christian church must fight – but it must fight on the basis of the *unum necessarium*, the Lordship of Jesus Christ, and nothing else. To fail to do this is to fail to be the church of Jesus Christ in the world. The tendency of the church then, as now, to peripheralize its own distinctive insights into the political and cultural situation was called into question by Barth. The German church treated National Socialist culture as the major premise, and Jesus Christ as the minor premise, of the theological syllogism, and tended to develop a new natural theology based upon the 'orders of creation'[36] of the German state. Barth's protest against an autonomous natural theology – perhaps most evident in his famous *Nein! Antwort an Emil Brunner* (1934) – is partially grounded in his conviction that the authority of divine revelation is subverted through an appeal to the state and its institutions (particularly its laws)[37] as its 'point of contact'. For Barth, liberal Protestantism was impotent to challenge National Socialism, precisely on account of its quasi-normative understanding of the function of culture in relation to theology: 'culture' was virtually identified as the sole (external) criterion by which the authenticity of the life and doctrine of the church could be judged. What was required, in Barth's view, was an *internal* criterion, a criterion which was consonant with the word of God, by which the church could judge German culture, instead of *being judged* by that culture.[38] A religion based upon a culture has covert hidden interests in the survival of that culture, and has neither the theological resources nor the will to criticize it. Similarly, the intuitive reaction of some theologians against Nazism was robbed of potency through the absence of any positive *theological* foundation.

The establishment of the theological foundation by which the 'errors of the "German Christians" of the present Reich Church government' might be exposed and judged must be regarded as substantially due to the insights and personal influence of Barth himself. The Barmen Declaration of May 1934 encapsulates Barth's insistence upon the centrality and material sufficiency of God's self-revelation in Jesus Christ to the life and doctrine of the church:[39]

> Jesus Christ, as he is attested for us in Holy Scripture, is the one Word of God which we have to hear and which we have to trust and obey in life and in death.
> We reject the false doctrine, as though the church could and would have to acknowledge as a source of its proclamation apart from and besides this one Word of God, still other events and powers, figures and truths, as God's revelation.

The historical importance of this declaration is evident. But a more pressing question concerns the contemporary relation of church and society. Upon what basis may a prophetic critique of society be made from within a church which shares so many of its presuppositions? Barth pointed out the tendency of the church of his own day to fail to appropriate its distinctive theological foundation – which Barth identifies with Jesus Christ – in its engagement with social and political issues.

The need of a coherent theological basis for a critical engagement with social and political issues is adequately demonstrated by the ethical inadequacy of the liberal tendency to enthrone or absolutize present experience as revelatory.[40] Consider Tom Driver's assertion that present experience – such as stepping out of a bath – *is* the 'word of God'.[41] This uncritical attitude towards present experience is nothing other than the elevation of the experience of the individual, or the group to which an individual belongs, to a primary status in which it is regarded as revelatory and endowed with the authority of 'God'.[42] Such a theology is defenceless in the face of, for example, the German Christians' claim that their Nazi experience of Hitler and his vision for the German Reich was revelatory and normative. Driver's bathtime experience of 'an energy that has no name' shows little promise as a theological tool which might permit discrimination between Nazi values and those of liberal democracy. Its radical subjectivity disarms it for all save the most superficial engagements with society. Is Driver's experience to be regarded as normative, the criterion by which the content and authenticity of everyone else's present religious experience, and hence theology, is to be evaluated? For Barth, there was only one such criterion, an *external* criterion – and the Barmen Declaration affirmed this to be Jesus Christ himself.

Barth himself, of course, was not completely consistent in applying his Christological insights politically. For example, his defence of the democratic political system appears to be based upon a confusion of the three persons of the Trinity with the original three Swiss cantons. But at least Barth tried to give a theological basis to his passionate defence of democracy as an authentically Christian political system – whereas there is a distressing tendency on the part of many European and North American Christians to accept this culturally-given political system as 'given' for both secular and ecclesiastical decision-making.[43] As Reinhold Niebuhr realized, on the basis of his reading of the North American situation in the light of Holy Scripture, both culture and society had to be regarded as fallen.[44] There is a tendency on the part of many churchmen inadvertently to elevate cultural presuppositions to the status of a 'word of God', which the church must hear and obey (a development which appears to have occurred through default rather than intention). Lesslie Newbigin comments thus on his cultural assumptions during 38 years' missionary work in India: 'I look back with real penitence on the occasions when . . . I censured some things and commended others on grounds which – I now realize – were not evangelical but merely cultural.'[45] It is for this reason that Barth's recall of the Confessing Church to its sole basis in the one word of God, Jesus Christ, is of such significance: it represents a serious attempt to ground the social action and criticism of the church *theologically*, in order that the church may have a basis independent of the contemporary social structure from which to criticize it.[46]

IV

In this paper, we have been concerned with some of Barth's insights concerning Jesus Christ for the life of the Christian church. Too often, Barth is treated simply as a theologian, a combatant in a war of ideas. But it cannot be overemphasized that Barth's relevance extends to the life of the church in the world, and that he has a continuing relevance to the life of that church as it seeks to engage with and positively criticize the social structures of society. We may feel able to criticize Barth's choice of his theological foundation upon which social criticism should be based – but the German church conflict of the 1930s must be regarded as establishing the necessity for such a theological foundation in the first place. The church cannot be permitted merely to endorse or to lend a spurious sanctity to the presuppositions of contemporary society, but must learn to criticize them on the basis of its own criteria.

Equally, Barth's insistence that theology is a function of the church, rather than an autonomous academic discipline, poses a powerful challenge to prevailing contemporary conceptions of theology, deriving from the legacy of the Enlightenment, and – like an intellectual Declaration of Independence – allows us to rise up and challenge, perhaps even to overthrow, the tyranny of this movement which has held theology captive, perhaps as a willing prisoner, for so long.[47] It is currently fashionable, particularly within English theological circles, to treat Barth with some derision – but let us hope that there are many who, like him, will be prepared to swim against the theological current of their day and age. For, as Barth himself knew, it is by swimming against the current of a river that we finally reach its source – which for Barth is, as it always has been, none other than Jesus Christ. Christian theology and proclamation must, like John the Baptist's extended finger in Grünewald's Isenheim altarpiece, point away from themselves to the God who made himself known – who *wills* to make himself known – in Jesus Christ.

3

Karl Barth on 'The Work of Creation'

A Reading of *Church Dogmatics*, III/1

W. A. WHITEHOUSE

In 1946 I received a copy of *Kirchliche Dogmatik*, III/1, published in the previous year, and I dared to publish a report on the content in a short-lived periodical sponsored by my youthful contemporaries. My acquaintance was confined to the first half-volume of 'Prolegomena' and a summary of volume II, on 'The Doctrine of God', written by F. W. Camfield. There were no secondary sources to explain what was going on. My rudimentary familiarity with its linguistic and cultural context was formed through contacts with the German Confessional Church before and immediately after the war. As for the particular subject-matter, the relation of God and creatures, I had compared what Aquinas taught about this with the modern suggestions emanating from A. N. Whitehead, in a one-year post-graduate exercise done under pressure in 1940 – and examined, I am proud to say, by Austin Farrer. When, forty years later, I look back at that *Presbyter* article, I am vastly impressed by Barth's evident power to communicate to so ill-prepared an amateur what he had to say. But – and here is the point of this gratuitous piece of autobiography – I welcome the opportunity to revisit the scene of those juvenile antics in this context of centennial celebration, with the English text now at our disposal; though I do so with a daunting awareness of critical expertise from many hands to which I am not adequately sensitive, and of new styles in theological scholarship which I respect but cannot profess to have mastered.

There are, of course, four parts to Barth's volume III on the doctrine of creation. I shall confine attention to the first part, Christian evaluation of 'The Work of Creation', which is the establishing by divine action of the world about us with our human species as part thereof. The second part deals with humanity; the third with providence (and evil) and with the reign of God from heaven; and the fourth with ethics to be derived from the command of God the Creator. All this, as doctrine of creation, is distinguished from the doctrines of God, of reconciliation, and of redemption. The distinctions and entailed inter-relationships are expounded in the last section (§24) of the second half-volume on 'Prolegomena' (*CD* I/2) under the topic of 'the Dogmatic Method'. God, self-expressed in his atoning act in Jesus Christ, is 'the open centre at the heart of theology', an 'open ring' circumscribed by the Word of God which stands as the common origin of all these lines of doctrine. The metaphor of open ring, with circumference and radiating lines, occurs in *Church Dogmatics*, I/2:869; Stephen Sykes elicits the point at issue with graceful precision on pp. 199f. of *The Identity of Christianity*.[1] Each line has its own integrity; and I propose to watch Barth at work over the first stretch of the doctrine of creation and let the principal (and debatable) features of his Christocentric epistemology of faith emerge from this concrete instance of dogmatic method.

I

Whence does this world about us derive? Are we in a position to know? If so, how; and with what degree of certainty? And, incidentally, is this way of referring to the whole cosmic phenomenon – 'the world about us' – misleadingly tendentious? Why should all things be assessed with any special reference to humanity on earth?

Barth deals with these questions with uninhibited confidence. By his own sovereign decisions and actions *God* acquaints mankind with his primordial actuality. 'The insight that man, together with all the reality distinct from God, owes existence and form to God's creation is achieved . . . only in faith in Jesus Christ' (*CD* III/1:3), Jesus, the Son of God who is the Word by which God brings mankind as partners into knowledgeable relationship with himself – a relationship properly depicted as elective covenant. This is the theology expressed in the Letter to the Hebrews, chapter 1. We have to be *told*, and have *been* told, whence the world about us (and we with it) derives; and within the logic of this communication we attend to the sagas of world-creation found in the first two chapters of Genesis. These invite us to look at the universe and to look at mankind as elected to covenant-partnership with God, from two related points of view. What is done in creation provides conditions for the intercourse between God and mankind, intercourse 'made possible by it technically, which follows it externally and temporarily, and which continues its history inwardly' (*CD* III/1:229); and what is done in creation also provides an initial expression of what is to be established when the works and ways of God reach their final goal. To these three phrases of reflection Barth adds a final section (§42), dealing, as I construe it, with the *cultural bearing* of the insight thus derived from Christian faith in God the Creator.

Forty years on from its composition, that last section could well be sharpened and perhaps re-shaped to deal more explicitly with the cultural significance of the enterprise of science (*vis-a-vis* the universe) and of the enterprise of theology (*vis-a-vis* God), and to meet newly emerging symptoms of paranoia menacing to our world's political and cultural well-being. The two sections (§41.2,3) based on the sagas in Genesis pose questions for any Christian theologian about proper critical respect for origin-stories dealing with the world about us and our place in it – stories not informed by the findings of modern scientific enquiry and governed throughout by Abrahamic (and then Christian) faith in God.[2] And, of course, an initial decision to start, not from the world as we find it to be in experience but from the Word of God, (§40), is open to a charge of cultural atavism. Let us revisit each of these four phases of reflection.

II

The starting-point for a reply to the question of origins which affirms an act of God, *creatio*, is faith in God the Creator. It is only as an element in Biblical proclamation – in 'God's Word and work attested by Holy Scripture and the confession of the church' (*CD* III/1:42) – that *creatio* carries any noetic certainty. To that proclamation it is *integral*, and its integral significance for Old Testament covenant theology is equally evident in the New Testament context where the ground for noetic certainty stands disclosed. Barth's first concern is to defend and to clarify this methodological axiom. His sustained critique of theological habits which trace out some other way to the divine creative Author need not detain us here. Any *creatio* to which they point is ill-defined by comparison with the act ascribed to God in Christian faith, and their affirmation of it lacks comparable certainty. Does Barth's exposition of the substance of Christian faith avail to mark it off from the tentative findings of human speculation as adequately and uniquely *definitive* for *creatio*? And does that *credo* establish itself in an honest human mind with noetic *certainty*? These are the main questions with which we are provoked to test what Barth does on pp. 11–94 where he paves the way for subsequent examination of the Genesis sagas. They can hardly be answered in a five-minute review of those pages!

The *articulus fidei* which affirms God the Father as Creator of heaven and earth has three elements: God, Creator, and the created product. The linguistic usage of Holy Scripture serves to direct us to the distinctive substance of the affirmation in all three respects. The article propounds a concept of creation 'which we are not free to fill out at will' (*CD* III/1:11). The God of whom it speaks is the Father, self-determined in the eternal generation of the Son and one with him in the Holy Spirit. *Creatio* is his further act, elected and posited in the free omnipotence of that love which is God's being, and so has some analogy to the eternal begetting of the Son by the Father whilst differing from this in its contingency and historicity. It establishes something other than God; and as an *accomplished* act it bears some analogy to the founding (*krisis*) of a public project by a decisive act of will, marked in all respects by free grace. By designating this founded gift as 'heaven and earth', this dogma secularizes the whole of the world about us as a finite totality beyond which there is no reality apart from God himself; a totality, moreover, in which man with his noetic and responsive capacity finds a central role. The basis for this dogma is available through the Scriptures of God's covenant with mankind, in a *form* which lends to its substance its unique distinctiveness. This form derives from Biblical confidence that 'the election of grace is the eternal beginning of all the works and ways of God in Jesus Christ' (*CD* 11/2:94) – a topic already clarified by Barth in the third part of the doctrine of God (*CD* II/2, chapter VII). One highly debatable aspect of this form is that *creatio* must be represented, neither as necessary in eternal principle nor as implicit in the constitution of that which comes to be, but as 'a concrete act of God and therefore a historical reality filling time' (*CD* II/2:61). And it is an *accomplished* act – 'part of a travelled road that cannot be travelled again'[3] – and can be affirmed only in the literary genre of story, of pre-historical history.

The second question is about noetic certainty for any honest human mind (see *CD* III/1:31–41). Such certainty will not be found outside the household of faith. Barth's principal concern is that it should be there within the household, acids of modernity (ancient and modern) notwithstanding. But, lest such certainty be no more than arbitrary credulity, he directs attention to that faith in Jesus Christ which 'contains within itself the knowledge of the secret of creation, the Creator and the creature' (*CD* III/1:31); and we observe how *krisis*, glossed by the adjective *kainē*, is used in New Testament expressions of that faith to account for radically renovated existence, lived out in acquaintance with God's presence, with confidence in his omnicompetent power, his right to sovereignty and his unfailing grace. Through Jesus

Christ, in whom God's elected works and ways by covenant with mankind reach their consummation, human beings are made sure of God and of these elected works and ways. This paves the way for the use of *krisis* in passages like Galatians 6:15, and this in turn validates Old Testament witness to the origin of the whole cosmic project and of God's interest in it. This is hardly the poetic certainty which so-called free-thinkers covet. It is not even the rational probability of Joseph Butler, based on assessment of powers evident in the reality open to human perception, of rights evident in the constituents of the world about us, and signs of benevolence in that to which it owes its origin. That such noetic certainty should find expression in worship and in obedience – with language more realistically intended than that merely of liturgical rhetoric – is integral to life lived with Christian faith. If it is to be tested for intellectual probity, this will be done by the process known to theologians as *fides quaerens intellectum*; and this brings us to Barth's proposal that this process be directed by 'the Biblical history of creation', which is 'pure saga, distinguished as such from "history" on the one side and myth on the other. Precisely in this form it is a constituent part of the biblical witness and therefore itself a witness to God's self-revelation' (*CD* III/1:90).

III

Barth's prescription for *fides quaerens intellectum*, applied to Christian faith in the Creator and *creatio*, is to allow the related sagas in Genesis, chapter 1–2, 'to say what they have to say' (*CD* III/1:77–94, *passim*). These sagas, humanly speaking, derive from resources of 'divination and poetry', and the resources of 'physics and metaphysics' are less prominent in their construction than we might wish. When Barth is under review, we should consider this proposal in as detached a way as we can; and however great may be one's admiration and gratitude for the 235 pages of exegesis, there are questions about methodological adequacy which are not dispelled by the remark that 'there are more things in heaven and earth – and even in the human capacity of perception and presentation – than are dreamed of' in the philosophy of what he calls 'spiritual invalids' (*CD* III/1:91). I have already described the content of the sagas as an invitation to look from two related points of view at the universe and at mankind within it elected to covenant partnership with God. What is done in creation *provides conditions for the intercourse* between God and mankind; and it also *provides an initial expression of what is in view* – of what is to be established when the works and ways of God come to their climax. Somewhat reluctantly I must undertake a lightning tour of each saga, guided by Barth's careful exposition.

Genesis 1:1–2, 4a. For anything other than God there is an initial possibility of monstrous disorder, chaos ineffectually overlaid by brooding but frustrated aspirations for order (*ruach*); a *past* possibility, ruled out by *Deus dixit*, but still hauntingly there as a threat for the universe if and when it comes under final divine judgement. (See Jeremiah 4:23–27 and Isaiah 34:1–4, where the precise threat is cancelled by promised deliverance.) Light – not identified with luminants, to correct any cult of astral deities – is established as a constituent in what is to be, and as a prime condition for cosmos-making works to be done with knowledge and with lasting grace. And times for creaturely eventuality, phenomenally evident in the sequence of day and night, provide an 'external basis' for that covenant-existence with God to which Israel – and all mankind – will be summoned in the days and nights of history. (See Jeremiah 33:19–22 for the connection.) So do the separations made within the potential chaos, yielding as they do 'guarded space'; where, for living creatures yet to be fashioned, sky is symbolic of some place of presence for God – and his heavenly creatures – within the created project but 'above'; and dry land on earth below is guarded against threat from terrestrial oceans, under heaven which guards the whole project against destruction by supposed celestial oceans –

symbolic, in both instances, of chaos held at bay; though *total* liberation from the threat emanating from what God has in fact ruled out is deferred until the project is consummated. (Persons liberated to live with cosmology in the tradition of Galileo have considerable difficulty with symbolic divination which requires them to entertain the thought of a cosmically localized operational headquarters for God, and to construe atmospheric and astronomical effects around this planet in these terms.) The dry land is instructed to clothe itself with vegetation, a self-perpetuating form of life which is sustained by an obedience of which the earth is capable, irrespective of natural provisions not yet mentioned. (This aetiology of vegetation, made in contrast with that for subsequent forms of life, asks too much of us; and though it may serve to demythologize the mother-goddess of Earth, too much of her *persona* haunts this bit of divination.) The astral luminaries which, from a terrestrial point of view, furnish the sky, are (notoriously) confined to a demythologized role of timing the light within which the project takes its ordered course. Once they are in place the stage is set for beasts. The strong word for 'create' is now used for the first time since the saga's opening sentence. Beasts are created first in those areas of the cosmic structure most hazardously close to the frontiers against chaos, regions unsuited for regular human occupation. There they are explicitly blessed, authorized to breed and flourish. Tintoretto has a picture of birds and sea-creatures streaming away from the Creator's hand which, for me, encapsulates the joy with which Barth greets this element in the saga. And so to the creation and blessing of land-animals, and among them the human species in the duality of man-woman relationship, for whom blessing includes a call to dominion over all fellow-beasts in the pursuit of a shared vegetarian life.

The thrust of Barth's essay in 'letting the saga say what it has to say' emerges, I hope, in this sketchy account, and I have included a few tell-tale phrases which hint at his appreciation of it. There is room for nit-picking in the detail of his exegesis, but that is hardly the main issue. There are grounds for suggesting that this view of the cosmos and its *creatio* is distorted by time-bound ignorance of fact, by selectivity in the interest of some arbitrarily related faith, and by fictitious divination of factors unperceived by honest minds alleged to suffer from 'spiritual invalidity'. And those who published the saga as a document of faith provide no answer to the question principally generated by any decent university education: Can you take responsibility for what you have chosen to say? These are all difficulties which must be negotiated in the course of posing the main question: Does this saga satisfactorily amplify, sustain and confirm human faith in the Father of Jesus Christ as Creator of this existing cosmic project; and is that project properly appreciated as 'external basis of the covenant'?

Genesis 2, 4b-25. The thrust, the gist, of this complementary saga is that man is necessary for 'the perfecting of the earth; the redemption of its aridity, barrenness and death; the meaningful fulfillment of this God-given hope' (*CD* III/1:238 f.); man, predestined for covenant-partnership with God in a dialectic which the people of Israel were privileged to know by living it out under conditions of a fall from grace *not* elected by God. With major reflections on anthropology postponed (to *CD* III/2), we are invited to consider afresh how world-creation 'promises, proclaims and prophesies that which, in his grace and finally and supremely in the giving of his Son, God plans for man and will not delay to accomplish for his benefit' (*CD* III/1:231). This theme is common to both sagas, but in this only it governs the structure, and the thrust of 'will not delay' emerges in the specific content.

The cosmic project is viewed from an earthly centre. Its historicity and its location are presented, in 'saga' fashion, as partially identifiable yet now veiled in secrecy. (Can we, one asks, suggest date and location for it other than in imagination – and so, perhaps, evade the saga's central thrust?) The centre is 'on earth', and its sole initial component, arid dust, is in need of irrigation, and of man as cultivator.[4] Irrigation is made possible, with elementary regard for cloud-formation by evaporation; and man, 'earthy but breathed upon by God' (*CD* III/1:243) in a special intimacy of role-giving presence, is formed as a living being. Then comes the planting of a Garden in Eden, with its rivers and trees, and the servant-role for man specified in terms of permission and prohibition which set him free to live in the service of God. We are left wondering about the two special trees. The first, so Barth suggests, is 'a *sign* of the presence of God which guarantees life for mankind' (*CD* III/1:), a sign there to elicit conscious and constant gratitude. The second one is a revelation that there is a judicial wisdom, unique to God and deadly for man should he aspire to expropriate it. (On pp. 263–266 Barth takes time to challenge other interpretations, notably any which find in the second tree a risky element, 'a bridgehead left to the kingdom of darkness' by a Creator content to tolerate for his own good reasons a potential threat from within to the whole project) (*CD* III/1:263). This initial expression of what is to be established when the works and ways of God reach their eschatological consummation includes climactic provision for humanity to live in *human* partnership. Man must have a created companion who is 'a Thou as truly as *he* is an I, and he is to it a Thou as truly as it is an I' (*CD* III/1:290). What is said about the production of such a companion – one to whom Adam is related 'as to another part or member of his own body', in whom he finds something lost from himself – veils the real secret of the will and work of God in the deep sleep of Adam's anaesthetized passivity; but, given the capacity for reflection proper to aetiological saga (in which at this point I find that I am somewhat deficient), the 'four basic pillars' of the man-woman relationship emerge in the light of such *creatio* (*CD* III/1:290 f.) The relationship between man and woman is honoured for its own sake, and not merely with reference to parenthood and posterity, in a style found only rarely in the Old Testament, notably in the Song of Songs. In this saga, Israel's experience of life in covenant-partnership with God is drawn into the substance of the *creatio*-affirmation. From what Barth has called the 'dialectic' found in that experience, the two trees acquire symbolic reference to God's sustaining of life for mankind by Gospel and by Law. And for humanity there is direct experience of inter-human partnership in sexual duality which carries analogical correspondence to that covenant, and in its own way testifies to the status of the covenant as 'the internal basis' of creation.

IV

At the beginning of Book Two in his *History of Europe*, entitled 'Renaissance, Reformation, Reason', H. A. L. Fisher records the passing of a culture 'shaped by the surviving prestige of the Roman Empire and the overpowering authority of the Roman Church'.

> To this Roman and clerical outlook upon the world, the sixteenth century, the first age which may be regarded as distinctively modern, offered the sharpest contrast. The lay mind, fortified by the free use of the vernacular languages and by the full recovery of Greek and Hebrew, had come into its own. The close interrogation of nature, which was to lead to the development of modern science, had begun. Painters examined the human frame, surgeons dissected it . . . The discovery . . . that the earth revolved around the sun steadily secured adherents. A new lay culture, aristocratic in origin, for it had chiefly grown up in the courts of Italian despots, was made a general possession through the invention of printing. Strong and continuous as were the theological interests, they were now balanced by an exciting body of new knowledge, having no connection with theology, and the fruit of mental processes which theology was unable to turn to account. With a sharp gesture of impatience Europe turned away from the vast literature of commentaries and glosses which the pedants of the later middle ages had inscribed 'in letters of opium on tablets of lead'.[5]

What *cultural* status may we accord to Barth's theological account of the doctrine of creation? Is it vitiated by a conservative itch to put the clock back, under the cloak of modern effort to move forward in this twentieth-century crisis for post-Renaissance culture? Is it, potentially, a significant contribution to human culture in the broad sense, or is it no more than an ideological *tour-de-force* for some few within the cultural ghetto of the Europeanized Christian Church who enjoy that sort of thing? (The operative words in that question are 'no more than'.)

For us there is a question prior to these, namely the question about its Christian theological integrity. Some comparison with previous essays of a similar character and of acknowledged cultural influence may be pertinent. In finding his own bearing Barth profited from critical attention to Basil, followed by John of Damascus, in the East, and to Ambrose, followed by Augustine and then by Thomas Aquinas, in the West (*CD* III/1:64, 173). There is one surprising omission: the unfinished *Collationes on the Six Days* by Bonaventura in the thirteenth century. His modern editor, José de Vinck of Louvain, says, quite fairly, that 'there is here the clear and even luminous expression of *the existential presence of God among men through every manifestation of being*'.⁶ How, at times, I would love to be translated into the company of that Seraphic Doctor of the Church and to pursue the *itinerarium mentis in Deum* which leads to a Franciscan vision of the world charged in all its manifold detail with the grandeur of God! To find about me a world, and within me a mind, 'organized, trinitarian, symbolical, numbered, meaningful, hierarchical', to be *enjoyed* with faith and love and hope!⁷ Cultural development and theological discipline combine to rule out that particular prospect. Do they admit of anything comparable, with a capacity to enliven human imagination in salutary ways?

'A clear and even luminous expression of the existential presence of God among men, through every manifestation of being' – does Barth take us in this direction, and if so in what form and with what adequacy? His contention is that from the content of the divine revelation attested to us in Holy Scripture we have knowledge of God and of the work of creation as the object of Christian faith. We know 'the Lord who alone can be the Creator at the beginning of all things. Who is this

Lord? He is the God of Israel, who in Jesus Christ has loved man, and sought and found him . . .' (*CD* III/1:332). Yes, but what prospect do we have of tracing lines from this centre to every manifestation of being, and from every manifestation of being discerned by close interrogation of nature in modern fashion back to this centre, with cultural relevance for all our contemporaries? Barth criticizes Basil and Ambrose (in their *Hexaemera*) for helping the biblical narratives to speak 'by clothing what we think are the far too naive and scanty words of the Bible with the fulness of our own natural science, with which we seek to harmonise them', as does also Thomas Aquinas (*CD* III/1:64). And in his ebullient exposition of the creation of fish and birds, he censures the Church fathers when 'in their commentaries and sermons they try on the one hand to make use of all the natural science of their day and on the other to attach to its constituent parts the most diverse edifying and naturalistic allegorizings' (*CD* II/1:173). Should we therefore 'turn our backs resolutely on all scientific and pious considerations' (*ibid*.), not only when trying to listen properly to Genesis (which is fair enough) but also when, having listened, we have opportunity to improve the cultural diet of a society besotted with technological and mercantile enterprise, from our own diet of properly formed faith in the substance of this Christian doctrine of creation? It is with these questions in mind that I have looked again at the last 85 pages of the *Church Dogmatics*, III/1(§42), which speak of 'benefit' – benefit spelled out under thematic headings which declare that 'in the limits of its creatureliness, what God has created may *be* as it is actualized by him, and *be good* as it is justified by him' (*CD* III/1:330). Will further reflection, based on these refined abstractions, enable us to say something which evades H. A. L. Fisher's borrowed censure on 'letters of opium inscribed upon tablets of lead'?

In debate with Marcion, with 'modern pessimism' (Schopenhauer), and with possible modern 'optimism' (Leibniz), Barth draws out from the *articulus fidei* a beneficial certainty about a 'genuineness' in the world that we are empowered to appreciate – about its stability in *truth*; and about *goodness* intrinsic to its substance. He did not take the opportunity (which I think is there) to invite us also to reflect on *beauty*, encountered within what is otherwise its somewhat bleak natural context.[8] Theology may still rightly aim to provide a basis for the cultural critique of scientific enterprise and of ethico-political enterprise and of aesthetic enterprise on the part of human beings in society. Such theology might even find expression in a form sketched more than fifty years ago (and for the most part ignored) by one of our own most adult theologians, R. S. Franks, in *The Metaphysical Justification of Religion* – a justification glimpsed when the triad of fundamental values are given their place, together with the *holy*, in a quadrate constellation.[9]

We hear, from the Word of God, spoken of old to the fathers by his spokesmen in Israel – and in these last days by a Son whom he appointed the heir of all things, through whom also he created the world – that our existence, in and with the world about us, happens in the space and time established between an accomplished work of God (*creatio*) and its goal in an accomplished covenant of God with mankind to which all creation has relevance. This Word must prevail to correct the manifold lies in the soul which corrupt human culture – those deceptions in the highest recesses of the self from which the deceived person has the least power of delivering himself. Such deceptions are apt to enslave human beings, sometimes in Thrasymachean forms ('might is right') as in the laboratories of industrial-military complexes, or in spiritual forms developed in natural theology or philosophical speculation when claims are made for 'the Tao of Physics' (Fritjof Capra) or for the salvific wisdom of ecology. Can we learn again how to serve in the saving mission to be directed against involuntary possession by falsehood, but without lapsing into arbitrary dogmatism?

Barth's contribution to such learning, in *Church Dogmatics*, III/1, was, ostensibly, to let the Genesis sagas say what they have to say; and I have done no more than hint at what is distinctive in the theology that emerges therefrom, and at difficulties which inhere for us in the 'saga' form. What status can we give, for instance, to purported recollection of a lost Eden, to which the world about us is still related in varying degrees of approximation? Must we cultivate new respect for the resources of divination and poetry so evident in the construction of those sagas; and can we amplify them from resources of physics and metaphysics with greater perception than that attained by the authors of past *Hexaemera*? (The *Hexaemeron* form, incidentally, is not one to be recommended as a vehicle for this expression of *fides quaerens intellectum* in our present culture.) Perhaps, as the Creationism crudely resurgent among supporters of the present American administration seems to suggest, the whole programme is so riddled with cultural archaism that we no longer have the spirit to sustain it. Barth's challenge so to do is a matter for substantial celebration.

PART III
PHILOSOPHICAL THEOLOGY

4

No Other Foundation

One Englishman's Reading of *Church Dogmatics* Chapter v

COLIN GUNTON

I *The Shaking of the Foundations.*

For the most part and despite exceptions, the English find it difficult to come to terms with the theology of Karl Barth. A recent paper by Daniel Hardy identifies the strongly naturalistic bent of English thought as the chief culprit:

> ... English norms (sc. of knowledge) involve the use of naturalistic human knowledge as determinative of what can be believed. Employing these norms in interpreting Schleiermacher and Barth, however, makes them – and indeed most important theology – seem ... either to conflict with, or to stretch the bounds of, what is considered 'possible'.[1]

Naturalism's predominance brings it about that where Barth is concerned a frequent English reaction is one of puzzlement that someone should commit intellectual suicide in so spectacular a fashion. It is indeed difficult to take seriously one who appears to be hell-bent on intellectual self-destruction.

But it is also true that English naturalism is a variation, albeit a particularly dismal one, on a common Western tradition of rationalism. The dominance of ways of thinking created by the Enlightenment in recent times has made the appropriation of the work of a theologian like Barth doubly difficult, and the American Baptist theologian Bernard Ramm is surely right in seeing a major feature of Barth's programme to be an attempt to out-think that movement.[2] This paper takes its orientation from Ramm's suggestion. A first task, accordingly, is to examine the particular Enlightenment themes which provide the background for Barth's thought; against that background we shall then move to examine some of the features he shares with others who seek to develop alternative directions.

The first general feature of the Enlightenment tradition is its individualism. The model thinker is Descartes, the one who sits alone, attempting to decide in solitude what may and may not be dignified with the name of knowledge. One of Descartes' working assumptions was that his route of knowledge would be more secure if he threw off all that he had obtained from his teachers and accepted only that which commended itself to his naked intellect. Since his time that has been the norm: what I as an individual can or cannot demonstrate, albeit with the use of the appropriate rational methods and criteria. Today individualism is one of the things that all right-thinking people reject, but it is important to be aware that influential representatives of non-individualistic epistemology remain rare: we are not sure if we know what it really involves. That is particularly true of recent theology, marked as it is by the oft-lamented absence of ecclesiology. Alluding again to English lack of comprehension of Schleiermacher and Barth, Hardy comments that 'While both conceive their primary focus of attention as the Church's faith, the English understand this as *individual* faith found in members of the Church'.

The second feature is the Enlightenment's characteristic view of the relation of mind and reality. It is an epistemology of spatial distance, and has been depicted variously by its critics. For Rorty, it is characterized by its view of the mind as a kind of mirror reflecting only those parts or aspects of the world it is fitted to reflect, our 'Glassy Essence', deriving ultimately from Plato's *theoria*.[3] For Polanyi it is the idea of the godlike, disembodied spectator – a visual image again – with a bird's-eye view of what is happening 'below', rather like Aquinas's view of God's knowledge as the view of a landscape from a mountain (*Summa Theologiae* 1.14.3).[4] A particular *picture* is associated of how the subject of knowledge is related to the object: mind and thing confront each other statically, at a spatial distance from each other. The achievement of Berkeley – another thinker the English tend to misunderstand – was to attempt to replace that picture with another which attempts to make more sense of the relation of knower and known than that between inanimate object and intellectual subjects.[5]

The third feature of the modern tradition to which I want to allude is its foundationalism. This is the doctrine, which Ronald Thiemann's recent study has shown to be deeply engrained in recent theological thought, that there are certain fundamental truths, concepts or axioms, known intuitively, which must be shown to underlie any putative expression of 'objective' knowledge.[6] *Knowledge* is that which is built on the foundations; anything else is not 'real' knowledge. The quest for foundations is an almost universal feature of post-Enlightenment Western thought, with the result that it is very difficult for us to disentangle ourselves from it. There is a deepseated belief in the existence of an *intuitively* intellectual basis for all thought. There are differences from thinker to thinker in conceptions of what the foundations are – such as in the differences between the philosophies labelled rationalist and empiricist – but foundationalism was, until very recent times, all-pervasive nevertheless. There is a theological critique in Ronald Thiemann's recent work, in which it was argued that foundationalism vitiates the thought of three such diverse theologians as Locke, Schleiermacher and Torrance. Whether or not Thiemann is justified in all that he says, his book is another indication of the all-pervasiveness of the phenomenon.

In sum, it can be concluded that according to what was until very recently the almost unquestioned mainstream doctrine, knowledge is something (1) possessed by an *individual*, who (2) stands over against something which is conceived to be spatially distant. The spatial distance is bridged by either bringing the mind into conformity with the world ('realism') or the world into conformity with the mind ('idealism'). In either case (3), the intellectual bridge between the two is provided by the foundational axioms which are conceived to link the mind with the world. In the next section, we shall begin an exploration of whether and how far it is right to read Barth as a theologian who shared in the process of questioning the Enlightenment approach.

II *Towards an Alternative Foundation.*

In the remainder of this paper, I wish to argue two theses. The first is that Barth's theology is in part a conscious attempt to replace the Enlightenment project with something different. It was not altogether successful, for there are many remnants of the old syndrome, so that the achievement is something of a *tour de force*, plucked from the intellectual air by an act of intuitive genius and giving rise to half-justified accusations like that of Bonhoeffer that Barth's is a 'positivism of revelation'. The second is that the Enlightenment project has failed, because it does not register with the way we actually go about the world cognitively, and that therefore Barth's theology is to an extent justified by its fruits.

The defence of the first thesis depends in part upon some borrowings from the thought of Michael Polanyi. There has developed in recent years something of a Polanyi cult, accompanied, as is often the case with cults, by an equally disdainful refusal on the part of those who do not share in it, to take him seriously. I do not wish to share that cult, but to draw from him certain aids to reflection, and in particular, to begin with, a broad contrast between two fundamentally different approaches to knowledge, which can be called the critical and the post-critical. The former, as we have seen, has among its distinguishing features that it is an epistemology of spatial distance. In such an epistemology, the essence of knowledge is the proposition, in which the distant object is described in words which attempt to mirror what is there. The emphasis is on 'knowledge that' rather than knowledge by acquaintance.

In the Polanyian approach, the reverse is the case. The central metaphor here is that of 'indwelling'. The knower knows the world by indwelling body, tools, concepts and the like, which, by being known tacitly, become the bridge by which other parts of the world can be known. It is tempting to speculate that the origin of the metaphor – and it must be remembered that it is a metaphor, so that the limits of its explanatory power are recognized – is ultimately in the Fourth Gospel, where we find an extended use of the notion of knowledge by indwelling. (It is when this fact is overlooked that there is talk of a 'gnostic' bias in that gospel.) The Father and Son know each other by mutual and asymmetrical indwelling. Briefly to look forward to Barth, we can already here discern a theme emerging: for Barth, the fundamental reality of our being is our indwelling in Christ. But, to leave that on one side, the point for our purposes is that in place of an ontology of spatial distance, we find one of *acquaintance*. Knowledge is a relation of knower and known before it is propositional. Here there is a link to be seen with the famous Polanyian slogan: we know more than we can tell. Knowledge is something achieved by personal beings with the flexibility to adapt themselves to the world around and to express part – but only a part – of the relationship conceptually.

The crucial presupposition of such a conception of knowledge is that the relationship is prior to any conceptual expression of it. It is therefore not possible to justify the relationship *a priori*. You cannot prove that you have it before you come to speak about it. According to Polanyi, all knowing is a form of faith seeking understanding: faith in his case meaning a committed orientation to and indwelling within the world and our language. There is no other route to knowledge. It must be stressed that what is being attempted here is not a proof of the position being taken, although there is surprising support for something of the kind in recent philosophy.[7] Rather, a framework is being constructed with the help of which Barth's distinctive theological epistemology can be approached.

The concept of knowledge as a relationship of indwelling in

a specific subject matter has a number of important consequences. In the first place, it is subversive of all epistemologies of spatial distance because it presupposes that the world is not distant. We live in it, and in our words and concepts as part of it. Second, it is subversive of the choice between realism and idealism as the Enlightenment tradition presents and attempts to compel it, because it presupposes on the one hand that the world is the kind of reality that can be known (that is to say, related to); and on the other that we are the kind of beings that indwell the world rationally. Again, to indicate in advance that such a consideration is not irrelevant to the interpretation of Barth it is only sufficient to refer to his important paper from 1929, the time when he was developing his mature theological method, 'Schicksal und Idee in der Theologie'.[8] Here Barth is quite explicit that theology must take elements of truth from both realism and idealism if it is to come to terms with the actual relation of the knower to God.

Third, the Polanyian conception of knowledge in terms of indwelling presupposes at once the actuality and limits of propositional knowledge. Knowledge is not as such propositional; but propositions are a way in which to express the articulate level of our knowledge. By contrast, the Enlightenment has hoodwinked us into believing that there are two classes of proposition, those adequate to the world – because they are justified according to the canons of the foundational axioms – and everything else. In face of this increasingly discredited view, a Polanyian theory claims both the success and the relative inadequacy of all conceptual expression. Fourth, and as a development of the third point, a post-critical conception of knowledge liberates us for an appreciation of the diversity of possible forms of knowledge which derive from the diversity and variety of forms of relationship. Not all relationships are the same, and therefore different ones generate different forms of articulate expression. (That is, of course, another anti-foundationalist point.)

Some of the differences can be brought to mind if we consider the different measures of reciprocity to be found in human cognitive activity. At one extreme, we find relationships in which there is minimal reciprocity, for instance a laboratory experiment upon a chemical. Even that, however, does not reduce the object of knowledge to pure passivity if it is to create conditions in which nature can, so to speak, give up her secrets to the enquiring mind. In other words, there is rarely if ever a time when the knower is purely active, the object entirely passive. There is a measure of reciprocity even there, and we can, without mere anthropomorphism, speak of asking questions of nature.[9] A good way further along the spectrum, in the case of our knowledge of other people, a greater, perhaps a complete, reciprocity, is required. People, unlike some things, cannot be compelled to give up knowledge of themselves, at least so long as we treat them as persons and not things. Moreover, we are often alienated from our neighbour by suspicion, fear, guilt, pride and the rest, so that we sometimes cannot know them at all, repentance and forgiveness apart. The knowledge of our neighbour is a gift, to be given and received freely and in full reciprocity if it is to be worthy of the name. The implications of this for theology are immense if we conceive it as taking shape in personal relations or sets of relations, and here Polanyi is notoriously weak, for he failed to extend to theological knowing the insights he had developed elsewhere. But there is still one more lesson we can learn from him.

Something has already been made of the fact that a major feature of Enlightenment thought is its individualism. What alternative does the post-critical thesis have to offer? It is the doctrine that without a community – its traditions, its language, its structures of authority – there can be no knowledge. Without, that is to say, other people in our present and past, without a common language, there can be no articulate knowledge. Knowledge is not only personal, but takes form in interpersonal relationships. The fact is demonstrated by Polanyi in the section of *Personal Knowledge* entitled 'Conviviality', but is now increasingly a feature of other writing. The conclusion, then, is that in the absence of intuited intellectual *foundations* built, so to speak, into the structures of rationality, we have another foundation: the communities, for example, of science or of literary interpretation. It is in and through communities of persons that knowledge becomes possible and takes form. The community is in that respect the only foundation, because it is the matrix within which, as a matter of fact, our cognitive enterprises become possible.

III *Karl Barth:* Coram Deo

On the face of it, and sometimes somewhat deeper, Barth's epistemology is but a repetition of the modern syndrome which was charted in the first section of the paper. Ronald Thiemann rightly sees that the epistemology of the *Commentary on Romans* bears the marks of the modern tradition. First, there is the imagery of spatial *distance*: 'God is transcendent insofar as he stands outside of or on the boundary of ordinary human existence'.[10] Second, this spatial transcendence carries with it a particular epistemology:

> A position which stresses both God's sovereign transcendence and his knowability is hard pressed to give an account of how we can come to know such a God. Barth's solution . . . is to grant to God's Spirit the mediating power to bring divine object and human subject together. The Spirit of God dwells within the believing interpreter and bestows the capacity to know the unknowable.[11]

The epistemology of the *Commentary on Romans* is an epistemology of spatial distance: to know God is to be enabled, by means of a timeless theophany and the agency of the Spirit as *deus ex machina* to cross from ignorance to knowledge.

If we are to understand the programme of Barth's mature work we must realize that, whether or not his later account of the matter uses the benefit of hindsight, the concept of transcendence was at this early stage programmatic or therapeutic rather than theoretical, an attempt 'to turn the rudder to an angle of exactly 180 degrees.'[12] As Steven Smith has written, 'Had the "Wholly Other" been a doctrine of God, rather than a device for placing theology in the right position before God, Barth could not have looked back on his *Romans* more than thirty years later with so much approval.' Similarly, it would be wrong to view 'Barth's theology as a philosophy in disguise, as a preoccupation with the abstract transcendence beyond man's power of knowing. . .'[13] The development from the dialectics of the early Barth to the conception in the book on Anselm of theology as faith seeking understanding has often been charted. Accordingly, if the Anselm book really was as important as Barth repeatedly says it was for his understanding of theological method, we must expect to find after it an emerging conception which builds upon and transcends the therapeutic dialectics of the 1920s. Something of what it became will come to light if, in the light of the discussion of personal knowledge in the previous section, we examine some of the elements of the treatment of the knowledge of God in *Church Dogmatics* II/1.

For Barth, despite the frequent assertions or at least suggestions to the contrary in the secondary literature, human knowledge of God is not the conditioned reflex of the automaton. It is free personal action in relation, deriving from an indwelling in Christ and taking the form of thanksgiving, awe and the ordered employment of human concepts. Let me begin with some of the evidence that he sees theological knowledge as a genuinely human action. He speaks, for example of 'the movement, the human action which we call the knowledge of God' (*CD* II/1: 204); in it 'we are definitely active as the receivers of images and creators of counter-images' (*CD* II/1:182). The stress is on the action rather than the results or some completed body of propositions: something very like what we have seen to be in a Polanyian epistemology the limits of our conceptual articulations of knowledge. 'Our viewing and conceiving of God and our speaking of Him will never be a completed work showing definitive results . . .' (*CD* II/1:208). In this respect, Barth uses language which is quite startling in its claims for the extent of the human side of the enterprise: 'In and by this way man comes to stand before God, in a situation in which he can perceive and consider and conceive God . . .' (*CD* II/1:31f., cf p. 194: 'a real human viewing and conceiving').

The passages cited so far are, of course, taken out of context, always a dangerous procedure and particularly dangerous in this case. But they serve to set the scene as well as to overturn some misconceptions. Barth intends to set before us a conception of the knowledge of a personal God by free and thinking persons. The talk is of active human knowledge in the context of a relationship, one indeed in which there is a measure of reciprocity. 'There is . . . a reciprocity of relationship between [God] and these objects. Man . . . can therefore perceive and consider and conceive God . . .' (*CD* II/1:58). Again, the words are carefully extracted, but they make the point that here is personal knowledge, knowledge taking shape in a particular relationship: 'the event between God and man which we call the knowledge of God' (*CD* II/11:179).

But, inevitably, it is an asymmetrical reciprocity. How could it be otherwise? We have seen that there can be no true knowledge of people if they choose to hide themselves from us or if we are alienated from them. Unless you reveal yourself to me, I shall not know you. Without revelation, there is no knowledge, not only of God but, I believe, of anything at all. Yet to introduce the topic of revelation in a discussion of Barth can hide more than it reveals. There are a number of reasons for this. The first is that concentration on the undoubtedly high noetic content of Barth's theology can obscure other important features, without whose inclusion we shall not see the whole. Even in the part volume with some claim to be the one most dominated by noetic considerations (*CD* IV/3), Barth is insistent that, even when speaking of the knowledge of God, we are in the realm of personal relationships rather than being concerned with the conveying of information. We recall that in personal knowledge, knowledge by acquaintance is primary, propositional expression secondary:

> We cannot impress upon ourselves too strongly that in the language of the Bible knowledge . . . does not mean the acquisition of neutral information, which can be expressed in statements, principles and systems, concerning a being which confronts man, nor does it mean entry into passive contemplation of a being which exists beyond the phenomenal world. What it really means is the process or history in which man, certainly observing and thinking, using his senses, intelligence and imagination, but also his will, action and 'heart', and therefore as whole man, becomes aware of another history . . . (*CD* IV/3:183).

The second reason for wanting to give minimal attention to Barth's numerous appeals to revelation is that we shall be tempted to take as the whole what it undoubtedly is in part, an attempt to cross an otherwise uncrossable epistemological gulf, what Thiemann has called 'the epistemological bridging of a spatial gap.'[14] If we are to understand Barth's theology, and in particular its movement beyond familiar epistemologies, it will profit us to pay attention to the features of his thought which revise the theology of the *Commentary on Romans*.

In order to know God, we must be where he makes himself known. For Barth, that is in Jesus Christ according to the witness of the prophets and apostles. The eternal God's presence to the world in time is what makes knowledge of him actual. Again, we must be careful. As Robert Jenson long ago pointed out, there is in Barth a tendency to conceive Jesus Christ as a timeless metaphysical idea.[15] The interesting features of Barth's thought, however, are those which transcend this relic of Augustine's neoplatonism. First, there is the claim that the form of knowledge corresponds to the personal relationship in which it takes shape. As I have suggested, our knowledge of each other depends on the way in which we are or are not able and prepared to make outselves known. Barth rightly sees that the shape of our knowledge of God must correspond to the covenantal relationship in which we stand. We are, as a matter of fact, those who are elect in Christ for fellowship with God but wilfully deny our election. The knowledge of God, then, can become actual only as that fellowship with God is realized and restored by atonement. This consideration is a real if much underplayed feature of Chapter v of the *Church Dogmatics*. But the fact that there is too much stress on revelation, too little on reconciliation, does not invalidate the general point:

> Because God forgives us our sins we know that we need forgiveness, and that we are sinners. And because God views and conceives Himself in His Word we know that He is not viewable and conceivable in any other way . . . (*CD* II/1:192).

Knowledge must take shape in the actual relationship.

Similarly, it has been almost a truism for Christian theology that relationship with God, especially for the sinner, comes as the free gift of the Holy Spirit. If *knowledge* is one aspect of the actual relationship with God, then knowledge too must be the gift of the Spirit, as the theologies of both Paul and John abundantly illustrate. Again that is a prominent, if in some ways underplayed, feature of Barth's argument: 'it is the work of the Holy Spirit that the eternal presence of the reconciliation in Jesus Christ has in us this temporal form, the form of faith, which believes this truth' (*CD* I/1:159, cf p. 200). For Barth, as for Kierkegaard, *faith* is the appropriate word to use in giving expression to the kind of relationship we have with God. Unlike Kierkegaard, however, he did not wish to deny that it is also knowledge. As for Polanyi, so for Barth faith *is* a kind of knowledge, the only form that this particular kind of knowledge can take. But although, given the fact that this is the knowledge of the creating, reconciling and redeeming God, it is a unique kind of knowledge, it is not without continuity with other forms of human knowing. Barth is insistent on that also: the Spirit does not override but perfects nature. Not only does this relationship make legitimate the use of human words in theology (see *e.g. CD* II/1:223ff), but also, 'The fact that it has God not only for its object but also as its origin . . . does not mean either the abrogation, abolition or alteration of human cognition as such, and therefore of its formal and technical characteristics as human cognition', (*CD* II/1:181). The knowledge of God, then, and the theological method flowing from it, is understood by Barth to be a form of personal relation, that between the creator and his erring but forgiven creatures. It is 'a positive relationship, *i.e.*, one in which there exists a real fellowship between the knower and his knowing on the one hand and the known on the other' (*CD* II/1:224). It is the kind of personal knowledge legitimated by this particular relationship.

A second feature of Barth's treatment is that he takes some, though again a somewhat underplayed, account of the communal matrix in which theology takes form. In one respect, he by no means underplays the matter, for there can be few theologians who have taken so seriously the requirement to listen carefully to other voices in the tradition, and to include in the conversation many of the unbelieving voices that recent centuries have witnessed. One way of reading Barth's theology is as a conversation, albeit at times rather one-sided, with a broad tradition of thought of many kinds:

> . . . we cannot be in the Church without taking as much responsibility for the theology of the past as for the theology of our present. Augustine, Thomas Aquinas, Luther, Schleiermacher and all the rest are not dead, but living. They still speak and demand a hearing as living voices, as surely as we know that they and we belong together in the Church.[16]

We may instructively refer again, in contrast, to Daniel Hardy's characterization of the typical English approach to theology. 'In England, singular figures from the past do not – as persons – normally have a "lasting" influence on their successors, in the sense that they can be considered to have an importance beyond their time.' Despite some exceptions, 'the more common attitude is neatly summarized, "Who do these dead men think they are?"'[17]

Similarly, it is part of Barth's genius to have realized that in an era of the shaking of the foundations, Christian theology can take place only as the theology of a community. The movement from *Christian* to *Church* Dogmatics signals the movement from the epistemology of the *Commentary on Romans* to that which we are now exploring. The notion that theology is based in the community is present in *Church Dogmatics*, II/1, though in rather muted form. 'All speaking and hearing in the Church of Jesus Christ entirely rests upon and is connected with the fact that God is known in the Church of Jesus Christ; that is to say, that this Subject is objectively present to the speakers and hearers, so that man in the Church really stands before God' (*CD* II/1:3). Barth's conception of theology as serving the proclamation of the Church, for all its inadequacies, must first be seen as a step forward if its significance is to be appreciated. When John Howard Yoder writes that 'The church precedes the world epistemologically'[18], he is making not a Barthian remark so much as one made possible because Barth has been.

But that leads to a problem, and to a third area of discussion. How, on such an account, do we avoid the charge of arbitrariness, of sheer assertion? To a certain extent, the objection has been met already: if the language is the language of a community, extended in both time and space, then that is the only *a priori* justification it requires. What other foundation should there be than that laid by the prophets and apostles? And yet it is necessary to face the question from the other end also. Given that the language is the speech of a community, is there no way of providing some account of why we think we are talking about something rather than simply projecting from uncertain experience? Barth rightly rejects appeals to anything outside the theological circle as a ground for that circle. That would be to return to foundationalism. If that is not required in other disciplines, why should it be necessary here? (That is not, of course, the way Barth put or would want to put the matter.) Moreover, if this knowledge takes the form of faith, what right have we to ask for guarantees deriving from outside faith (*CD* II/1: 247ff.). Despite this, however, it is right also to ask for a measure of *a posteriori* justification. A theology must be judged by its content, if not by appeal to foundations outside it.

At this stage, I want to take from Thiemann another point, that in theology, there can be *a posteriori* assessment of a cumulative or holistic kind wherein appeal is made to different but overlapping considerations.[19] Similarly, 'the theologian asks' writes Barth, paraphrasing Anselm, 'to what extent is reality as the Christian believes it to be?'[20] There are many possible ways in which that question and the matter of the holistic assessment of a theology may be approached. It may be thought that Barth has employed too few forms of argument in support of his contentions, while most modern theology in its desperation seeks too many. But there are two areas where his theology is matchless in its depth and richness.

To approach the first, we must keep before our eyes the fact that Barth is a disciple of Anselm, and it is as a relentless quest for the *perfection* of God that his positive contribution to theological epistemology must be assessed. Both the intellectual brilliance and the difficulty of Barth's theology derive from the way in which concept is piled upon concept in an attempt to allow the truth, goodness and beauty of God to take form in rational human language. There is no coming to terms with Barth's theology without the taking of immense pains to 'think after' it.

There is in Chapter v of the *Church Dogmatics* a number of places where Barth's development of concepts can be illustrated. One is the way in which the concept of the hiddenness of God is treated. For Barth this is not, as it has often been in the tradition, a mere limiting concept, that which emerges when we project into God our inability to know him. Because God is actually known in the community, our conceptuality must be controlled by our knowledge, and not made a projection of human inability to know God. For this reason, Barth builds upon a hint of Anselm's that the task of theology is *rationabiliter comprehendere (Deum) incomprehensible esse* (*Monologion 64*, cited *CD* II/1:185) to argue that God's hiddenness is not a function of his *distance* from us, for that would be to return to precisely that concept of spatial transcendence which he has been trying to avoid, but must be understood ontologically in terms of his judgement and grace (*CD* II/1:191f). It is then the *ontological* rather than *spatial* otherness of God which comes to expression in our awareness of the asymmetrical personal relationship between creator and creature.[21] It is not being claimed that Barth is necessarily right in all he says here: the point is that he does enable us to examine the arguments and the conversation with the tradition and so to make some kind of assessment of whether his is an appropriate development of the content of Christian talk of God.

The second way in which Barth offers to us his theology for an *a posteriori* assessment of its content is found in his concern to give responsible conceptual expression to the object of theology: to give reasons why it is God that we know and not some idol or idea of our own constructing. We have seen that in the dialectics of the *Commentary on Romans* the Holy Spirit tended to be treated as the means of crossing theologically an otherwise unbridgeable epistemological gulf. We have seen also that for Barth God is known only through the Spirit. What has changed? Much in every way. There, it was a means to claim a kind of knowledge of the intrinsically unknowable; here it is the opposite, a means to knowledge of Him who is knowable in himself. Some account has been given in the secondary literature, particularly by Jüngel,[22] of the way in which Barth's trinitarian doctrine is a means of giving appropriate expression to the personal being of God, developing a conceptuality which will allow him to be at once objectively real while truly free and personal. Barth is himself aware that he is seeking to avoid both the Scylla and Charybdis of contemporary epistemology: 'We do not say all that so as to commend some sort of realism or objectivism' (*CD* II/1:13). Rather, the programme is to give a basis in God's trinitarian objectivity to himself for his personal knowability by us. It is because God is knowable in and to himself in the life of the Trinity that he can become object to us, though object only in the ways so carefully delimited in the way we have charted. There is therefore a direct parallel between the personal knowledge of the world which was outlined in section II of this paper and the personal knowledge of God which is the theme of the *Church Dogmatics*. Both of them attempt to transcend realism and objectivism in the received sense, because their programmes are both designed to transcend the old dualisms. This means that in Barth's theology it is not the intention that the Holy Spirit should function as the means to cross an otherwise unbridgeable epistemological gulf, though there is as a matter of fact a personal gulf which cannot be crossed without him. That gulf, however, has already been crossed in Christ, and, indeed, in God's eternal election of all humankind. The Holy Spirit gives what is there to be given because God becomes 'an object . . . in such a way that in His objectivity He bestows . . . by the Holy Spirit the light of the clarity that He is God . . .' (*CD* II/1:12).

IV Some Assessments

It is when we examine the trinitarian dimensions of Barth's theology that we find at once his greatest strengths and weaknesses. They are the key to his theology as a whole. Here, however, we shall centre attention on them as they bear upon the epistemological stance that Barth has taken. In it there are, on the one hand, the features I have already reviewed: a brilliant awareness of the requirements of a theological epistemology and an accompanying movement out of the shadow of the Enlightenment. In place of the static, propositionalist, individualist and foundationalist, we have a conception of knowledge which seeks to be dynamic, personal and communal. On the other hand, it cannot be denied that some of the development does have an air of unargued assertion. There are two main reasons for this, and, therefore, two main places where there are questions to be asked. The first is to be found in the contrast Barth makes between the knowledge of God and of other objects. Here he is strangely Kantian. 'We have all other objects as they are determined by the pre-arranged disposition and pre-arranged mode of our own existence' (*CD* II/1:21). But do we? The wider the gulf is made between theological and non-theological knowing, the more will theology appear, especially under modern conditions, to be no more than a tilting at epistemological windmills. Can one be an anti-Kantian in theology and a Kantian elsewhere without intellectual schizophrenia and an appearance of theological special pleading? It would be a mistake to build too much on that one perhaps careless statement, particularly in view of the fact that the later Barth appears to have been more careful.[23] But the question remains whether Barth would have profited more if he had spent less time polemicizing against positions he believed to be invalid, more on considering in greater depth the mutual light thrown by theological and non-theological epistemology on each other. The very strength of Barth's theology, its singlemindedly *theological* character, can become its greatest weakness.

The second problem is to be found in the doctrine of God itself. Much has been made in recent discussion, especially by Moltmann and Pannenberg[24], of the modalist tendencies of Barth's trinity. While their account is badly one-sided because it fails to take due account of Barth's critical revisions of western trinitarianism, it does sometimes appear as though Barth is suggesting that God is more of a thrice-repeated I than one whose being is constituted by the communion of Father, Son and Spirit. Furthermore, there are times when the Holy Spirit appears to exist as no more than the means of the Father's and Son's knowledge of each other, or even to drop out of the transaction:

> In and for Himself He is I, the eternal, original and incomparable I . . . God is object in Himself and for Himself: in the indivisible unity of the knowledge of the Father by the Son and the Son by the Father, and therefore in his eternal and irrevocable subjectivity (*CD* II/1:57).[25]

I do not wish to join the speculation on the Hegelian or other provenance of this modalist tendency, so much as to remark briefly on its impact on our topic. A God whose being consists in the communion of the three persons – and here readers of John Zizioulas' *Being as Communion*[26] will recognize the basis of what is here being developed – will provide a foundation for a conception of theology which is truly the work of a community. There is very little actual pneumatological or ecclesiological content in Barth's major treatment of theological epistemology, and that must remain a serious weakness. Individualism is not entirely vanquished. There is, moreover, an element of the theological virtuoso about Barth, despite his warnings about the danger in the case of Schleiermacher.[27]

However, that is not the note on which to end. What we have seen in the parts of Barth's work which have been called upon is the great distance he travelled in the direction of a theological epistemology with which to break the stranglehold of the Enlightenment on modern culture. In face of the division of the intellectual world into 'reason' and 'faith', and of the playing of the one against the other, he has begun to develop a post-critical epistemology of faith seeking understanding, learned from Anselm but shaped for modern theological conditions. The original title I considered for this paper was something like, 'A move in the right direction'. I hope that I have shown that to use such a title would be greatly to underestimate the distance which was travelled by one who has done so much to enable the church to develop the kind of theology that is needed now that Christendom is no more.

5

Karl Barth's Hermeneutics

WERNER G. JEANROND

Introduction

Before we analyse Karl Barth's contribution to theological hermeneutics we might wish to gain clarity about what we mean by the term 'hermeneutics'. 'Hermeneutics' has become one of the key-words in 20th century intellectual discourse. It is almost impossible to discuss any philosophical or theological topic today without at least referring to implicit or explicit hermeneutics at work; and every theologian of importance, and thus worthy of discussion and celebration, is bound to be assessed partly in terms of his or her contribution to the field of hermeneutics. On the one hand, I feel slightly pretentious in taking part in such a fashion, yet on the other hand, I am convinced that the question of hermeneutics is of great importance for all critical theological thinking.

However, there are dangers with every fashion, particularly the always increasing terminological confusion. Babylon has hit even hermeneutical debates! I see four major areas of confusion in the current usage of the word 'hermeneutics'. First, many people confuse hermeneutics with its subject matter. But hermeneutics means 'theory of interpretation' and not 'interpretation' itself. Hence theological hermeneutics is not identical with theology, but reflects upon procedures, methods and implications of the understanding of texts in theology. Secondly, some people confuse the terms 'epistemology' and 'hermeneutics'. Of course, all hermeneutics have to do with epistemology, yet it would be wrong to say that the two are identical. The original purpose of hermeneutics is to reflect upon the understanding of human utterances in verbal or artistic language, that is upon the understanding of texts and works of art, whereas epistemology is concerned with the act of knowing in general. Thirdly, some are unclear about the boundaries of hermeneutics. They often mix up what I would like to call 'macro-hermeneutics' and 'micro-hermeneutics'. 'Macro-hermeneutics' explore human understanding in general in the light of the interpretation of texts; 'micro-hermeneutics' explore the acts and possibilities of text-interpretation in particular and it avoids any quick ontologizing. It goes the long route of interpretation, to use a dictum by Paul Ricoeur to which we shall come back later.[1] Fourthly, some people expect hermeneutical reflection to free them from the ambiguous and often paradoxical situation of human existence which it has just disclosed. These have misunderstood that the liberation which results from our insights into the possibilities and limitations of text-interpretation can only be a liberation *for* further and possibly new acts of understanding and not a liberation *from* such activity.

In view of these confusions I would like to propose that we understand by 'hermeneutics,' first of all, the reflection upon the conditions and possible methods of the human understanding of *texts*.

The answer to the question why theology has to deal with hermeneutics and why it has to enter the contemporary debates on hermeneutics is trivial: Christian theology is by nature concerned with the interpretation of texts. The texts of the Hebrew Scriptures and the New Testament, and the texts produced by the church, such as confessional and organizational statements, need to be interpreted again and again by every generation of Christians. While it is obvious *that* theology is by nature hermeneutical, it is less clear *which* theory of interpretation is the most adequate for theology. How shall we interpret our texts? To what extent do our subjectivity, our prejudices and our expectations condition or even determine the act of reading, and to what extent do we allow the text to challenge our ways of reading? How can we describe most accurately the relationship between text and reading? Is there always only one and the same sense of a particular text to be disclosed by the reader, or are we confronted with the possibility of a pluralism of legitimate interpretations of the same text? Does such a pluralism threaten a community of readers such as the Christian church which sees its origin and shape largely determined by the understanding of a particular set of texts?

That theology needs some theory of interpretation is an old insight, and we all know that theologians throughout the history of the Christian church have tried to develop adequate theories of interpretation. All theologians were more or less aware that they moved within a hermeneutical circle when they read their texts: they always had already some idea of the sense of the whole text which was then either modified, validated or corrected in the act of reading itself. And, more recently, it was Martin Heidegger who reminded us anew that we should not try to escape from or resist this hermeneutical circle in which we think, rather we should accept it consciously as the always given condition of all human understanding. 'What is decisive is not to get out of the circle but to come into it in the right way'.[2] Heidegger's insight means for us Christian theologians that we should not regret the textual foundation of theology, rather we should accept our hermeneutical condition and do our micro-hermeneutical task first – that is, the interpretation of our texts – before we move on to our macro-hermeneutical task – that is, the exploration of the understanding of our universe in the light of God's revelation in history. Only if we critically and self-critically develop our theory of interpretation, can we hope to reach a more appropriate theological understanding of God's revelation and of his relationship to us and the world.

We shall pursue our study of Karl Barth's hermeneutics within the context of this search for an adequate theory of theological text-interpretation.

I shall begin with a brief indication of the major sources for our study. Then I shall present an outline of Barth's hermeneutical reflections. Thirdly, I shall examine his hermeneutical proposal with critical eyes. And finally, I shall assess

Barth's hermeneutics in the context of the continuing debate on hermeneutics.

1 *Context and Development of Barth's Hermeneutics*

The life of Karl Barth is well documented and generally well known. Eberhard Busch, Eberhard Jüngel and others have provided us with sufficient biographical details[3], and the current German edition of Barth's complete works[4] allows us many insights into his concerns and his search for new and more adequate ways of proclaiming the Word of God.

The young pastor in Safenwil was faced with the task of preaching the Word of God to his congregation. This effort directed his attention in a fresh way to the texts of the Bible. This was to remain the context for Barth's life-long theological reflection: his rediscovery of the biblical texts and his interpretation of these texts for his troubled times.[5] Among the first fruits of this rediscovery were his talk, 'The Strange New World in the Bible,'[6] and, of course, the two editions of his commentary on Paul's letter to the Romans[7] Moreover, all the volumes of his *Church Dogmatics* were written with this same intention: to serve the church in its proclamation of God's Word. Barth the Professor always remained faithful to the concerns of Barth the Pastor: his academic theology deals with the practical task of responsible preaching. His theory was always to be a theory for the praxis of the Church. Of course, the university teacher gained a greater awareness of the heritage of his Reformed Tradition, especially of the powerful scriptural emphasis of the Reformers. Yet, the exploration of the background of the Reformed Church did not add a new qualitative dimension to his theological programme. Barth's task was from the beginning, and remained thereafter, 'evangelical theology'.[8]

At various places in his opus Barth discusses this practical task of biblical interpretation in a more theoretical way. In our analysis we shall concentrate mainly on such theoretical statements in both parts of Volume I of his *Church Dogmatics*, *i.e.* the prolegomena for a church dogmatics, where he treats the hermeneutical problems in greater detail.⁹ But we shall also consult his *Epistle to the Romans*, especially the various prefaces,¹⁰ and we shall look at the dialogue with his life-long friend Rudolf Bultmann, which gave rise to various discussions of hermeneutical problems.¹¹

In this essay I do not wish to provide yet another discussion of Barth's theological journey, from his student experiences in the German tradition of Liberal Theology to his rejection of this tradition in the light of his discovery of the biblical God. Rather I would like to examine and assess more systematically the lasting hermeneutical presuppositions of Barth's theological work.

II *Proper Hermeneutics According to Barth*

The hermeneutical question arises for Barth not from a mere methodological concern which could lead to an adequate method of theological thinking, rather it entails the ultimate material question of theology, namely: Who is God and who am I? Thus, Barth's hermeneutics is not an introductory reflection before actual theology begins. It is part of theology proper and, thus, part of dogmatics. Therefore Barth begins his *Church Dogmatics* with the hermeneutical-theological question: What is the Word of God and who am I in relationship to God's Word? The hermeneutical question is for Barth the question of how to talk adequately about God's revelation in history (*CD* I/1: 187ff.).

Barth's particular revelation–hermeneutics can be best understood if compared with Rudolf Bultmann's approach to hermeneutics.¹² Bultmann searched for an adequate description of the human situation in which the biblical texts are allowed to speak today and in which these texts confront the individual human existence. Thus, he attempted to clarify the formal (*i.e.* linguistic, cultural, geographic etc.) and perspectival conditions (*Voverständisse*) of the process of biblical interpretation. He insisted that there cannot be an understanding of these texts without such particular presuppositions. Therefore he suggested, following Heidegger's recommendation, that the reader must recognize these conditions in order to become better aware of the various obstacles in his/her way of reading these texts.[13] However, Bultmann, like Barth, believed that the final understanding, the ultimate appropriation of God's Word in Jesus Christ by the reader is in fact God's own achievement in the reader. Yet Bultmann sees God at work in the human process of interpreting the biblical kerygma.[14]

Barth rejects Bultmann's hermeneutical approach to the biblical texts. He sees Bultmann as a victim of philosophical and other decisions which can lead to the illusion that any human method of interpreting the Bible could be sufficiently qualified to grasp God's revelation. God must never become the object of our methods, of our hermeneutics, our interpretations.[15] For Barth, God must always remain the subject who interprets us (*CD* I/1:295f.).[16] As God speaks in history, God interprets history. According to this order, the human activity called for here is not an appropriation of the Word of God, but a way of corresponding best to it while submitting to interpretation by it. Thus, 'revelation is not a predicate of history, but history is a predicate of revelation' (*CD* I/2:58).

Already in the various prefaces to his *Epistle to the Romans*, Barth had described our relationship to the biblical texts with the old Germanic term 'Treue'.[17] This faithfulness to the text does not exclude a critical awareness of the general relativity of all human words, even the Pauline ones. Here Barth and Bultmann could agree.[18] Yet Barth's concern is not limited to a detailed historical and exegetical study of words, sentences or concepts. Rather he aims at bringing to light the subject matter of the text. Therefore he demands that the historical-critical exegetes should be more critical[19] in order to be able to see what the subject matter of this text really is and demands from us. According to Barth the historical-critical exegetes are too modest in their hermeneutical efforts.[20] Barth sees the ultimate theme of biblical texts as follows:

> God is in heaven and you on earth. *This* God's relationship to *this* man, *this* man's relationship to *this* God is for me the theme of the Bible and the sum of philosophy at once.[21]

Barth's hermeneutics begin where Bultmann's hermeneutics might eventually lead to, namely with the recognition of God's revelation in history. Barth understands the Bible as witness to God's freely given revelation, But Bultmann tries to analyse the process of human understanding first. Barth's hermeneutics is material, Bultmann's formal. Barth rejects the imposition, as he sees it, of formal hermeneutical principles on the human appreciation of God's revelation; Bultmann rejects the material imposition, as he sees it, of a particular theological dogmatics on every effort to begin the process of understanding.[22] To use the distinction introduced earlier in this essay Barth starts with a macro-hermeneutics, Bultmann with a micro-hermeneutics which Barth rejects as too modest.

For Barth, an appropriate reading of the Bible must avoid engaging in human talking, *eisegesis*. Rather, the interpreter should listen to the human words of the Bible through which God's word *might* reveal itself.

> God's revelation in the human word of Holy Scripture not only wants but can make itself said and heard. (*CD* I/1:471)

But how does Barth know that God's revelation can and does make itself heard through the mediate and never immediate witness of these texts?[23] He answers:

> We believe in and with the Church that Holy Scripture as the original and legitimate witness of divine revelation is itself the Word of God. (*CD* I/2:502).

This faith must precede our exegesis and our theological reflection. Therefore, Barth can say that theology is always under the Bible.

When the Scriptures do become for us the Word of God, God's revelation, then this is itself, according to Barth, a miraculous event of God's freedom. It can only be accepted in faith (*CD* I/2:506). Outside this faith and the Word which has called for faith there is no firm ground. Barth condemns that biblicism which wrongly identifies the letter and spirit of the text (*CD* I/2:506–12). The Bible is not infallible, it is a human book, yet a book which witnesses to God's transcending Word. The presence of the Word of God transforms the reality of the book, but this transformation does not mean that it is by the power of the book that revelation actually happens. The authority of the Bible is that this revelation can happen, but the event of revelation is God's free activity and not the Bible's. Barth supports this insight with his doctrine of the Holy Spirit: 'The witness of Holy Scripture is therefore the witness of the Holy Spirit' (*CD* I/2:538).

The only appropriate response to the event of revelation is obedience (*CD* I/2:543). And the church as the community under the Word of God must therefore be a church of obedience (*CD* I/2:575f.).

Barth underlines the written nature of the Bible; because of it the Bible can continue to resist all efforts of domestication and distortion. So the Bible's openness and potential for reformation of the church is protected (*CD* I/2:583ff.).

The freedom under the Word of God is the freedom of all Christians. All Christians are invited to participate in the explanation of the biblical texts. Yet all Christians must accept the fundamental rule for all appropriate explanation of the Bible:

> the freely performed act of subordinating all human concepts (*Vorstellungen*), ideas and convictions to the witness of revelation supplied to us in Scripture. (*CD* I/2:715)

Thus, the basic mode of biblical interpretation for Barth is subordination. Barth qualifies this rule further when he says that subordination does not mean disposal and destruction. Rather it

> presupposes that that which is subordinated is and remains present as such. However, subordination means *Hintanstellung*, discipleship, flexibility of the subordinated to the superior.[24]

Subordination and obedience are the key terms which Barth

uses in order to clarify the absolute priority of Scripture over against all of our emotions, axioms, systems, philosophies etc. No method of interpretation, no special hermeneutics could ever disclose God's revelation. Therefore, the only remaining response for the reader of the Bible is obedience and the willingness to let the Bible interpret him or herself, to let the holy Spirit speak the word of judgment about the reader through the text.

The reason for this fundamental rule for the interpretation of Scripture Barth finds in the content of Scripture.

> The content of the Bible, and the object of its witness, is Jesus Christ as the name of the God who deals graciously with man the sinner. (*CD* I/2:720)

For Barth the recognition of this content excludes all autonomous activities of our own thinking.

> the testimony of the Bible . . . and the autonomy of our own world of thought is an impossible hermeneutic programme. (*CD* I/2:721)

This principal rule also determines the three practical dimensions which Barth now recommends for the detailed explanation of the biblical texts:

1) *Observation* aims at the literary and historical presentation of the structure and sense of the text (*CD* I/2:722ff.).

2) *Reflection* aims at thinking along with the text and assessing the text (*CD* I/2:727ff.). Here Barth agrees that no reader can think along with the text without certain hermeneutical keys. The crucial point here for Barth is not that we do approach the text with certain modes of thought (*Denkweisen*) or even philosophies, but that these philosophies are only of an experimental nature, and that they must not determine our reading.

> I shall have to bear in mind the difference between my mode of thought and that of Scripture, the essential unfitness of the means employed by me. I shall have to remember that grace is implied if my attempt and therefore my mode of thought can become useful to this end. (*CD* I/2:731)

3) *Appropriation* (*CD* I/2:736ff.). This third dimension of

biblical interpretation corresponds to the classical concept of *usus scripturae*. It is concerned with the *applicatio* and that means with assuming the biblical witness into one's own responsibility. Application does not mean, however, that we *use* the Scriptures for our own purposes but, rather, that we should allow ourselves to be taken over by the Scriptures for God's purposes. Total faith is the only adequate human response to the Word of God.

Can we accept this hermeneutics today?

III *How Critical is Barth's Hermeneutics?*

Karl Barth's hermeneutics are passionate hermeneutics. He is passionately concerned with protecting the biblical texts against the 'uncritical' claims of those historians and exegetes who pretend to have understood a text when they have analysed it as a historical document. Barth demands a better criticism.[25] True criticism – according to Barth – means to take the sense of the text seriously, and, in the case of the biblical texts, that means to take seriously that the text is critical of the reader. The biblical text causes a crisis in the serious and attentive reader.

Eberhard Jüngel has shown how Barth gained the material criterion for this hermeneutics through his reading of Paul's Epistle to the Romans. Barth's interpretative experience with this text led him to accept the axiom that 'God is God' which he then applies to all the biblical texts. Jüngel reminds us that this axiom is in fact an insight of Natural Theology. But, unlike in the tradition of doing so-called Natural Theology, Barth's tautology 'God is God' certainly does not act so as 'to secure the existence of a godhead, of a divine essence, but to emphasize the radical difference between the divine essence, the Godness of God, and all ungodly essences.'[26]

This axiom of the divinity of God is the axiom through which Barth wishes us to read every text, not only biblical and religious texts. That is why he could say that we do not really need a specific theological *Wissenschaft* and that all the sciences that are engaged in explanation and understanding could ultimately do the business of theology. In other words, biblical hermeneutics do not need to be different from general hermeneutics. Only because general hermeneutics do not agree with this basic axiom do we need biblical hermeneutics in order to be reminded of the subject matter of all honest understanding (*CD* I/2:725–727).

This axiom 'God is God' conducted Barth's reading of *Romans*, whereas his *Church Dogmatics* is guided increasingly by the axiomatic insight that God did reveal himself in Jesus Christ in order ultimately to show his eternal love for us human beings. This latter insight is no longer born from Natural Theology, but from Barth's particular hermeneutical experience with the New Testament texts. Thus, while the major reading perspective of *Romans* was more or less apologetic, the guiding perspective of his *Church Dogmatics* was based on his specific reading experiences. However, here too an axiom is at work which provokes our critical attention, namely the axiom that the biblical text interprets itself. What does that mean?

In his battle against Liberal Theology, Barth wished to restore the authority of the scriptural text in order to make sure that the particular theme, the subject matter of this text can mediate itself. All of his negations of whatever philosophical description of the hermeneutical situation (from Schleiermacher to Bultmann and Ebeling) serve to emphasise God's free revelation in Jesus Christ and the work of the Holy Spirit in each event of proclamation. However, Barth's ultimate hermeneutical concern does not change from *Romans* to the end of his life: the theme of the text (*die Sache des Textes*) must make itself known to us.

This is, of course, also Bultmann's principal concern. Yet, whereas Barth claims to know the only possible outcome of all truly biblical interpretation (the obedient witness to the self-revelation of God in the Logos) Bultmann suggests that we interpret the biblical texts in order to see what they have to say to us today. Both theologians wish to protect the texts from *eisegesis*: Barth through his effort of unmasking all ideological misreadings, Bultmann through his call for a self-conscious and self-critical openness for the text. Both hermeneuts are aware of the human condition of reading. Both reflect upon the necessity for perspectives and the dangers of ideologized horizons. Yet they differ sharply in their starting point. For Bultmann the connecting point between God and us is the hermeneutical process itself, whereas Barth begins already with the positive fact of God's revelation as witnessed to by the text. Barth starts ultimately *extra nos*, Bultmann *intra nos*.

Comparing Barth's hermeneutics with Bultmann's, I do, of course, not wish to suggest that Bultmann's theological method is without problems. It would lead beyond the scope of this essay to provide the reader with an equally extensive assessment of Bultmann's hermeneutical programme and its difficulties. Such an assessment would need to discuss the unhappy term 'demythologizing', the ahistorical nature of Bultmann's existential interpretation, the confusion between such different levels of biblical critique as the scientific, philosophical and theological ones,[27] and other weak points of his programme. Yet within the context of this essay it is particularly important that we recognize that Bultmann's principal progress beyond Barth lies in his insight that every reader or listener of the biblical text has to enter the hermeneutical process itself, the hermeneutical circle.

> This is why there is a circle: to understand the text, it is necessary to believe in what the text announces to me; but what the text announces to me is given nowhere but in the text. This is why it is necessary to understand the text in order to believe.[28]

Thus, the crucial question is: How can we estimate whether Barth's macro-hermeneutics is adequate if not through our own readings of the text themselves? In other words, in order to see if Barth's universalization of his particular hermeneutical experience is legitimate we must go the long way through the texts. No macro-hermeneutics without critical micro-hermeneutics! Without such a continuous test Barth's criterion for biblical interpretation, God's revelation, remains indeed mere positivism, as Bonhoeffer had suggested.[29]

Barth's great achievement was undoubtedly to have drawn our attention to the *theological* message of the biblical texts. But he did not help us to see how we can disclose this message today, how we can read the texts, and how we might legitimately read the texts in different way with different results. Barth did not tackle the problems of such a legitimate pluralism.[30] And why should his assertion of the rôle of the Holy Spirit exclude our reflection upon the most adequate method of studying the biblical texts?[31] Barth's passionate vote for the difference between God and human beings might not only have failed to appreciate the importance of the humanity of God, as he later admitted (1956: 'Die Menschenfreundlichkeit Gottes'), but also the basic hermeneutical condition in which we recognize this difference.[32]

His legitimate fear of all the ideological and systematic distortions of biblical interpretation which he saw at work in Liberal and Natural Theologies led him to misunderstand Bultmann's equally legitimate reflection upon the condition of human understanding. The exchange of views between Barth and Bultmann in 1952 shows once again in great clarity how Barth rejects Bultmann's reflections on the hermeneutical condition as an illegitimate determination of the text.[33] As Barth had outlined already in his earlier book on Anselm, the foundation of any good theology must be the prevenient *credo* of the theologian.[34] Therefore he feels the duty of rejecting any theological programme which starts below or outside this determination by faith. Bultmann recognized correctly that Barth's ontological presupposition differs radically from his own. And with Bultmann we must ask Barth[35]: Why should an open discussion of the presuppositions of our approach to our texts *determine* our understanding? Of course, all our interpretative efforts are *conditioned*. Yet if the discussion of this condition is a truly open discussion, I cannot see why God's Spirit should not be able to lead us to an appreciation of the truth of the Bible through this discussion.

IV *Karl Barth's hermeneutics and the contemporary debate on interpretation theory*

Although the hermeneutical discussion has gone on beyond the contributions of Barth and Bultmann, their concerns continue to occupy much of today's debate. The discussion between the theologians Barth and Bultmann is mirrored in the discussion between the philosophers Hans-Georg Gadamer and Paul Ricoeur.[36] Barth and Gadamer on the one hand represent a universalist trend in hermeneutics, Bultmann and Ricoeur on the other hand represent a methodological movement.[37] The misunderstanding between Gadamer and those philosophers and theologians who have been criticizing him for his continuous rejection of methodology in hermeneutics reminds us of the misunderstanding between Barth and the Bultmann School. For Barth and Gadamer there can be no doubt that the truth (Gadamer) or the Word of God (Barth) will make itself known to all human beings who are willing to open themselves obediently to the theme of the text. For Bultmann and Ricoeur, there can be no doubt that all human understanding occurs in a particular context, within particular world-views, according to particular linguistic rules, so that methodological modes of explanation are required in order to unmask possible misunderstandings of the text, or even systematic distortions both within the text itself and as Jurgen Habermas has pointed out, in our communicative situation.[38] Thus, our understanding and its presuppositions must be critically examined, validated, corrected or possibly rejected altogether. Therefore, all understanding requires some methodological explanation as its critical companion.[39]

Gadamer's hermeneutical maxim that the interpreter has to enter the tradition of the text and the history of the text's effects,[40] and his claim that the hermeneutical process culminates in the fusion of horizons (the horizon of the interpreter and the horizon of the text)[41] has provoked a massive and lasting protest: hermeneutics must be critical, for it cannot maintain a naïve faith in the innocence of either the text or the process of reading; and all critical hermeneutics must come to terms with this need for correctives in every act of interpretation.[42] Yet Gadamer continues to insist, as Barth used to do, that the truth of the text discloses itself, and that no method can guarantee its revelation.[43] This is where the misunderstanding grounds: the event of God's revelation or the disclosure of the text's truth can, of course, never be guaranteed by any methodological consideration; however, methodological reflection can prepare the reader to act more responsibly in the process of interpretation.

In this context it is interesting to note that both Barth and Gadamer reject Friedrich Schleiermacher's hermeneutics, Gadamer because of its alleged Romanticism,[44] Barth because it misses the theological axioms which he, Barth, insists must be accepted before good interpretation could begin.[45] Both Barth and Gadamer fail to appreciate Schleiermacher's penetrating insights into the process of human communication and into the conditions of understanding. Barth's lecture on Schleiermacher's hermeneutics does not even begin to deal with Schleiermacher's theory of the dipolar nature of interpretation (the grammatical and the psychological interpretation of a text),[46] and Gadamer misrepresents significantly Schleiermacher's contributions to hermeneutics in *Truth and Method*.[47] This misrepresentation has been corrected only recently after Paul Ricoeur[48] and Manfred Frank[49] rediscovered Schleiermacher's hermeneutics again for the modern debate.[50] Ricoeur in particular appreciates Schleiermacher's concerns for a critical and responsible hermeneutics and develops his grammatical interpretation further.

Like Schleiermacher, Ricoeur rejects all ontological presuppositions of text-interpretation. Ricoeur proposes that we avoid ontological shortcuts and instead begin the long route of searching for the truth through interpreting all relevant and promising human expressions.[51] For him, ontology can always be only broken ontology (*ontologie brisée*).[52] Ricoeur does not share Gadamer's identification of the result of the hermeneutical experience with the ultimate disclosure of truth. Similarly, Bultmann had rejected Barth's identification of all hermeneutics with Christian ontology and instead insisted, like Schleiermacher, that theological hermeneutics does not differ in principle from all other hermeneutics.[53]

The difference between both hermeneutical trends can also be seen quite clearly if one compares the different models of truth at work in each of these hermeneutical theories. Gadamer and Barth operate on a correspondence model: the reader has to be obedient to the self-revelation of truth and to behave correspondingly. Bultmann and Ricoeur operate on a disclosure-transformation model: the reader has to be critically attentive to the text and its possible disclosure of revelation/truth in the act of reading. Both trends, however, emphasise that the recognition of truth should lead to a practical transformation of the interpreter's self-understanding. Bultmann and Ricoeur speak of the revelation of new modes-of-being-in-the-world, Barth and Gadamer of the revelation of a new praxis of life which calls for correspondence in the interpreter's life.[54]

Yet our critical question to Barth remains unanswered: are all the disclosures of revelation really what they pretend to be and are all resulting transformations of the interpreter's life good? In other words, is every transformative experience of the Word of God really an experience of God's Word? What is the function of the community of interpreters in view of the possibility of conflicting interpretations and transformations?

The invocation of the Holy Spirit in this context does not save us from our human predicament. Rather, we should invoke the Spirit to guide us through the process of our life-long interpretation.

Barth does not tackle the problems of human misreadings, misunderstandings of the texts, for he is not interested in the functions of language. As Eberhard Jüngel sees correctly, Barth's hermeneutics are hermeneutics of revelation and not hermeneutics of signification.[55] But how can we talk about God's Logos if not through the medium of our language and its often ambiguous processes of signification? Barth himself presupposes and uses these functions of language, but he neglects to appreciate their significance and implications for our understanding of texts. Instead he aims at the whole, at the interpretation of the universe in the light of his personal hermeneutical experience of revelation. Through his own reading of the Scriptures, his own observations, reflections and appropriations, he reached the theological and ontological axioms for his interpretation. While he still recommends these dimensions of interpretation to us, his axioms would already determine too much of the outcome of our own reading. Nowhere does Barth deal with the possibility and the consequences of a pluralism or even conflict of possible interpretations. This fact and his fear of distortions as well as his rejection of explicit theological methods must weaken our trust in his own particular retrieval of the biblical message.

Yet, when we accept the possibility of distortions and when we try to strive for a more critical analysis of our hermeneutical condition, then we are preparing the way for a more adequate and responsible interpretation of the biblical texts. This methodological preparation, however, does not in itself determine our reading of the texts, but it does make us more aware of the presuppositions always already at work which, if they are not unmasked, may indeed determine our reading. Only through such methodological critique can we try to prevent old and new ideologies from distorting our interpretations, and only so can we really make sure that Barth's insights into the ideological character of many theologies bear lasting fruits.

The biblical texts, as Barth says, have proved to be witnesses to God's revelation for many generations of Christians. They might continue to do so for us as well, if we are willing to interpret them adequately. However, adequate interpretation – and here again Barth is right – must be more than the philological and historical analysis of the texts.[56] It must also be the open, self-critical, text-critical, non-ideological effort of retrieving the sense of the text. Barth claimed that the text's true sense is God's self-revelation in human history. So let us all read the texts and see if Barth was right. If we do not presuppose Barth's theological and ontological axioms and begin to read the texts ourselves, we might find out for ourselves that theology is indeed as attractive an enterprise as Barth has claimed.

The appreciation of Barth's valuable theological insights, of his fears and shortcomings, and most of all of his faith might help us today to assess our own hermeneutical possibilities and limitations accordingly, and to pray to God's Spirit for the grace of guidance in our theoretical and practical search for the ultimate sense of this universe.

PART IV
ETHICS AND POLITICS

6

Hearing God's Command and Thinking about What's Right: With and Beyond Barth

NIGEL BIGGAR

On 1 August 1914, Karl Barth's theological world shook. A socialist pastor of an industrial parish in the north of his native Switzerland, Barth was stunned to learn that, on the very first day of the First World War, almost all of his theological mentors in Germany had rallied in public support of Kaiser Wilhelm II. On that day, it was made clear to him just how easily religion could assume the form, as he later put it, of 'intellectual 42 cm. cannon'.[1] He had encountered the ethical and political complaisance and fecklessness of his liberal theological heritage.

Barth attributed the ethical failure of liberal theology at the outbreak of war to the inadequacy of its exegetical and dogmatic presuppositions.[2] Equipped with this diagnosis, he set off in search of an alternative set of presuppositions, one capable of spawning and nourishing a Christian ethic sufficiently robust to stand on its own peculiar feet, and so to exercise a critical and transformative influence upon secular culture.

It was in the course of this pursuit that Barth stumbled into what he later called 'the strange new world' of the Bible; and it was here that he made a threefold and seminal discovery.[3] He discovered, first of all, that God is in heaven and Man on earth; that is to say, that the ways of God are simply not the same as the ways of Man; that one cannot presume to infer the nature of God even from what is considered to be the very finest in human thought and practice; that God cannot properly be made in Man's image.

The second feature of the Bible's world that arrested Barth was that, as God is not primarily the embodiment of a moral ideal or an explanation of human existence, nor is he primarily an object of human thought. Rather, God is a living and active and personally spontaneous reality. He is subject rather than object. Indeed, he is preeminent Subject. He acts long before he is ever acted upon. He *is*, before he is thought about.

The first two things, then, that struck Barth as he wandered into the world of the Bible were theological: they had to do with the nature of God. The third had to do with Man or, rather, with his action: it was ethical. And it was this: that in all that he does Man acts well only when he acts in response to the deeds of God. This responsiveness is the formal nature of right action.

The threefold discovery that Barth made when he encountered the Bible in the middle of the Great War was to remain at the heart of his thought throughout its development in the 1920s. Then, combined with a Christological focus and qualification, it provided the foundation upon which he set about building the *Church Dogmatics* in 1930. It therefore constituted a major part of the set of theological presuppositions out of which Barth began to construct his own ethics. Further still, it is directly responsible for the nature and the crucial role in Barth's ethics of the concept of knowing what is right by hearing God's command. Because God is not Man writ large; because God is active and personal subject; and because it is, therefore, proper for the human creature to act responsively, the first act of anyone who would know what he should do must be that of *listening* to what God commands here and now. It must *not* be that of engaging in abstract thought about the Good and about principles and rules. It must *not* be that of interpreting a normative text, theological or philosophical, objective or subjective, Scripture or Tradition, law-code or story. The first act of anyone who would know what he ought to do must *not* be one of reflection, but of hearing. This is the primary significance of Barth's concept of the command of God – a concept that is basic and central to his ethical thought, and to which it therefore lends a quite distinctive tone.

When I say 'distinctive' here, I mean it primarily in relation to the thought of Aquinas, Luther and Calvin. For all of these, direct moral illumination by the Holy Spirit – which I take to be the equivalent of Barth's divine commanding – is auxiliary to the prudential application of principles to cases. More or less radically, it aids practical reason, whether this takes its cue primarily from Natural Law or from Scripture. *Prima facie* it would appear, then, that in his concept of a divine command which is to be heard and obeyed rather than reflected upon Barth aligns himself epistemologically with the Spiritualists or with the enthusiastic wing of Anabaptism, for whom the Spirit's revelation is wont to supersede the written Word and reasonings therefrom. It would appear that Barth is a sort of ethical charismatic. It will, however, be one of the tacit arguments of this essay that Barth, although certainly distinctive in the central role which he assigns to the hearing of God's command, is nevertheless much closer to the Thomist and magisterial Reformation traditions than is usually supposed. Here ends the historical theological excursus.[4]

Barth's idea of hearing God's command, as it is commonly understood, has not proven hugely popular among subsequent exponents of Christian ethics. This is so, I think, for at least two reasons. First, it seems to betoken a moment of essentially private revelation; and because essentially private, therefore irrational. It appears to lie beyond the scope of public debate, being susceptible neither of rational justification nor of rational criticism. Either you believe my claim to have heard a command of God, or you do not: there is no way in which we can argue or reason about it. The first objection commonly raised against Barth's concept of hearing God's command, then, is that it is fideistic.[5]

The second depends on the first. Since God's command cannot be articulated in terms of principles or rules that hold from one situation to another, and about which we can debate, it precludes the formulation of precise moral guidance. If we would know what we ought to do, Barth seems to be saying, then we must simply listen to what is said here and now: there is no given body of general moral norms upon which we may rely, and which we may seek to relate to the particular case before us. The second common objection to the concept of God's command, then, is that it precludes normative ethics.[6]

Both objections just described I believe to be considerably mistaken; but before I address them, I would like first to commend some of what I regard as the virtues of Barth's concept, and thereby to present some reasons as to why one should be concerned to retain and promote it in Christian ethics. My list of virtues numbers five.

The first, and perhaps predominant, virtue is that it contradicts any theory that presents the process of coming to know what is right *primarily* in terms of interpreting a normative text. (I use the word 'text' here in a very broad sense to denote anything that can be interpreted or 'read', whether written or unwritten. It may, therefore, be the Bible or some classic of Christian literature; or it may be some feature of the current life of the Church or of our own experience. A text is something that can be interpreted.) To describe our apprehension of what is right in terms of our hearing God's command is to deny that our relationship to the Good is *simply* that of interpreters to a text, of active subjects to a relatively passive object. It is to deny that our ethical role is primarily that of a technician, applying his expertise to the inert matter of a text and constraining it to produce its meaning. Rather, it is to assert that to come to know the Good is, fundamentally, not to be in control – not to be the centre of activity – but, rather, to find oneself encountered by the living reality of the sovereign and personally spontaneous God. It is to assert that, in the moment of moral decision, we humans are not alone in the world with ideas, whether our own or someone else's or however wise and true; but, rather, that then, as in every moment, we stand and act in a relationship with the Person of the God who has elected from eternity to be with us in his Word.

The denial of a technical concept of interpretation and the

correlative assertion of a receptive moment in the hermeneutical process cannot, of course, be claimed as a peculiar virtue of Barth's concept of divine command. What the divine command does add to the dialectical hermeneutics of philosophical provenance is the unambiguous assertion that there are always more than two partners to the hermeneutical dialogue; that, besides the text and the interpreter, there is the God who wills and works to reveal himself through the text. Further, by identifying this God with Jesus Christ, it reminds the interpreter that he is not only contingent creature but deliberate sinner, and so disposes him to be vigilant against his own persistent tendencies to justify himself by assimilating the meaning of the text to himself, by permitting it merely to recite what he has already approved of.[7]

So much for the first virtue of Barth's concept. All the others, as I reckon them, follow from this one. Indeed, the second has just been alluded to: namely, that the concept of God's command insists that, if I would know what is right, I must acknowledge my status as a creature, as a sinful creature, as a sinful creature reconciled to God by God. This means that I am bound to approach the Good through a certain ethos: in humility, in penitence and with gratitude. The act of apprehending what is right, then, is not a purely theoretical exercise. It involves the whole of my existence; it requires me to assume a certain fundamental set of dispositions.

The third virtue of the concept of God's command is that it brings worship and prayer right into the very heart of Christian ethics. For Barth, authentic *ethos* is not separable from correspondent practice; so the genuine assumption of the dispositions of humility, penitence and gratitude necessarily expresses itself in acts of worship and, *par excellence*, prayer. Indeed, Barth proposes prayer as 'the primal and basic form' of the Christian ethos and the 'archetypal form' of all good acts (*CD* III/3:89). This is because it is 'the one free act of man in which he confesses that the initiative lies with the freed of God rather than with his own freedom' (*CD* I/1:698) in other words, the necessary form of all good acts; of all human acts that respond to, correspond with, follow after the acts of God.

As a fourth virtue, I commend the fact that the concept of apprehending what is right by hearing God's command demands of the one who would know an openness, a constant readiness to hear something new, something different, something arresting, something that takes by surprise, something that provokes change, something that converts. It demands of the person who would know what is right an active willingness to review and revise her moral assumptions and convictions. But not only her assumptions and convictions: also the ethos and practices that they sanction, even rationalize. Since God is a living and active and spontaneous Person; since God is not Man; and since we know what is right by hearing what God says to us here and now, we cannot presume to know already the content of his command. It is our proper role to correspond, not to predict. We follow; we do not precede.

The fifth and last virtue of Barth's concept of God's command that I should like to commend is that it precludes ethical elitism. Since apprehension of what is right is not, in the first place, a product of ethical reflection, of analysis and interpretation, but rather of a prayerful and open hearing, it does not presuppose on the part of the knower the possession of highly developed powers of abstract reasoning. Knowledge of what is right requires primarily that I put myself in a position to listen to what is told me. Such a posture is no more natural to an academically trained expert than to anyone else. The promotion, through the concept of hearing God's command, of the existential and dispositional dimension at the expense of the theoretical, militates against a socially authoritarian or aristocratic understanding of the process of acquiring moral knowledge. Knowledge of what is right is not the preserve of a special, highly educated social class; it is not a moral form of *Gnosis*.

So, there stand five grounds upon which I commend Barth's concept of hearing the command of God, and five reasons why I think that such a concept should be promoted in Christian ethics.

I am now going to turn to the two objections commonly raised against it, which I mentioned earlier and which I shall spend the rest of this essay addressing. These are: first, that it denotes a private revelation that transcends rational discussion and implies a purely, as it were, charismatic epistemology; and, second, that in its rejection of normative ethics, it renders the formulation of moral guidance impossible.

It seems to me that both of these objections stem from an understanding of Barth which has been largely shaped by a reading of Chapter VIII of his *Church Dogmatics* (II/2) in the light of the second edition of his *Epistle to the Romans* and, perhaps, his 1922 lecture, 'The Problem of Ethics Today'.[8] They depend, that is, on texts in which Barth wages quite ruthless war against normative ethics as but one more, or even the original, form of human self-justification. Correspondingly, these objections either neglect altogether Chapters XII (*CD* III/4) and XVII (*CD* IV/4)[9] where, in spite of his protestations to the contrary and under the guise of what he calls 'special' ethics, Barth himself clearly engages in normative ethics; or else they treat these normative ethical chapters too readily as demonstrating that his concept of God's command is not viable. The fact that, in the end, even Barth was compelled to resort to normative ethics, they take as sufficient ground for dismissing both his critique of it and the notion of hearing God's command with which he seeks to replace it. They suppose, in other words, that there is in Barth's ethics a sheer and radical contradiction.

I judge this conclusion to be both premature and mistaken. It is premature because it fails to ask certain very pertinent questions. For example, does Barth anywhere in the later 'special' ethical chapters of the *Dogmatics*, upon one of which he was still working in the early 1960s, repudiate the concept of God's command and the corresponding critique of normative ethics that he had formulated in Chapter VIII, as early as 1942? Or, at least, does he anywhere acknowledge a contradiction between his earlier concept of God's command and his later 'special' ethics? Moreover, does not Barth indicate that he regards both these elements as quite compatible? And does he not provide some explication of the grounds of this compatibility?

Because those who interpret Barth's 'special' ethics as simply subversive of his concept of divine command fail to ask these questions, I judge their conclusion to be premature. And because Barth never in his later writings repudiates his earlier stance, and is quite deliberate in offering grounds upon which the one may be integrated with the other, I judge their conclusion to be considerably mistaken.

Note that I say 'considerably', not 'absolutely'. In other words, I admit that this conclusion does enjoy a measure of validity; which I shall identify in due course. Immediately, however, I will proceed to explain in what ways the two common objections to Barth's concept of God's command fail to do him justice.

The first point to be made against the objection that Barth's command of God denotes a thoroughly private and irrational revelation is that in Chapter VIII of the *Church Dogmatics* (III/4) Barth expressly denies that what he means by the notion of hearing God's command is the receipt of 'a kind of direct and particular inspiration and guidance'. 'This', he says, 'is not what is meant' (*CD* III/4:15).

What, then, *is* meant? Pursuit of the answer to this question leads us immediately to my second point: that Barth's concept of hearing God's command is not to be abstracted from his doctrine of the Word of God and of its relation to Holy Scripture. God's command is God's Word in its imperative form; and the hearing of God's Word is never separable from the reading of Scripture. If Scripture may not, simply, *be* the Word; then, equally, nor may the Word be *apart* from Scripture. Barth is not an ethical Spiritualist. Therefore, if we would hear what God commands us, we must listen in the context of biblical exegesis. We hear the command of God only through and under Scripture.

But if God's command is but a form of God's Word, then

we must hear it, not only in the light of Scripture, but also in the Church. This is my third point; and it is one that is, I think, sufficiently important and sufficiently ill-appreciated as to warrant substantiation by extensive quotation from Barth himself. It is, according to Barth, one of the distinctive features of God's Word that it unites sinful, partisan human beings in a common subordination to itself, in a community of hearing and receiving:

> Where there is any attempt to break loose from the community of hearing and receiving . . ., any attempt to hear and receive the Word of God in isolation – even the Word of God in the form of Holy Scripture – there is no Church, and no real hearing and receiving of the Word of God; for the Word of God is not spoken to individuals, but to the Church of God and to individuals only in the Church. The Word of God itself, therefore, demands this community of hearing and receiving (*CD* I/2:588).

What this means for our hearing of God's command is that

> here and now the command of God must be proclaimed by one man to another who must hear it through him; that the very case of conscience in which each must act for himself means for both that they should talk and listen to each other. It can please the Holy Spirit – and it continually pleases Him – that not merely ethical advice and direction but the very command of God should be given in a very concrete form immediately from one man to another or to many others (*CD* III/4:9).

We hear God's command under Scripture and we hear it in the Church; that is, we hear it in conversation and debate with our fellow-hearers of God's Word as it is attested in Scripture. These fellow-hearers may be contemporary or they may not: the Church is not only present, but also past. So, readiness to hear God's command requires that we open ourselves, under Scripture, to the traditions of the Church.

And yet the extent of our openness must be greater still. We are to hear God's command in the Church. But if in the Church, also in the world, because the Church is inseparable from the world on three grounds. First, the Lord of the Church, Jesus Christ, is also the Lord of the World. So, we find that 'in all ages the will of God has often been better fulfilled outside the Church than in it . . . because Jesus, as the One who has risen from the dead and sits at the right hand of God, is in fact the Lord of the whole world, who has His servants even where His name is not yet or no longer known and praised' (*CD* II/2:569). Second, the Church is inseparable from the world because it is representative of the true humanity and therefore the divinely appointed destiny of all human beings: by virtue of the universal reconciliation effected in Jesus Christ, it represents 'the true being of all men who are not yet as they are, but will be' (*ChrL*, pp. 21–22). Third, the Church and the world are inseparable because the final and therefore real bounds of the Church are not yet quite patent. Therefore,

> as Christians and therefore as those who are called we are constrained to be absolutely open in respect of all other men without exception . . . No man who is called does not also have to see and understand himself as one who still has to be called and therefore as one who stands alongside and in solidarity with the uncalled. . . . For all the seriousness with which we must distinguish between Christians and non-Christians, we can never think in terms of a rigid separation. All that is possible is a genuinely unlimited openness of the called in relation to the uncalled, an unlimited readiness to see in the aliens of today the brothers of tomorrow (*CD* IV/3:493–94).

Those 'who are already called and recognizable as such' must be open to others because they share with them the common status of sinner and so stand in common need of divine grace (*CD* I/2:431–32).

Because of the universal sovereignty of its Lord, its role as representative of universal reconciliation and its current status as sinner and pilgrim, the Church is bound to regard the non-Christian as a virtual, if not actual, member of the community of hearing. The Christian, then, must open himself to hear and receive the divine command through the thought, speech and practice of the indifferent and the godless: for 'it may be', Barth writes in *The Christian Understanding of*

Revelation, 'that the Lord has bidden those outside the Church to say something important to the Church. The Church therefore has every reason not to ignore the questions and warnings of the outside world.'[10] Since Barth is popularly held to be relentless in his negation of any positive dialogue between Church and world, it is worth invoking the witness of Hans Urs von Balthasar who, in his classic account of Barth's theology, considers him to be 'as open to the world as any theologian could be.'[11] And this, from a Roman Catholic.

God's command is the imperative form of God's Word. God's Word must be heard under Scripture; and because under Scripture, therefore in the Church; and because in the Church, therefore in the World. It is clear, then, that what Barth does not mean by his concept of hearing the command of God is a moment of purely private revelation. It is not a form of solipsistic monologue. Hearing takes place in dialogue – primarily with Scripture and secondarily with one's fellow-hearers, both past and present, both actual and virtual. There *are* public criteria that one can bring – indeed, *must* bring – to bear on another's claim to have heard a command of God. These criteria derive, in the first place, from Scripture, Christologically interpreted; but also, in the second place, under the control of Scripture from the natural and social sciences. Clearly, the public forum in which rational consideration of a claim to have heard a command of God occurs, is limited. It is limited to that community which acknowledges as its ultimate authority, as the final criterion of what is rational, the Word of God in Scripture. The members of this public must listen to and may learn from what outsiders have to say; but they will do so finally on their own proper ground, subject to their own final criterion. The scope, then, for public and rational justification and critique is certainly not infinite; but it is, within limits, not only possible but mandatory.

I move now from the first common objection to Barth's divine command to the second: namely, that, in its rejection of normative ethics, the concept of hearing God's command renders impossible the formulation of moral guidance.

Against this second objection, I note, to begin with, that Barth expressly denies that, in order to hear the command of God, one must render oneself an ethical *tabula rasa*, emptying one's mind of all its moral concepts and norms. Understanding God's command does not require us, first of all, to leave all our pre-understandings about what is good and right at the door. It does not stipulate as its rite of initiation the sacrifice of normative ethical intellect. Indeed, for Barth, such a sacrifice would be not merely impossible, but even sinful; for it would constitute an attempt to step outside both our creaturely contingency and our sinful corruption *as a precondition* of meeting God. It would, in other words, be an act of self-justification; a striving to avoid the miracle of God's grace to ignorant and corrupt humanity (*CD* I/1:247). So, if we would hear God's command, we must be prepared to do so from within our limited and fallen humanity, not beyond it. We must come to the place of hearing, penitently and prayerfully, but with our heads nevertheless full of norms and principles and rules. We must expect God's command *through* our normative ethics, not outside them. We can, in fact, expect nothing else.

Barth admitted that the hearing of God's command does not require us to wipe our intellectual slates clean of all their normative ethical notes. Further, he also recognized the need to provide precise moral guidance and, accordingly, he himself engaged, albeit covertly, in that more logically rational form of normative ethics which treats norms as principles and derives rules from them; namely, casuistry. In Chapters XII and XVII of the *Church Dogmatics*, Barth may be found to abstract general principles indirectly from the text of Scripture and directly from his dogmatic system; and from these principles to derive moral rules. So, for example, from the principle of the nature of Man as both male and female he derives the rule that homosexuality is outside God's will (*CD* III/4:166); from the principle of respect for the gift of life, the rule that life may not be taken wantonly or maliciously or faithlessly (*CD* III/4:398); and from the principle of non-conformity to the godless and lordless powers that dominate the world, the rule that devotion to any political ideology may never to be absolute (*ChrL*, pp. 224ff.).

Further still, Barth's affirmation here of a casuistic ethics does not constitute a contradicition of his earlier critique. For, it is clear that when Barth equates ethics with original sin, he means by it a closed, rationalist system that moves with inexorable logic from first principles through rules to particular cases. By sinful ethics he intends an absolutist form of casuistry.

It is equally clear that Barth does not believe that all kinds of normative ethics are necessarily casuistic in this absolutist sense. He quite evidently believes that it can avoid being a closed, mechanical, absolutist system; that it can avoid being rationalist. He believes that normative ethics may recognize that the final gap between rule and case cannot be closed by logic alone; that there is a point at which moral reason ought to stop and listen and respond to what is given it. He believes that normative ethics may be open and responsive to a voice that is not its own and which says to it something strange.

Which brings us to my final point in defence of Barth's divine command against the second common objection: namely, that Barth patently regards a certain non-rationalist form of normative ethics as perfectly compatible with hearing God's command. He sees their relationship in the following terms. I know what is right – what I ought to do – here and now, only in the moment that I hear God's command. The purpose of normative ethics is to provide me with general guidelines as to the content of that command. It cannot predict the exact nature of what will pass from God to me in the event of that encounter, but it can prepare me to recognize the sound of the divine voice. I cannot, therefore, extrapolate from a given set of principles or rules exactly what God will command. The role of normative ethics is, then, strictly preparatory and preliminary. In the end, I must always move from thinking to hearing, for it may well be that God will command something 'exceptional' to my customary rules.

I have mentioned four grounds upon which I reject the complaint that Barth's command of God makes the provision of moral guidance impossible. Now I turn to the one point at which, in my opinion, this complaint holds.

Barth does not regard engagement in normative ethics and the hearing of God's command as mutually exclusive activities: normative ethics is preliminary to the moment of hearing; the moment of hearing relativizes normative ethics. So far, so good. The particular term which Barth chose to describe this relativizing or limiting function of the command of God is, however, problematical. For, to describe God's command as limiting normative ethics by threatening it with the possibility of a sheer *exception* to its rule, is to limit it at the expense of making it redundant. If there is always the possibility that God may command an irreducible exception to my ethical rule, something that stands forever beyond the comprehension of my ethics; if my normative ethical reflection has no necessary or dependable connexion with what God will or will not command, then why should I bother with it at all? If the function of God's command is conceived in these terms, then normative ethics is suffered to perform only after it has been sterilized. It is allowed to go through the motions, provided that it has already been bereft of the capacity to make a difference.

It may be said in Barth's defence, however, that he does not always talk about the exceptional command as a sheer and irreducible contradiction of a given rule. He is at pains, whenever he contemplates a concrete instance of a so-called exceptional command, to stress that it is not absolutely contrary to the given principle nor subversive of the derived rule, but constitutes, instead, an unusual meaning of the former and a qualification of the latter. So, for example, when he mentions the possibility that God might command us to leave our families and follow a prophetic vocation, he insists that such an exceptional command would not be a violation of the rule that we should honour our parents (*CD* III/4:260). Likewise, he argues that, when commanded, the taking of human life is not contrary to the rule of respect for the gift of life, but rather an unusual form of its meaning (*CD* III/4:397–98). In these cases, what Barth means when he speaks of an 'exception' to a rule is not so much a sheer and capricious contradiction before which normative ethics must bend an unthinking knee, as a revelation in the light of which ethics sets about reforming itself. God's command says something that causes ethics to reinterpret a principle and to reformulate the rule derived from it, and to do so more or less radically. God's command limits ethics by correcting it, not by reducing it to nonsense.

Nevertheless, we have to acknowledge that Barth may also be found to insist quite vigorously that an exceptional command is such that ethics cannot come to rational terms with it (*CD* III/4:411,413). He insists that it stands as something irreducible alien and incomprehensible. At this point, then, the complaint that Barth's concept of the divine command effectively scuppers normative ethics is cogent. Although he clearly recognized the inevitability and necessity of normative ethics; although he himself practised a tentative form of casuistry; and although he evidently regarded this casuistic form of normative ethics as having some contribution of relative worth to make, he failed in the end to formulate its relation to God's command in such a way as to maintain what he affirmed of it.

I can think of two closely related reasons for this failure. The first is his relentless repudiation, in theory, of system and method as such.[12] It is a constant refrain of Barth's theological thought that the Word of God cannot be captured or possessed by any human concept or theory, however basic; it cannot be absolutely identified with any one principal concept or set of them. Systems and methods, whether theological or ethical, require the identification of God or the Good with such a principle or set. That they do not necessarily require that this identification be absolute, Barth often appears not to notice. Therefore, in spite of all his direct and indirect, theoretical and practical affirmation of normative ethics, Barth never relinquished a lively suspicion of it as a systematic and methodical enterprise. Even though he practises a form of casuistry – even though he formulates moral principles, derives rules from them and connects these to cases – he never ceases to think of casuistry as the original sin.

Which brings us immediately to the second reason for Barth's failure to integrate adequately divine command and normative ethics: the fact that he shared with most Protestant ethicists since the 17th century a misconception of casuistry as the epitome of rationalist ethics; as a necessarily closed logical system, utterly mechanical in procedure and absolutist in pretension (*CD* III/4:7ff.).[13]

I call this a *mis*conception, because casuistry has not always – perhaps, even usually – pretended to provide an absolute, self-sufficient method of deciding what is right. It has not presented itself as consisting in an inexorable one-way movement from principles through rules to cases. It has not claimed to be able to bridge the gap between specific rules and particular cases by logic alone.[14] Instead, if Kenneth Kirk's account is to be believed,[15] casuistry has often approximated the open model that Paul Ramsey has proposed in his famous essay, 'The Case of the Curious Exception'.[16] Here Ramsey argues that the casuist is always properly engaged in the process of modifying old and generating new rules in order to find appropriate ways to express a given principle in the light of new, morally significant data. The rational movement from principles to rules to cases is not closed and mechanical and predictable – not rationalist – but open and vital and creative.

Had Barth explicitly acknowledged such a form of casuistry; had he distinguished with consistent clarity between system and ideology, method and mechanism, reason and rationalism, he could have found a way of formulating the relation of God's command to normative ethics that does not affirm the former by rendering the latter pointless. He could have conceived of normative ethics as intrinsically open to revision, and of the command of God as corrective in relation to it. He could have thought of the command, not as an irreducible exception – a sheer outlaw – but as a new morally significant datum that provokes the modification of an old rule or the invention of a new one, and thus qualifies or explicates in a new way the meaning of a given principle. He could have conceived of God's command as contradicting normative ethics, not in order to strike it dumb, but rather to teach it to speak differently.

As it is, Barth did not make these distinctions clearly and consistently. Therefore his ethical thought does suffer from a measure of tension between his concepts of God's command and normative ethics. So, if we would affirm both coherently, we must go beyond Barth. But not far beyond; for the tension that afflicts his ethics is not nearly severe enough to vitiate it radically. It does not take much revision of Barth to be able to affirm normative ethics – even casuistry – in a manner compatible with a concept of hearing God's command. And such revision as it does take has already been alluded to, in one place or another, by Barth himself.

If, as I propose, we go a long way with Barth and a little beyond him, we may avail ourselves of a moral reasoning that is both rigorous and docile, precise and open. We may benefit from the rational rigour and precision of casuistry – which I count no small advantage – without surrendering ourselves to rationalist ideology and idolatry. We could do this, because our casuistic reasoning would be bounded by the need and call and duty to listen for the command of God. We would, therefore, be reminded that, when we set about abstracting our moral principles, deriving rules from them and connecting these with concrete cases, we do so in the midst of a relationship with a reconciling and redeeming Creator, and so as sinful and reconciled creatures, whose moral intellects stand in constant need of enlightening grace; and that we ought, therefore, to reason humbly, penitently and gratefully in the context of acts of worship and prayer.

Accordingly, we would also be reminded to hold our reasoning prayerfully open to development and correction in the face of morally significant data, which we have either not taken into account or have taken into account improperly; and that, while such new moral data may require merely the modification of a very specific rule, it may equally demand the radical reformation of a basic principle and so of the whole of a system.

Finally, the need to listen for the command of God would remind us that such new moral data always meet us under Scripture and in the Church; and that we must accordingly prepare ourselves to receive them through the counsel and example of our Christian sister and non-Christian brother, whether educated, articulate and logical, or merely faithful, imaginative and shrewd.

7

The Christian in Revolt: Some Reflections on *The Christian Life*

J. B. WEBSTER

I

Of Barth's last writings, the volume of posthumously published lecture fragments *The Christian Life*[1] is the least well-known outside German-speaking countries. Published in Switzerland in 1975 as part of the Barth *Gesamtausgabe* intiated by the *Karl Barth Stiftung*, it contains a methodological section on 'Ethics as a Task of the Doctrine of Reconciliation', which would have formed paragraph 74 of the *Church Dogmatics* if Barth had authorized its publication before his death. This material would, therefore, have come before the better-known (but by English readers still generally neglected) fragment on 'Baptism as the Foundation of the Christian Life', published in Zürich in 1968 as part IV/4 of *Die Kirkliche Dogmatik* and translated into English in the following year.[2] In addition to paragraph 74, however, *The Christian Life* also contains three paragraphs (76–8) which structure their exposition of the ethical life of the Christian believer around the introductory invocation and the first two petitions of the Lord's Prayer. It is these three paragraphs which provide the main focus of my remarks in this essay.

As always with Barth's writings on ethics, we face a question: why is it that what Barth is attempting to do is generally so difficult of access? Barth's ethical writings display a set of preoccupations and a style of approach which differ very considerably from much recent English or American writing in Christian ethics. The difference lies partly in the way in which Barth places what he is doing *vis-à-vis* moral philosophy. In some (though not all) contemporary styles of Christian ethics, the boundaries between Christian ethics and moral philosophy remain very fluid: there is commonly a transferability of procedure and content from one field to another, and a certain reluctance to attend to the distinctive doctrinal and religious aspects of Christian moral policy. Barth, on the other hand, adheres not without a certain stubbornness to the two-fold principle enunciated in all of his treatments of ethics in the course of the *Church Dogmatics*: (1) Christian ethics is *theological* ethics in the sense that it is not guided by notions of human nature, action or goodness other than those yielded by a dogmatic consideration of revelation in Christ; (2) Christian dogmatics is *ethical* dogmatics since it is concerned with the covenant established between God and his human partners.

The second of these two principles is frequently passed over in more casual critiques of Barth, where he is sometimes represented as unremittingly hostile to affirmations that human action has any substance. A more detailed analysis than we can offer here would show how difficult that critique is to sustain in view of some of the fundamental moves which Barth makes in the *Church Dogmatics*. Indeed, the alert reader is constantly surprised by the fact that Barth has a much fuller and rounder account of the human moral agent than we are often led by his critics to expect. This account is, moreover, very different from the much more slender theories of the moral self to be found in some analytical ethics. 'The agent, thin as a needle, appears in the quick flash of the choosing will'[3] – Iris Murdoch there acutely characterizes the way in which the duration of the self as a background to its activity almost entirely disappears in some recent work in the area: the enduring regularities of the self vanish into the quandary situation. As one reads through *The Christian Life*, it soon becomes evident that Barth, too, is immersed in a search for categories to describe the self as a weighty reality, continuous between its moments of choice and formed not simply in the instant of decision but by its convictions about the realities outside itself to which it must give assent.

If this is at all a correct account of Barth's intentions, then the common appraisal of him as vitiating the status of human persons as responsible selves needs to be called into question. Willis, for example, prosecutes a common line of argument when he claims that in Barth's grounding of human nature in the humanity of Jesus Christ 'man's status as subject and agent is threatened . . . by . . . an insufficient distinction between God and man'[4]: human action is absorbed by the divine action in Christ. Barth's last writings show with great force that such a charge is too undifferentiated to be successfully prosecuted. As we shall see, Barth's account of the relation between Jesus Christ and human nature cannot be reduced to a single pattern: the texts contain a variety of arguments, not all of which obscure human agency and responsibility. Moreover, Barth shows that the easily-drawn antithesis between grace and morality becomes much less sharp when grace is characterized in certain ways: as an invitation to act, for example, or as a summons to courage. In his *Study in Ethical Theory*, Donald MacKinnon suggested that 'we have to ask what becomes of (a man's) action if he takes the law of that action from outside himself to the extent not only of acknowledging that he receives *ab extra* its principle, but that he must regard its very accomplishment as something which he has received. True, he may point, as Paul does, to the range of his endurance; but is it his own? Is it tolerable for a serious morality to speak of "our sufficiency as being of God"?'.[5] Barth's last works are a sketch of such a serious morality.

II

In what ways is it possible and appropriate to conceive of Jesus Christ as the origin of human freedom, status, responsibility and maturity? And how may such freedom and status (and the acts in which they are realized) properly be said to be our own when their origins and even perhaps their fulfilment lie beyond us? Barth's exploration of these questions in paragraphs 76–8 is prepared for by the methodological reflections in paragraph 74 and the treatment of baptism in paragraph 75. Some brief remarks on each of these earlier sections are in order.

(1) In the context of the doctrine of reconciliation, special ethics serves to demonstrate how far the command of the one God is centrally the command of the Lord of the covenant, in which the action of sinful man is determined, ordered and limited by the free grace of the faithful God manifested and operative in Jesus Christ. (*ChrL*, p. 3)

Barth's exposition of the thesis proceeds by examining four related issues: the character of the commanding God; the character of the man who is responsible to him; the situation in which they encounter each other; and the nature of both the commandment and the obedient response. Superficially, it seems that Barth pushes to its limit the notion of God as one who commands, in the face of whose heteronomy there is no space for morality as a project chosen and undertaken by human selves. On such a reading it would be easy to pursue the familiar argument that heteronomy subverts morality, since only self-initiated projects can be the object of responsibility, only values created rather than imposed can be moral. As we read, however, it becomes clear that Barth's language of command contains sophisticated rebuttals of such arguments, and is in no way intended to reinforce a kind of infantile reliance on an external will which admits of no self-reflection on the part of those who obey. He is not so much proposing a purely deontological ethic, that is, as suggesting that the Christian moral life has grounds beyond the act of choice; the Christian life is bound up with an intelligent apprehension of and response to what the believer takes to be the case about the world. And so the divine command does not issue in the obliteration of human willing so much as in its formation, in specifying the constraints upon the will and laying out the area of its operation. Barth's notion of divine command is rich and supple, and cannot easily be dismissed as simply an aggressive external agency. Three leading themes in paragraph 74 bear this out.

The first is the theme of 'partnership' or 'encounter': 'God and man are two subjects in genuine encounter. God and man do in fact confront one another: two partners of different kinds, acting differently, so that they cannot be exchanged or equated' (*ChrL*, p. 27). In the partnership motif there surfaces one of the fundamental themes of Barth's last work: the distinction between God and man, a distinction in which the inalienable reality of each partner is affirmed. The 'togetherness of God and man', Barth goes on to argue, cannot be envisaged 'as anything other than one of distance and distinction' (*ChrL*, p. 28). For 'what would responsibility mean if the man who is responsible to God did not truly and genuinely stand *over against* him?' (*ibid.*). Certainly human responsibility is not such that we are obliged to maintain the covenant of ourselves. But to say this is not to make our actions otiose so much as to set us free in relation to them; they are born neither of hubris nor of anxiety about self-maintenance, but rather flow from achieved status which issues in free action: 'When the man who labours and is heavy-laden is summoned to obedience, it creates for him *anapausis*, sabbath refreshment, rest' (*ChrL*, p. 31).

Second, Barth takes up his controversial account of Gospel and Law: 'the command of God will infallibly make itself known as the law of the gospel' (*ChrL*, p. 35). In his 1935 paper on 'Gospel and Law', as well as in his treatment of the ethics of creation, Barth has already expounded the law as 'the form of the gospel', rather than as a source of knowledge of sin *extra Christum*. His argument that the gospel always has 'the form of law, commandment, demand, claim'[6] has been variously censured – as a sort of monism in which Father and Son are the only real agents (Thielicke[7]); as an attempt to smuggle deontological thinking into the gospel ethos (Niebuhr[8]); as further evidence of the dominance of epistemology over soteriology in his work (Wingren[9]). However just some of these criticisms, the heart of Barth's argument here is that human persons under grace remain agents. Ruling grace is commanding grace, in the sense that grace establishes a community of agency between God and his human covenant partners. As Jüngel comments, 'Barth's version of the relationship of gospel and law is . . . concerned with this correspondence, this analogy between God and humanity, an *already* ontological correspondence between the existence of God as pure act and the existence of the human person who is self-defined in action'.[10] Set within the context of election to the covenant, the law is no longer primarily accusatory. Rather, it incorporates into the relationship between God and his creatures the imperatival aspect which makes the recipients of grace more than mere beneficiaries.

Third, Barth chooses the rubric of 'invocation' (*Anrufung*) as the term to describe the Christian life as creaturely response to divine grace. After reviewing several alternatives, Barth settles on 'invocation' because it states most clearly the relationship of grace to responsive human action that forms the central theme of the ethics of reconciliation. To say that the Christian invokes the gracious God is certainly to envisage human persons as *subsequent*, since invocation is 'the normal action corresponding to the fulfilment of the covenant in Jesus Christ' and in invocation the Christian 'acts as one who is referred wholly to God and has absolute need of him' (*ChrL*, p. 43). Yet the gracious God so invoked is not the inhibition of action or the removal of its necessity, for 'God has turned to him [the Christian] and summoned him to this venture', so that in invoking God 'man in his whole humanity takes his proper place over against God' (*ibid*.).

(2) Paragraph 75 fills out these formal remarks by an account of Christian baptism. In essence, Barth distinguishes sharply between baptism with the Holy Spirit, which is exclusively God's own act, and baptism with water, which is the corresponding human act of obedience and allegiance. This distinction, maintained over against the weight of the Reformed tradition, 'even Calvin' (*CD* IV/4: ix), contains *in nuce* an entire account of the relation between divine and creaturely agency. The divine act of baptism with the Holy Spirit is creative and evocative; it generates the Christian life begun in water baptism which signifies the recovery of the-

Christian's identity as worker in partnership with the Lord of the covenant. Following through what Barth calls 'my radically new view' (*ibid.*) involves him in denials: of the practice (or at least the abuse) of infant baptism, and above all of the sacramental status of baptism with water. What lies behind the denials, however, is an affirmation: at conversion, the Christian is miraculously and yet firmly set on his feet.

Perhaps the most significant feature of Barth's argument is the variety and complexity of his Christology and the kinds of arguments that he seeks to base upon it. On the one hand, he insists on the vicarious nature of the humanity of Jesus Christ. The Christian life initiated in baptism rests upon the status of Jesus Christ as 'the Representative of all men', the one who acts 'in the name and stead of all' (*CD* IV/4:13). But Barth is keenly aware that to root the Christian life in Christ as vicarious historical subject may so lodge its reality in an external accomplishment that it lacks any recognizable human substance. 'How', asks Barth, 'can that which he was and did *extra nos* become an event *in nobis*?' (*CD* IV/4:18). His answer to that question is not so much a retraction of his Christological grounding of human action as its further refinement, through the elaboration of 'a true Christocentricity' (*CD* IV/4:19). The key term in his proposal is that of 'correspondence' (*Entsprechung*); no account of 'the ethical problem of the Christian life' can be allowed which fails to talk of 'a human activity corresponding to the divine activity' (*CD* IV/4:19 – '*eines dem Handeln Gottes entsprechenden menschlichen Handelns*'). The conceptuality of 'correspondence' is central to Barth's proposal here because it articulates a sense of God and man as distinct and yet related agents whose identities may not be run together and whose roles may not be exchanged or confused or collapsed into each other. The history of Jesus Christ is thus not *only* substitutionary, such that all subsequent histories simply look back to a perfected achievement. His history generates imitation: it 'includes the fact that, as it took place there and then, in the history of that One, it also takes place here and now, *in nobis*, in the life of the many' (*CD* IV/4:22).

Crucially, then, Barth is exploring a different kind of Christology from what might be expected of him – a point that can be illustrated from T. F. Torrance's critique of Barth in his distinguished essay 'The One Baptism Common to Christ and his Church'.[11] Torrance finds Barth's final account of baptism 'deeply inconsistent'[12] with the incarnational and trinitarian structure of the rest of his thought, because it underplays the vicarious character of Jesus' obedience in his own baptism, into which the Christian enters at his or her own 'baptism': 'There is *one baptism* and *one Body* through *one Spirit*. Christ and his Church participate in the one baptism in different ways – Christ actively and vicariously as Redeemer, the Church passively and receptively as the redeemed Community'.[13] In the end, Barth and Torrance part company because the latter allows little substance to the notions of covenant partnership and reciprocal agency which are deeply embedded in the structure of Barth's account. Torrance, indeed, explicitly repudiates what he calls the trapping of grace 'within a reciprocity between God and man'.[14] Behind this lies a deeper incompatibility at the level of Christology: where Torrance sees the acts of Jesus as solely vicarious, Barth sees them as representative acts which are nevertheless more than simply completed events containing proleptically our involvement: they are 'really an imperative' (*CD* IV/4:67).

So Barth's point unfolds as one about human *maturity*. Grace does not furnish us with excuses for inaction. Hope in Christ and his gracious provision for human sin in his death and resurrection is not such that it sanctions a drift into the kind of dependence where our actions make no significant contribution to the fabric of our lives. Baptism is not fate; in it, candidate and community are not 'the instruments and objects of an event which storms past them' (*CD* IV/4:132). Offering oneself for baptism is neither regression nor resignation: it is consent. Here, in this call to courage and hope, the Christian is not 'put under tutelage, but addressed and treated as an adult' (IV/4: 22f).

III

In the course of some talks to students on the theme of 'the Christian life' which he gave in 1926, Barth remarked that 'the question about the Christian life as a question about what happens to us, about our own little Ego, is a special one that very well deserves to be asked'.[15] Thirty-five years later, in his final attempt to write about sanctification, Barth is still asking the same question, still seeking a way of portraying the Christian life as a perceptible form of voluntary agency.

(1) 'A Life in this Vocative' (paragraph 76)

His account in paragraph 76 begins with a remarkable series of short meditations on the word '*Vater!*' as he seeks to show that the *lex orandi* implies a *lex credendi* which in turn contains a *lex agendi*. *Vater!* Why is the word of such singular significance? In summary form, Barth's argument is that the vocative is fundamental to the theological grammar of the word, since its case specifies both the priority of God as subject and agent and human subsequence in relation to him. In that Christian language about God is primordially vocative, it retains reference to the antecedent subjectivity of God: invocation of God is 'invocation of the self-acting Subject-Father' (*ChrL*, p. 53)

So far the *lex credendi* which the *lex orandi* contains. But what of the *lex agendi*? There is much here which suggests that the Christian life, whose determining motif is invocation of God as Father, is wholly taken up with God as the 'self-acting Subject' and not with Christian subjectivity and agency. Such an impression is certainly reinforced by the second part of paragraph 76 (pp. 69–85) where, in turning to 'the children of the Father', Barth offers an extended reflection on the graciousness of human sonship of God:

> The freedom of the children of God to do what they are commanded to do is purely and simply the work and gift of the grace that is addressed to them and recognized by them. Because it is grace, the freedom cannot be one that is inherited or

won. On any other basis and with any other origin it would be a pretended and false freedom, a secret and even an open non-freedom. Grace is the presence, event, and revelation of what man cannot think or do or reach or attain or grasp, but of what is, in virtue of its coming from God, the most simple, true and real of all things . . . (*ChrL*, pp. 71f)

Because the authorization and entitlement to invoke God as Father lies wholly in the incarnational co-fraternity of Christ with humanity, 'our divine sonship, and with it the freedom to make use of it, is in no sense to be sought in ourselves but in him, and it is in him that it will always be found' (*ChrL*, p. 76). Deploying the notion of the Word's assumption of humanity in this way brings Barth close to disrupting the sense of the substantiality of human agency which, in the end, he is seeking to maintain. And so, tellingly, the language of infancy begins to appear: Christians only encounter God 'as those who are inept, inexperienced, unskilled, and immature' (*ChrL*, p. 79); the Christian meets God as 'a newly registered pupil' (*ibid*), or as 'beginner' (*ChrL*, p. 80); 'in the sphere of the covenant the decisive people are not the tested masters but the unproved pupils' (*ChrL*, p. 81). All of this is intended as a refusal of the Christian life as skill, as grace routinized to 'a learned and practised art' (*ChrL*, p. 79). But it would not be impossible to argue that here Barth has begun to slip into one of the traps of language about divine paternity, namely its encoding of regression.

How, then, can he simultaneously propose that the covenant is one 'which God did not just establish between himself and man but in which man was called and impelled to play his own free and active part' (*ChrL*, p. 74)? His chief resource in shaking himself free of some of these entanglements is the flexibility of his Christology. The whole of the meditation on the vocative structure of Christian ethics is undergirded by the notion of Christ as substitute, in the benefits of whose assumption of human nature Christians share. Alongside this vicarious humanity model, however, there is a significantly different account of the relationship between Christ and humanity, in which Jesus Christ is an *exemplar*. And so Barth can write, for example, that 'Jesus Christ founded calling upon God the Father – and made it binding upon his people – by doing it first himself, and in so doing giving a prior example of what he demanded of them . . . He took them up into the movement of his own prayer' (*ChrL*, p. 64). Here the two models combine: Christ's vicarious invocation elicits further invocation. The same is found in a series of statements: Jesus Christ is the one who 'enables, invites and summons' (*ChrL*, p. 63); Christians pray 'according to the permission, command and order of Christ' (*ibid*), 'after him and with him' (*ChrL*, p. 64) who is 'in the place and at the head of all men' (*ibid*).

The more that Barth focusses on prayer as human action, the more evident it becomes that the sufficiency of the vicarious humanity model is called into question. Both of Barth's substantial discussions of petitionary prayer in the course of his exposition of the doctrine of creation return frequently to this point[16]: once the propriety of 'asking' in the Christian's relationship with God is admitted, a duality of agency is presupposed and any notion of divine sole causality is disqualified. As he takes up the theme of invocation in paragraph 76.3, the same issue emerges: 'What [God] wills with and for these children is . . . history, intercourse, and living dealings between himself and them, between them and himself. They too have to enter into those dealings on their side. They have to actualize the partnership in history' (*ChrL*, p. 85):

> the God who is known as 'our Father' in Jesus Christ is not this supreme being who is self-enclosed, who cannot be codetermined from outside, who is condemned to work alone. He is a God who in overflowing grace has chosen and is free to have authentic and not just apparent dealings, intercourse, and exchange with his children. He is their free Father, not in a lofty isolation in which he would be the prisoner of his own majesty, but in his history with them as his free children whom he himself has freed. He does not just speak to them. He wills that he also be spoken to, that they also speak to him. As the Founder and the perfect Lord of this concursus, he wills their work as well. He for his part will not work without them. He

will work only in connection with their work. (*ChrL*, p. 103)

To affirm the reciprocity of human and divine agency is not a limitation of divine freedom, but rather its specification. A 'God condemned to work alone' is a prisoner of his own sovereignty, restricted in his capacity to engage in relationship. On Barth's account, God is not 'so omnipotent, or rather, so impotent, that as they call upon him, liberated and commanded to do so by him, he will not and cannot hear them, letting a new action be occasioned by them, causing his own work and rule to correspond to their invocation' (*ChrL*, p. 103).

What Barth has to say in paragraph 76 is, then, very instructive about the essentially unfinished nature of his theology. Even at the end of his life, his theological instincts were various, and he remained deeply suspicious of moves to suppress one or other of them by according preponderant significance to one factor alone. Moreover his writing here shows something of the unsettled character of his Christology, which has still not crystallized into a single theological principle, in the face of which all other theological work is a matter of mere corollaries.

(2) 'Hallowed be Thy Name' (paragraph 77)

> Father, do what thou alone canst do. See to it finally, perfectly, and definitively that thou and thy name are known – only known, and no longer in any place or to any person unknown. See to it that thy name is no longer desecrated but always and by everybody regarded as holy in the way that it is in fact holy as thy name that thou thyself hast sanctified. Dispel the fatal ambivalence of our situation. (*ChrL*, p. 115f)

– thus Barth's paraphrase of the first petition of the Lord's Prayer, which provides the text for paragraph 77, under the rubric 'Zeal for the Honour of God'. He expounds that petition as a cry to God to put an end to the régime of ambiguity, hesitancy and vacillation in respect of God which characterizes the public history of the world, the life of the Christian community and above all the personal life of the Christian believer.

It soon becomes evident as we read that Barth does not envisage the putting to an end of this 'ambiguous, divided and ambivalent situation' (*ChrL*, p. 115) as simply a divine self-sanctification; it is also a call to human persons to assume responsibilities and involves a purposive redirection of their wills. Much of the latter part of the exposition, most especially the fourth sub-section on 'the Precedence of the Word of God' is given over to an account of how human beings decide to do away with vacillation and consciously and voluntarily give allegiance to God. Certainly the third sub-section ('Hallowed be Thy Name!') argues with some passion (and against both Augustine and the Reformers) that the end of the régime of vacillation can in one sense only be brought about by an act which is God's and his alone: 'we have here a petition to God that he himself should sanctify his name and thus do in the matter what he alone can do' (*ChrL*, p. 156). But that being said and firmly understood, there remains a 'corresponding willing, acting and doing on man's part' (*ibid*) which the fourth sub-section (pp. 168–204) explores in considerable detail. Once again: *lex orandi lex agendi* – 'The order to ask God to hallow his name implies a command to do something ourselves in the matter' (*ChrL*, p. 168).

Christians are to act with a zeal for God's honour which 'corresponds and is analogous to his divine act' (*ChrL*, p. 170); their hallowing is 'analogous . . . to the hallowing of God's name for which we pray' (*ChrL*, p. 172). It is important to realize that Barth does not simply formally register the importance of an action corresponding to petition to God for him to work: he also seeks to portray something, at least, of the person of the human agent. His treatment of 'the Precedence of the Word of God' is, indeed, one of the most realistic attempts to portray Christian agency in the entire corpus of Barth's writings. 'Portray' is used deliberately. For Barth almost completely refrains from further theoretical discussion of the relation of virtuous human action to its transcendent ground. Instead, he fixes his attention upon the process whereby the Christian adopts and prosecutes a policy of life in resistance to the régime of vacillation. In this extended exploration of Christian resoluteness, as in the remarkable passage on 'the lordless powers' in paragraph 78, there surfaces something of the empiricism which, it is alleged, is absent from Barth's work. Certainly this is one of the passages in Barth's later work whose unschematic account of the moral life may remind the reader of an aspect of Butler's sermons.[17] Admittedly Barth does not often betray the same acute and detailed moral psychology as Butler, nor Butler's hesitations with regard to theoretical construction or general concepts. Yet there is a realistic acceptance of the limits of Christian resolution, a certain reluctance to set moral goals which are not realizable. The rubric which Barth chooses for the Christian's action which corresponds to God's self-sanctification – the *precedence* of the Word of God – is deliberately restrained, over against more exalted terms such as 'the *lordship* of God's Word' which Barth considers and then lays aside:

> The phrase 'precedence of God's Word' is perhaps a little weak, yet it is appropriate . . . when our task is that of trying to understand and characterize zeal for God's honour very plainly as an action which may be ascribed to us people, which is humanly possible . . . Would we not be guilty of doing something that is unfortunately all too frequent in the language of the church, namely, filling our mouths with grandiose speech, saying too little in too big words, if we were to tell Christians that they had to establish that lordship and practice that subjection in their own lives? Would this . . . be asking for something ethically attainable, something they could and would practice? To allow and give the Word of God precedence over other constitutive factors in their lives – that is something that *can* take place. It *can* be done.[18]

'Precedence', moreover, acknowledges that the Christian's choice and resolution to honour God's name is a choice which does not ignore other claims but which is set in the midst of them. There can be no question of the reduction of the moral life to a single principle, adherence to which constitutes the whole sum of obedience to God. And so the Christian's resolution to honour God does not obliterate or render uninteresting his other roles and relations, as '*Homo sapiens, Homo faber, Homo ludens*, as father, businessman, teacher, as patriot with obligations here or there, as thinker oriented more idealistically or more positivistically, as a man with this or that political or aesthetic gift, and simply as a sexual being, with all that that implies. So be it' (*ChrL*, pp. 179f). Set in this situation, necessarily and inescapably so, the Christian can only grant to God's claim 'the position that is its due at the head of all the factors that claim us, when we resolve at all costs to hear its claim first and only then, as determined by this claim, the claims of the other factors' (*ChrL*, p. 179).

Barth ranges, then, over some of the ways in which the Christian's deeds and decisions are limited, fragmentary, lacking in that finality and absoluteness which can be predicated only of God's perfect act. Yet for just this reason, the Christian may not be excused from acting. His acts are, certainly, 'interim steps' with 'no more than provisional significance and range' (*ChrL*. pp. 180f). But 'one thing . . . (the Christian) will never have cause or reason to do, namely to refrain from action like the lazy servant' (*ChrL*, p. 181). The treatment of sin in the earlier sections of the doctrine of reconciliation contains, we may recall, a long meditation on human sloth – a passage which is grounded in sober observation of human habit and of the sheer mediocrity to which men and women can condemn themselves.[19] Seen against this background, Barth's insistence upon the Christian's 'rebellion and resistance against the régime of vacillation' (*ChrL*, p. 174) takes on sharper contours:

> The Christian would be no true man, or would know himself poorly in his humanity if, apart from all that he sees outside himself, he did not see the whole stream of his own human thought and feeling, desire and will, flowing down strongly to the ocean wastes of compromise between light and darkness. But the Word of God, which has made him a witness to the light without shadow, wants from him the big but not impossible thing that precisely as a person, no matter what may be the result, he should not flow with the stream, but that following the lead of the Word and accepting its discipline, he should continually swim against it. (*ChrL*, p. 187)

The Christian acts, the Christian chooses in the face of all that is brought to bear upon him, and in this way he repudiates 'the status quo, the law of the recurrence of all things' (*ChrL*, p. 180). Barth's refusal of fate, we note, is not couched in the language of heroism, nor is it detached from realistic appraisal of the intractability of circumstance. But, nevertheless, human history is affected by conscious human purpose, and Christians more than any other people are to encourage what William Walsh calls 'resistance by the person to the encroachment of the context'[20]. The final, and perhaps the most remarkable paragraph of *The Christian Life* explores further how the Christian 'presents himself to other men of the world as a nonconformist' (*ChrL*, p. 204).

(3) 'Thy Kingdom Come' (paragraph 78)

As we read through the section on 'the lordless powers' early on in the final paragraph of *The Christian Life* (pp. 213–33), it is difficult to escape Barth's sense of the waste caused by human wickedness. Sin is not Promethean. It is impoverishment, belittlement brought about by a disordering of man's relation to himself. Sin is a dislocation of human identity; it dislodges man by disturbing an ordered set of relations in which he may find himself. He seeks an identity in abstraction from and in opposition to God's order. It is the deceit of sin that he believes such opposition to God is the path to self-mastery; but 'in no case does this result in his becoming the lord and master of the possibilities of his own life' (*ChrL*, p. 214). Like the sorcerer's apprentice, he finds that his own powers 'become spirits with a life and activity of their own, lordless, indwelling forces' (*ibid*):

> Parallel to the history of his emancipation from God there runs that of the emancipation of his own possibilities of life from himself: the history of the overpowering of his desires, aspirations and will by the power, the superpower of his ability . . . To be sure, he thinks he can take them in hand, control them, and direct them as he pleases, for they are undoubtedly the forces of his own possibilities and capacities, of his own ability. In reality, however, they escape from him, they have already

escaped from him. They are long since alienated from him. They act at their own pleasure, as absolutes, without him, behind him, over him, and against him . . . In reality, he does not control them but they him. They do not serve him but he them . . . If we are to see the disorder and unrighteousness which corrupt human life and fellowship, we must not only not deny, but consider very seriously, not merely man's rebellion against God, but also the rebellion unleashed by it, that of human abilities, exalting themselves as lordless forces, against man himself. (*ChrL*, pp. 214f)

The sinner, then, falls into hopeless self-alienation, rendering himself subject to pseudo-powers whose pretence to dominion simply masks the fact that 'they belong to him' (*ChrL*, p. 215). Man without God *suffers*, in every sense of the word.

The Christian is freed by God to be a rebel against these lordless powers. At no point is Barth's understanding of agency as fundamental to human nature more powerfully reaffirmed: it is the man of faith who rejects the régime of necessity, who is not satisfied with the passivity of the sinner under the forces he has unleashed; the Christian as it were disenchants the world by acting humanly in it:

> What they are commanded to do is to move against this plight, to enter into conflict with it. They are thus commanded to realize that it ought not to oppress people. This is not proper for it. It is no part of human nature. It is not a fate bound up with human existence. It is against nature. It is an alien dominion to which people themselves have appealed – this is their guilt – and to whose service they have given themselves. Hence it does not really have the dignity and legitimacy and therefore the ineluctability of a divine decree. From the pressure of this plight, people, if they are not free, can and should become free again . . . People who know God's will – and Christians should be such people – cannot in any circumstance accept this plight as an unalterable reality, even though no people, not even Christians, can overcome it or rescue humanity from the pressure of its rule. In all circumstances the Christian is summoned and is in a position to rebel against this plight, to rise up against it, to enter into conflict with it. (*ChrL*, p. 211)

But how can the *Christian* be a 'man in revolt'? A rebel, says Camus, is 'a man who says no, but whose refusal does not imply a renunciation. He is also a man who says yes as soon as he begins to think for himself'.[21] Rebellion, that is, concerns itself with the retrieval of the self and its worth: 'in every act of rebellion, the man concerned experiences not only a feeling of revulsion at the infringement of his rights but also a complete and spontaneous loyalty to certain aspects of himself'.[22] And so grace and revolt cannot coexist:

> The rebel is a man who is on the point of accepting or rejecting the sacrosanct and determined on creating a human situation where all the answers are human or, rather, formulated in terms of reason. From this moment every question, every word, is an act of rebellion, while in the sacrosanct world every word is an act of grace. It would be possible to demonstrate in this manner that only two possible worlds can exist for the human mind, the sacrosanct (or, to speak in Christian terms, the world of Grace) or the rebel world.[23]

The world of grace, the heteronomous 'sacrosanct' world, is always a place of diminishment and bondage. And so again: how can the Christian be a rebel?

Barth's account of 'the lordless powers' is one of the few significant treatments of revolt in recent theological literature[24], and is notable above all for the seriousness with which it registers the proper claims of human selfhood. Like Camus, Barth fastens upon the theme of revolt because of the primacy which it accords to human deeds. For Camus (and here he follows the analysis of Scheler) revolt is quite different from resentment in just this respect. Resentment is passive, self-involved, 'auto-intoxication' – 'the evil secretion, in a sealed vessel, of prolonged impotence'.[25] The mainspring of revolt, on the other hand, is 'the principle of superabundant activity and energy'.[26] Similarly for Barth the Christian's revolt is not a mere defensive gesture. It does not 'curve in upon itself' (*ChrL*, p. 206); it is not simply negative, simply the rejection of certain possibilities, but 'entry into the struggle for the actualization of a very different possibility' (*ChrL*, p. 207). For both Camus and Barth, that is, revolt entails the repudiation of historical necessity and a positive assertion of human work as the means to achieve a different reality. But there remains a deep divide over the question of the limits of human work. For Camus, human autonomy is, simply, absolute: 'rebellion plays the same role as does the *cogito* in the category of thought: it is the first clue'.[27] For Barth, it is quite otherwise: the Christian's protest against human diminishment and his attempt to realize a different order, is inseparable from his prayer: 'Thy kingdom come'. If the Christian maintains that neither 'the unrighteousness and disorder . . . of (man's) existence, nor the manifestation of this in the lordship of the powers which he has unleashed and which oppress and afflict him, can establish a definitive situation or represent an ineluctable fate' (*ChrL*, p. 234), it is only because he has been given freedom to call upon God. In the end, revolt takes its rise not in the actualization or preservation of the self, but in 'God's own revolt against the world he made'.[28]

Human revolt is rooted in prayer for the coming of God's kingdom. Barth devotes a good deal of space to defending the priority of divine action. 'Thy kingdom *come*' – the verb is of great importance, furnishing a focal term in Barth's exposition of how God's decisive deeds in establishing the kingdom relate to the deeds of his creatures. Prayer for the *coming* of God's kingdom presupposes that the kingdom is not within the range of possibilities realized by human action. It is 'the great new thing on the margin – yet outside and not inside the margin of the horizon of all the perceptions and conceptions of us people who are people of disorder' (*ChrL*, p. 237). The kingdom is transcendent, unrepresentable; it 'defies expression' (*ibid*). In ethical terms, this means that prayer for the coming of God's kingdom is prayer for God's own work; the kingdom is 'independent of human will and act and different from all the human works and achievements into whose sphere it enters. It is God's own independent action which limits all human history from outside, which is sovereign in relation to it' (*ChrL*, p. 246). More specifically, prayer for the coming of God's kingdom is a possible venture only on the basis of the presence of the kingdom in the person and work of Jesus Christ: '"the kingdom of God is at hand" means "the Word was made flesh and dwelt among us"' (*ChrL*, p. 249). In a set of paragraphs of considerable rhetorical force, Barth insists on the Christological *Er* and *Damals* – the absolute, irreducible singularity of God's being and acts which not only signify but are the kingdom:

> Jesus Christ is the new thing. *He* is the mystery that cannot be imprisoned in any system of human conceptuality but can be revealed and known only in parables. *He* is God acting concretely within human history. *He* is the one who calls those who know him to obedient willing and doing but who is and remains free from all human willing and knowing . . . Simply and solely *he himself*: accomplishing and completing God's work for the salvation of the world . . . (*ChrL*, p. 252)

> The New Testament writings . . . and with the New Testament writings the New Testament community, all look back to the past of the history of the coming of Jesus and to the past of the drawing near of the kingdom of God as to an incomparably and uniquely great *then* (*Damals*) . . . The *then* which in its inexhaustibility they keep before them either directly or indirectly as they look back to it is the presupposition of the prayer 'Thy kingdom come'. (*ChrL*, p. 253)

In view of all this, is not Camus' critique irrefutable? Is it possible, in the face of Barth's insistence on the perfection and incommunicability of divine action, to continue to talk in any real way of man as worker? Barth's response, implicit in the closing pages of *The Christian Life*, in the section entitled 'Fiat iustitia!', is a little tired, a little less taut than what has gone before. But it contains the elements of two main lines of argument.

First, there is a reiteration of the point made throughout his various discussions of prayer: prayer, which is itself responsible human action, cannot be divorced from a corresponding ethos. When Christians pray 'Thy kingdom come', 'then necessarily with their hearts and lips, caught up by what they pray, their whole life and thought and word and deed are set in motion, oriented to the point to which they look in their petition' (*ChrL*, p. 262). Prayer is not mere consent, not simply calling upon the strengths of Another, but that which actualizes the will and energies of the Christian and sets them upon specific paths.

But second, and more importantly, Barth tries to sketch a way in which the world of grace and the rebel world may co-exist. For Camus, the recovery of man entails the deposition of God; for Barth, the matter is more that of distinguishing properly between God and man, in such a way as to restore to man his proper, 'de-absolutized', humanity.[29] Barth is trying, that is, to construct a route between heteronomy and autonomy and so refuse a relationship of mutual contradiction between God and man. Thus he suggests that alongside prayer to God to establish his kingdom, there is also a properly human struggle for a properly human righteousness. The issue in proper and necessary human revolt is 'human, not divine righteousness' (*ChrL*. p. 264), since 'God's righteousness is the affair of God's own act' (ibid). But as with the refusal of sacramental status to baptism with water, so here: the apparent restriction of the scope of human action is not a jealous fencing of the divine preserve, but intended to the praise of human action as just that – *human*, and not quasi-divine:

> . . . precisely because perfect righteousness stands before them as God's work, precisely because they are duly forbidden to attempt the impossible, precisely because all experiments in this direction are prevented and prohibited, they are with great strictness required and with great kindness freed and empowered to do what they can do in the sphere of the relative possibilities assigned to them, to do it very imperfectly yet heartily, quietly and cheerfully. They are absolved from wasting time and energy sighing over the impassable limits of their sphere of action and thus missing the opportunities that present themselves in this sphere. They may and can and should rise up and accept responsibility to the utmost of their power for the doing of the little righteousness. (*ChrL*, p. 265)

Once again, the language of 'correspondence' provides a means of stating how divine and human action are neither identical nor mutually contradictory. The action of those who invoke God is 'kingdom-like' (ChrL, p. 266); in relation to and correspondence with God's own act, 'the action of Christians may in its own way and within its own limits be called a righteous action' (*ibid*).

On this basis, Barth hints at a concept of revolt which disentangles it from association with pure human autonomy. The plight of man is one in which his 'human right and dignity (is) being constantly overlooked, forgotten, broken and trampled under the lordship of the released and lordless powers' (*ChrL*, p. 266); it is proper that Christians should fiercely resist the impoverishment and corruption of human worth. But Barth is deeply, unremittingly hostile to human autonomy, which he reads as an evasion of the problem of self-loss, not an answer to it. 'Man himself *suffers*, and he fights tooth and nail against admitting this even to himself, let alone to others. He acts – this is the point of his disguises – as if he does not suffer' (*ChrL*, p. 269). Christian revolt, on the other hand, is the courage to identify and act in those spheres of life where we need not suffer, and, cheerfully and in good conscience, to leave all other matters to God. Once, that is, we begin to see grace as a divine undertaking which takes away from us our self-divinization and not the agency which is proper to creatures, it appears as a blessing and not an erosion. And so understood, the divine act of grace issues in a right human autonomy: an autonomy which is not human omnicompetence, but competence in those things which are our proper concern.

IV

Anything like a full appraisal of these last texts from Barth's hand is beyond the scope of this essay, which is primarily expository[30]. But an agenda of issues for reflection might be sketched.

Barth is sometimes represented by both admirers and detractors as consistent in a monolithic way, and his work thought to possess a degree of cohesiveness unparalleled in recent Protestant theology because of the substantive and methodological role accorded to Christology. But *The Christian Life* (and here it shares a feature with much of the rest of the *Church Dogmatics*) shows that 'Christocentrism' is too indefinite a term, covering too wide a range of affirmations about the person and work of Jesus Christ and their relation to human existence. Whilst the general place and function of Christology in Barth's work has been universally recognized, there is still a dearth of detailed accounts of its operation which are attentive to particular patterns of argument to be found in Barth's use of Christological material. Much can be gleaned from, for example, Charles Waldrop's study of the Antiochene and Alexandrian elements in Barth's Christology; but even here, the typology is rather too clearly polarized to yield a sufficiently precise descriptive account of how a range of different Christological affirmations are often combined in specific contexts.[31]

Barth's last writings are, however, of interest not only for the light they shed on his work, but also for the way in which they may help us give some specificity to a large set of questions about the relationship of grace to human agency, and to associated issues of the possibility of religious morality. The complexity of the issues here is easily obscured by slogans ('religious morality is infantile'[32]) which are simply inattentive to the details of particular religious convictions and their relationship to moral policy. In James Gustafson's fine book, *Christ and the Moral Life*, which is a presentation of 'how interpretations of the significance of the work of Christ are believed to entail certain consequences for the moral life'[33], he remarks that 'much closer and more detailed work needs to be done on particular crucial texts in particular authors'.[34] Certainly a close study of Barth's writings here would be a very significant task in observing with some precision how a set of theological convictions operates in a moral context. Barth shows that the (usually pejorative) term 'religious ethics' is banal, being devoid of content without qualifiers which point to particular traditions of argument.

More specifically, Barth may stimulate further reflection on the coinherence of morality and beliefs about the way the world is. Barth's theology is descriptive rather than apologetic or foundational. It is not, that is, inquiry into the transcendental conditions of a tradition of thought and speech about God so much as a description of such thought and speech. As Hans Frei remarks,

> Barth was about the business of conceptual redescription. He took the classical themes of communal Christian language moulded by the Bible, tradition and constant usage, in worship, practice, instruction and controversy, and he restated or redescribed them, rather than evolving arguments on their behalf . . . Barth had as it were to recreate a universe of discourse, and he had to put the reader in the middle of that world, instructing him in the use of that language by showing him how – extensively, and not only by stating the rules or principles of the discourse.[35]

Barth does not approach the tradition of Christian language by inquiry into its continuity with or grounding in other sorts of speech; he *uses* the language, attending to the logic of its habitual use and relying on what he took to be its inherent power to convict of its own meaningfulness. In terms of Barth's ethics, it is in this context that we are to understand its fierce particularism, its insistence that Christian ethics is not *Ethik*. The character of Christian ethics is determined by a series of events concerning Jesus Christ, and by the world which those events evoke and in which they are represented as possibilities for human living. The meaning of obligation is thus specified by reference to an irreducible world of discourse in which it is deployed and takes on a specific shape in Christian usage, a shape poorly perceived unless reference be made to theological convictions about God's action and creaturely existence.

Barth's ethics, like the theology of which it is a part, is hostile to abstraction; he rejects any idea that there might be a single, isolatable essence of 'morality' which can be extracted from the determinants of the habits and belief-structure of particular communities. This hostility to abstraction could also be seen as a radically *historical* attitude: Christian ethics is concerned with a particular set of events (the action of God in Christ) and the community which is brought into being by that action and thereby invited to enter into certain roles.

A number of recent writers have lent weight to Barth's particularism and his insistence on the theological character of Christian ethics. Some have argued the difficulty of establishing precise boundaries between religious and ethical language, since the description of the one seems inevitably to slide over into descriptions of the other[36]; others have brought to theology the emphasis on the cultural and social specificity of human intention and action which derives much of its authority from the later work of Wittgenstein.[37] Those who have prosecuted the latter line of argument have been strong in the advocacy of the role of community in moral formation, such that the self-descriptions of the agent cannot be understood apart from his belonging to a particular social setting in which a community perpetuates itself by training its members in the use of certain foundational narratives. Barth would, I suspect, have viewed some of this 'post-liberal' or 'intratextual' theology (the terms are Lindbeck's) with a measure of scepticism, partly for its implicit or explicit relativism, partly for its odd authoritarianism, partly for the ease with which it may abandon questions of the reference of religious discourse by concentrating so heavily on use and function. Nevertheless, with much of it he would have been at home.

More substantively, Barth may offer help in rephrasing questions about the relation of grace to morality. He is, as we have seen, deeply aware that the notion of grace can serve to corrode our sense of morality as a deliberate human project: the 'gift' character of well-doing is a profoundly ambiguous part of what Christian theology has to say about human existence. Barth's response to the ambiguity is to undertake a series of detailed examinations of the nature of heteronomy, by exploring how the history of Jesus Christ functions as a ground for the Christian life. By this, he is able to show with some success that, properly construed, the divine command is not an arbitrary external authority, repressive of growth into maturity and responsibility, but rather that which *both* accomplishes *and* (to use Gene Outka's terminology) 'elicits':

> Grace elicits rather than invades in that the agent must actively respond, not just passively receive. Grace elicits rather than infuses in that nothing fundamentally non-human is introduced as an extension of given human powers. The creaturely response considered in itself is never more than creaturely. Elicitation also differs from acquirement in that virtue is evoked and sustained from without; it is not simply self-activated and self-directed. The agent is drawn to do what he cannot do by himself.[38]

From the very beginnings of his rediscovery of the irreducibility of the divine in his urgent interrogation of Paul's Epistle to the Romans, Barth's theology is consistent in emphasising the *necessary* character of God. God *is*; God cannot be represented in patterns of language or action; his reality is impervious to our probings, and can only be received in its own inherent *Istigkeit*. But crucially for Barth, to be faced with such a reality which defies assimilation is not to be reduced to resignation, but rather to be summoned and impelled to purposeful action. His last writings are an attempt to describe both the action and the invitation which lies at its heart.

8

On Honour: By Way of a Comparison of Barth and Trollope

STANLEY HAUERWAS

I *Justifying the Comparison*

My aim is to show that Barth's main problem is that he did not read enough Trollope. Indeed I can find no evidence that Barth ever read Trollope. I am aware that this thesis may well strike many as a bit odd. How can I possibly think that any juxtaposing of two people as different as Barth and Trollope makes sense? After all, theologians and novelists generally do not mix. Moreover, they come from completely different times and seem to have quite different sensibilities about human existence – somehow I do not think Mozart was Trollope's favourite composer. Barth was formed personally and intellectually by confronting Hitler. Trollope faced the English postal service. In spite of such obvious obstacles I am determined to bring Barth and Trollope into conversation for no other reason than that I have learned much from each and, therefore, I cannot help but believe that there must be some sense in which they are complementary.

Such a comparison, of course, is fraught with difficulties, not the least of which is that neither Barth nor Trollope is easily summarized. Indeed one of the things I most like about Barth is that his position defies summary because he was so determinedly unsystematic, making it almost impossible to know what it would mean to be a 'Barthian'. Gerhardt Sauter reports that he jokingly tells his students 'You cannot quote Barth', because a countercitation can always be found from Barth himself. Sauter observes that this does not mean that Barth did not think consistently, but rather indicates that Barth's trend of thought is not a one-dimensional movement nor a clear progression. Barth saw that theology is incapable of saying everything at one time. So any attempt to wrap everything up into one concept which is continually unfolded simply will not work. Thus Sauter quotes Barth as describing his theology as trying 'to trace the bird's flight'.[1]

In that respect I think it is not so odd to compare Barth's work with that of a novelist. For just as any good novel cannot be captured by a summary of its plot, by a description of the characters, or by trying to say what it is about, so Barth's theology cannot be summarized. There is no substitute for reading the *Church Dogmatics*, just as the *Church Dogmatics* tries to remind us there is no substitute for reading the Bible.[2] As Hans Frei puts it, Barth was in the business of 'conceptual description: he took the classical themes of communal Christian language moulded by the Bible, tradition and constant usage in worship, practice, instruction and controversy, and he restated or redescribed them rather than evolving arguments on their behalf. It was of the utmost importance to him that this communal language, especially its biblical *fons et origo*, which he saw as indirectly one with the Word of God, has an integrity of its own: it was irreducible. But in that case its lengthy, even leisurely unfolding was equally indispensable.'[3]

If this is true, and I certainly think it is, then the procedure adopted in this essay is even more doubtful. For by concentrating on one aspect of Barth's ethics, and what appears to be a quite minor theme, it risks distorting his overall perspective. There is no way, of course, which can avoid the possibility of such misrepresentation. Rather, all that can be done is to ask the reader's patience to see whether comparison of Barth with Trollope does not in fact illumine Barth's method and help to locate some of the difficulties in Barth's ethics.

The method used is quite straightforward. Barth's discussion of the concept of honour at the end of *Church Dogmatics*, (III/4 (§56.3)) will be briefly presented. Then an attempt will be made to exhibit Trollope's understanding of honour by discussing one of his late novels, *Dr Wortle's School*. The latter is in many ways a more difficult task than the former as care will have to be taken not to turn Trollope's novel into a 'position' in the interest of schematic comparison. For, it is exactly the strength of Trollope's and Barth's understandings of honour to resist reducing honour to a formula or principle.

But why honour of all things? Honour is usually associated with what is owed to grandmothers in the South or what is still talked about but not embodied in military academies. It is my conviction, however, that no society can be without an account of honour. Moreover, if we live in an age when honour is no longer a working moral notion we are the poorer for it. By analysing Barth and Trollope on honour I, therefore, hope to develop some rather broad themes about why Christians have a stake in the notion of honour, as well as how that stake may help us understand better our relation to a world that no longer honours honour.[4]

There are, however, certain methodological reasons for focusing on the notion of honour. In a fine article 'Command and History in the Ethics of Karl Barth', William Werpehowski has challenged my criticism of Barth's alleged inability to provide a morally compelling account of the moral continuity of the self, or better, moral character.[5] As Werpehowski notes, underlying my criticism was a suspicion that the 'Barthian self is unable to express itself as shaped through history'.[6] My worry in this respect was and is very similar to Richard Roberts' analysis of Barth's account of time. As Roberts observes, for Barth 'human existence, and thus time which is "real so far as He wills and posits it a real existence" raises a difficulty inherent in the *Church Dogmatics* as a whole: How does this "real existence" relate to that existence experienced by the human subject as a mere percipient being?'[7] Or as Roberts puts it later, Barth's account of time – and with it, I think, his correlative sense of personal continuity – risks Docetism insofar as it is determined by an account of revelation whose temporality is not to be confused in any way with the time we experience as humans.

Werpehowski, drawing on Frei's insistence on Barth's programme of 'conceptual description', argues that my criticism fails to appreciate how Barth's account of continuity is congruent with our everyday sense of self. Barth's method is to locate the everyday within the Christian world through his description of the latter. For Barth 'the concrete invitation is freely and actively to conform one's personal history or "narrative" to the "narratives" of the creatures portrayed in Scripture, who themselves are depicted as constituted by a history of relationship with God. One is not only to ally oneself with them formally, in the awareness of having been given a commission, but one must also, in one's different time and situation, make the command and the mission given to them one's own, "not as something new and special, but as the renewal and confirmation of the task laid upon them (*CD* II/2:706)."'[8] Werpehowski substantiates his defence of Barth by noting that Barth extends the logic of the divine command in his account of vocation which includes the 'givens' of life – our age, our special situation, our personal aptitudes, and our specific 'field of ordinary everyday activity'.[9]

Summarizing his criticism of Barth's critics, Werpehowski argues:

> Barth incorporates a conception of 'history' which grounds reasons for action, character, and growth-in-continuity in his category of 'history of relationship with God.' The everyday conception of history, remember, explains the changes through self-expressing actions of a continuous subject. As *continuous*, Barth's Christian person stands loyal to the cause of Jesus Christ. As *changed* through his or her actions, he or she comes to a deeper self-understanding through a deeper understanding of God's plans for him or her. And as *changing*, he or she approaches concrete ethical events armed with a range of theonomous reasons which help to frame and limit the possibilities of obedient action. All the conditions are met for characterizing the Christian as one who does indeed express oneself through one's history. This history has an incarnational quality, in that the extraordinary history of relationship with God is manifested in and through the everyday history of self-expression, rather than having it manifested at the 'limit' or 'boundary' of the everyday.[10]

Now I must admit that Werpehowski almost convinces me. I

am sure he is right that the way Barth uses the language of command and/or act does not in itself entail a discontinuous account of the self nor a denial of moral rationality. Moreover, he is certainly right to direct attention to Barth's account of vocation at the end of *Church Dogmatics* (III/4), and I am sure that in my presentation of Barth's ethics I failed to appreciate the significance of that aspect of Barth's ethics. Yet I remain bothered by a peculiar 'abstractness' to Barth's ethics that gives his account of the moral life an aura of unreality. I hope to exhibit this unease by turning to Barth's account of honour, which is an extension of his account of vocation, and in particular, by contrasting Barth's abstractness with the concreteness of Trollope's *Dr Wortle*. By doing so I hope to test Werpehowski's defence of Barth on its strongest grounds since any account of honour seems to entail a self capable of constancy.

II *Barth on Honour* (*CD* III/4, §56.3)

It is a testimony to Barth's extraordinary imagination that he treats the question of honour. For as Peter Berger has suggested, the 'obsolescence' of the concept of honour is a correlate of the rise of a new humanism concerned with the dignity and rights of the individual. As Berger points out, the 'same modern men who fail to understand an issue of honor are immediately disposed to concede the demands for dignity and for equal rights by almost every new group that makes them – racial or religious minorities, exploited classes, the poor, the deviant, and so on'.[11] This new egalitarian emphasis has therefore tended to undermine the significance of institutional roles and inequalities of service that are crucial to sustain an ethos of honour.

Barth, however, maintains that while the forms of honour will change from time to time and society to society, no collective can exist without concepts of honour – that is, 'with their various standards, with their internal nuances and external frontiers, according to which the life of society and nations in their various groups, strata and classes, and also the personal life of the individual both in isolation and in relation to his fellows, usually tries to some extent to direct and regulate itself' (*CD* III/4:669). Indeed Barth argues that without a tacit or open acceptance of the concept of honour, man could not be man, whether we be isolated or in the company of others (*CD* III/4:669). In even stronger language Barth says, 'We may call honour the supreme earthly good. It may well be true that to lose honour is to lose everything' (*CD* III/4:663).

Moreover, Barth suggests that there is no reason for Christians to object to such concepts of honour.

> On the contrary, if the fact that there are, and that man, even as a transgressor, does not seem able to avoid forming and maintaining such concepts (however curious), we have to recognize the *character indelebilis* of the honour which God gives man by the mere fact that he is his Creator and Lord and man his creature. Even the oddest man attests this, whatever his intention or self-understanding, and however curious his concept of honour. So, too, does the most singular and questionable tradition or new invention in this sphere. All honour to it, alongside the views and opinions which seem more illuminating and authoritative and normative to us! There is basically no objection to the existence and validity of such collective and individual concepts of honour. Indeed, there is much to be said for them (*CD* III/4:669)

Barth's positive view of honour is correlative to his understanding of human existence in limitation. For honour is distinction – that is, honour is a claim to special, particular and specific recognition of a concrete and individual man. It cannot be a characteristic which can be attributed to the human race collectively.

> If the term is not to be empty, it must mean the honour of the concrete and therefore always the individual man, the dignity and estimation due to every man, but due to each as this particular man, not merely as a specimen of the race, but directly, personally and exclusively (*CD* III/4:655).

Of course, any honour, that is true or real can only be a

reflection of the honour God has done us by giving us our time and our vocation. In a typical Barthian mode we are told,

> If we are to be accurate from the outset, we must say that first and finally it (the honour of man) can be understood only as the reflection of the honour of God falling on every man as such, and especially of the fact that God is not arbitrary or false, but true to Himself as God, when He does man this great honour in His command. God finds and sees in every man as such something which certainly cannot be classified with the honour which He does him when He calls him to his service, which in comparison with this can be only an improper honour, but which is still an honour granted to man by God and therefore a true honour as such. It is the honour which God has done and still does every man in the fact that He was and is invested in virtue of the fact that he may have his existence as the creature of God and may be under His rule (*CD* III/4:651).[12]

'All honour of man is always God's honour' (*CD* III/4:654) but God allows us to participate in His honour. For God does not will to be God without man. Yet God's honouring of man has a twofold sense. There is the honour that comes to us as creatures of God and an honour which comes to us by our calling to the service of God. These two have been treated on the same plane by theologians with the result that there is an over-emphasis on the distinctively soteriological and ecclesiastical element and a hesitation to take seriously the general honour of man as such, or an over-emphasis on the latter element and a hesitation to speak of the special honour of the divine calling except as a form of the general human concept of honour. In contrast, Barth argues, 'theological ethics has to take seriously in their different ways both the honour of man as created by God and the honour of man as called by God. It has thus to understand the two as both unmixed in their distinction and yet inseparable in their inter-relationship' (*CD* III/4:653).

Thus any external honour depends on whether the honour that is acknowledged by others is based on a call from God, and so on whether the one honoured is occupied in the service assigned to him by God. Any human action that lacks the character of service is either not yet or no longer honourable (*CD* III/4:659). Of course, such honour may be misunderstood by others as there are a very large number of possibilities of lack of appreciation and misunderstanding. It is only in service that two men

> learn to know and respect one another, not by simply observing or thinking about one another, or even by living with one another, however great their concord or even friendship, in indolence or caprice, self-will or arrogance. Mere companions and comrades cannot appreciate either their own honour or that of the other. The honour of two men is disclosed and will be apparent to both when they meet each other in the knowledge that they are both claimed, not by and for something of their own and therefore incidental and non-essential, but for and by the service God has laid on them (*CD* III/4:659).

It follows, therefore, that man can be honourable only in pure thankfulness, deepest humility, and in free-humour (*CD* III/4:664). Because we know our honour does not belong to us we can only respond in thankfulness, manifesting the deep quiet and assurance that derives from the knowledge both of our own inadequacy and of God's faithfulness. That is why humour is so important, as it is the opposite of all self-admiration and self-praise. Humour is the profound recognition that all honour comes from God. The honourable man cannot help but be modest since honour is possible

> only in the sincere and complete withdrawal of the recipient before the Giver and His gift, only in the relaxation in which he wills to be only what he may become and to have only what he may receive, and all in the course and event of the divine action which his own action only follows, which it only serves, to which it only adapts itself, from which it cannot therefore loose itself, in the face of which it cannot want to play its own game (*CD* III/4:666)

Such modesty is completely compatible with healthy pride for it is but the positive recognition of God's honouring us by claiming us for service.

The fact that all wordly concepts of honour must be tested by the honour of God does not mean that the honour of service ascribed to man may not in large measure correspond to what is called honour by the world. It is not necessary, therefore, that the honour that comes to us from God must contradict worldly honour. As Barth points out, did not Joseph and Moses in Egypt, and David, Solomon, and Job receive superabundantly that which the world also regards as honour? And certainly Jesus as a child is said to have increased 'in wisdom and stature, and in favour with God and man,' as well as to have received all kinds of wordly honour in the exercise of his ministry (*CD* III/4:671).

But just as God is free to make worldly honour correspond to his honour, and therefore to our expectations and hopes, God is also free to have it otherwise. If there is no law 'in virtue of which man's honour before God must be continually and necessarily in contradiction and conflict with what he would like to regard as his honour from the human and worldly standpoint, there is also no law in virtue of which the two must normally agree' (*CD* III/4:672). We must recognize that God may force us to see that we have fashioned a small and limited idea of honour and that more is demanded of us than we or our environment have provided. In such a case we cannot be satisfied with personal or collective concepts of honour as they are all inadequate. We do not owe humility to such concepts; we owe it to God. God, moreover, may make higher claims for himself and therefore for others so that in the deepest humility we will have to have great courage. For God may well call us, like the disciples, to be raised higher than our society's concept of honour or we may be called, like Job, to an obedience that seems lower than the existing standards of honour (*CD* III/4:673).

More likely than the conflict envisaged by the call to a higher or lower sense of honour is that most of us will find the 'form of divinely willed and allotted honour in which there will be little or no evidence either to ourselves or others of either exaltation or abasement. The actual life of most men, and the main span even of those distinguished on the one side or the other, is passed at a mid-point, where the chief problem is not to persevere as consistently as possible, whether exalted or abased, in a clear conflict between the esteem intended for them by God and their own concepts of honour, but quite practically, *i.e.*, without such conflict, to be content actually to be honoured by God' (*CD* III/4:676). As Barth reminds us, those without problems are just as much needed in the service of God as genuine heroes and sufferers.

Since our honour is that bestowed by God does that mean that Christians are prevented from defending their honour against the words and acts of others? Certainly it means that Christians may accept, if not everything, at least a great deal. Barth observes that experience shows that most lies are short-lived and that what is written in the press is particularly short-lived. Barth reports that in recent

> theological history there is at least one instance of a man who is supposed to have died of a review written against him. But he had no business to do this. If he did, it is more to his own shame than that of the reviewer. Above all, it should always be regarded only as *ultima ratio* to allow ourselves to become entangled in judicial proceedings in respect of the so-called wounding of honour (*CD* III/4:679).

Nonetheless we may be commanded to take legitimate steps in confirmation or defence of our honour. For to fail to defend ourselves might prejudice our honour in the eyes and judgements of others and therefore in our own eyes. As a result, the service laid on us might be called into question. Since I am responsible for the discharge of my calling and vocation, I may be called on to defend my honour to protect them. But the way our honour is defended requires careful attention to what might entail at least an apparent compromising of our honour in our own behaviour. I must uphold it before myself before I can expect to be able to do so before others. In every way we seek to rehabilitate our honour we must appeal to something known to our detractors aiming in our action to restore fellowship on the basis of what is well known to us both.

> If others have no honour, what is the use of defending mine against them and before them? . . . He who seeks to secure his self-respect is thus asked: Do you respect yourself? Even more: Have you first respected before you wish to procure respect for yourself? And more again: Is it more important,

more urgent and more necessary for you to respect or procure respect for yourself (*CD* III/4:684).

Such is honour according to Barth. Effort has been made to present his account fairly and without commentary hoping to avoid distortions resulting from summary. Moreover, any critical commentary will be withheld until Trollope has been discussed. At this point I am content with the observation that Barth's account of honour is characteristic of his ethics in general, being a mixture of extraordinary insights about the status of the former. By discussing honour at such a general level, while noting it must take concrete form in this or that time or society, Barth is able to have his theological cake and eat it too. It seems to make sense, but I suspect that it does so because we fill up the formal analysis with our own categories without knowing how those categories are to be theologically controlled. What we need to know is how honour in this or that context may or may not be appropriate to the service to which we are called as Christians. Such concreteness is exactly what I hope to show that Trollope offers.

III *Dr Wortle's Honour*

Summarizing Barth is difficult but summarizing Trollope's novel – even one as spare as *Dr Wortle's School* – is impossible. Yet I think it worth the effort for this is a novel about honour, or at least about acting as a gentleman (which was for Trollope the same as acting honourably),[14] in which Trollope explores why honour may require us to act against the moral conventions of our society. That makes the novel particularly interesting for our purposes, since normally to act honourably is to act in accordance with the ideals of one's society. By placing Dr Wortle in a position that forced him to act contrary to societal convention, Trollope explores in this novel how honourable people extend their society's morality through being who they are.

The novel is primarily about two people – Dr Wortle and the Revd Mr Peacocke. Dr Wortle, we are told in the first sentence of the book, was a man much esteemed by others as well as himself. He combined two professions as Rector of Bowick as well as proprietor and head-master of a school at Bowick established as preparatory to Eton. His school was very successful, attracting students of the best families as well as providing Dr Wortle with an extremely good income. Dr Wortle was a man who would not bear censure from any human being though he did not look for controversy.[15] Thus he remained on good terms with his bishop so long as he was allowed in all things to be his own master. In short, Dr Wortle is quite successful and well-established; a man with an impeccable reputation, and a wife and daughter who adore and honour him in all things.

Dr Wortle's comfortable world is upset by his hiring Mr Peacocke, a former fellow of Trinity College, Oxford, to be an usher at the school as well as hopefully serving as curate. Mr Peacocke, though a well-respected classics scholar at Oxford, had left Oxford to be vice-president of a classical college in St Louis, Missouri. Five years later he returned to Oxford, with a beautiful American wife, looking for employment. It is surprising that Dr Wortle hired him, as being a Tory he hated all things republican as well as distrusting anyone that seemed to be a rolling stone. But Mr Peacocke's scholarship and teaching were excellent, he could at once be an usher and curate, and his wife could also serve as a matron. So, after many inquiries, Dr Wortle, as 'one who thought that there should be a place of penitence allowed to those who had clearly repented of their errors', (13) employed Mr Peacocke and his wife.[16]

Dr Wortle soon came to value Mr Peacocke's contribution at the school. Aware that Mr Peacocke's scholarship was 'deeper' than his own, Dr Wortle even allowed certain changes be made in the curriculum which everyone assumed was done at the advice of Mr Peacocke. It was apparent, however, that the relationship between Dr Wortle and Mr Peacocke went beyond their professional relation because the personal respect with which Dr Wortle treated Mr Peacocke seemed to imply that the two were equal – that is, that they were both gentlemen. Mrs Peacocke was no less valuable since, being every inch a lady, she performed her duties in an exemplary manner, even nursing a young lord when it was not among her duties.

There were only two matters that bothered Dr Wortle: Mr Peacocke began to preach only after being pressured to do so and the Peacockes refused to be entertained in Dr Wortle's home. While exemplary in every way, a mystery surrounded the Peacockes that was sufficient for Mrs Stantiloup, an enemy of Dr Wortle because he had sued her for her refusal to pay the full costs of her son's education, to create rumours about the five years in America. These rumours finally reached the ears of the Bishop so the Bishop, in the kindest manner, finally asked Dr Wortle to inquire about Mr Peacocke's lost years in America. These reports were based on nothing more than a lack of information but, as Trollope notes, 'so much in this world depends upon character that attention has to be paid to bad character even when it is not deserved. In dealing with men and women, we have to consider what they believe, as well as what we believe ourselves' (26).

Though thinking such suspicions were monstrous, unreasonable, and uncharitable, Dr Wortle agreed to make inquiry of Mr Peacocke; yet he continually put it off because he found it so disagreeable. Finally bringing himself to arrange an interview with Mr Peacocke he discovered that Mr Peacocke did have a story to tell; and in fact Mr Peacocke confesses that he had been considering asking Dr Wortle if he would do him the 'favour to listen to the story of my life' (39). Before doing so, however, he asked for a week to think the matter through. Dr Wortle granted his request, noting that

> of course I cannot in the least guess what all this is about. For myself I hate secrets. I haven't a secret in the world. I know nothing of myself which you mightn't know too for all that I cared. But that is my good fortune rather than my merit. It might well have been with me as it is with you; but, as a rule, I think that where there is a secret it had better be kept. No one,

at any rate, should allow it to be wormed out of him by the impertinent assiduity of others. If there be anything affecting your wife which you do not wish all the world of this side of the water to know, do not tell it to anyone on this side of the water (40–41).

The story that Mr Peacocke resolved to tell Dr Wortle was, in brief, that he and Mrs Peacocke were not in fact man and wife. Mr Peacocke had become acquainted with Mrs Peacocke in St Louis as the wife of a Colonel Lefroy, who with his brother were Southerners who had been ruined both financially and morally by the War between the States. Mrs Lefroy had been married to Colonel Lefroy when she was only seventeen because her father (who was also a ruined Southern planter) had died leaving her no way of supporting herself.

When Mr Peacocke became acquainted with Mrs Lefroy and the two brothers, there was a great scandal in St Louis about the cruel treatment the wife received from her husband. He was going to Texas to pursue his fortune with a band of desperadoes and he was violently trying to force her to accompany him. Certain persons in St Louis intervened to prevent this, Mr Peacocke being among them, so the brothers went alone to Texas. Mrs Lefroy was left to provide for herself and Mr Peacocke was among those who aided her. In the process we are told that a certain intimacy was created, but not of the sort that would be injurious to the fame of the lady.

Things continued in this way for two years until news came that Colonel Lefroy had been killed by a party of United States soldiers. It was not clear from the news, however, which Colonel Lefroy had perished, since both brothers bore that title. Seeing the distress of Mrs Lefroy in the face of such inexact news, Mr Peacocke went to the Mexican border to discover the truth. Mr Peacocke learned from the younger brother, Robert Lefroy, that the husband had in fact been killed. On returning he proposed marriage after which they enjoyed six months of married happiness.

Then Ferdinand Lefroy, the husband, suddenly appeared

in St Louis, confronting the Peacockes, and making himself known more generally. But just as suddenly as he appeared he was gone again. You can imagine the consternation of the Peacockes. She immediately said she must go, but Mr Peacocke refused, bringing her back to England as his wife and subsequently finding a position with Dr Wortle's school at Bowick. That is the story Mr Peacocke resolved to tell Dr Wortle, realizing that in the telling he must leave the school.

Before he was able to tell the story himself, however, there arrived in England Robert Lefroy, who presented himself to Mr Peacocke threatening to tell all unless compensated. At being refused by Mr Peacocke, he told the story to Dr Wortle, thinking that he might well pay to preserve his school from scandal. Mr Peacocke then asked for an interview with Dr Wortle during which the following exchange took place:

'Colonel Lefroy has been with you, I take it.'
'A man calling himself by that name has been here. Will you not take a chair?'
'I do not know that it will be necessary. What he has told you – what I suppose he has told you – is true.'
'You had better at any rate take a chair. I do not believe that what he has told me is true.'
'But it is.'
'I do not believe that what he has told me is true. Some of it cannot, I think, be true. Much of it not so – unless I am more deceived in you than I ever was in any man. At any rate, sit down.' Then the school master did sit down. 'He has made you out to be a perjured, willful, cruel bigamist.'
'I have not been such,' said Peacocke, rising from his chair.
'One who has been willing to sacrifice a woman to his passion.'
'No, no.'
'Who deceived her by false witnesses.'
'Never.'
'And who has now refused to allow her to see her own husband's brother, lest she should learn the truth.'
'She is there – at any rate for you to see.'
'Therefore the man is a liar. A long story has to be told, as to which at present I can only guess what may be the nature. I presume the story will be the same as that you would have told had the man never come here.'
'Exactly the same, Dr Wortle.'

> 'Therefore you will own that I am right in asking you to sit down. The story may be very long – that is, if you mean to tell it.'
> 'I do – and did. I was wrong from the first in supposing that the nature of my marriage need be of no concern to others, but to herself and me.'
> 'Yes – Mr Peacocke; yes. We are, all of us joined together too closely to admit of isolation such as that.' There was something in this which grated against the schoolmaster's pride, though nothing had been said as to which he did not know that much harder things must meet his ears before the matter could be brought to an end between him and the Doctor. The 'Mister' had been prefixed to his name, which had been omitted for the last three or four months in the friendly intercourse which had taken place between them; and then, though it had been done in the form of agreeing with what he himself had said, the Doctor had made his first complaint by declaring that no man had a right to regard his own moral life as isolated from the lives of others around him. It was as much as to declare at once that he had been wrong in bringing this woman to Bowick, and calling her Mrs Peacocke. He had said as much himself, but that did not make the censure lighter when it came to him from the Doctor, getting up from his seat at the table, and throwing himself into an easy-chair, so as to mitigate the austerity of the position; 'Let us hear the true story. So big a liar as that American gentleman probably never put his foot in this room before.' Then Mr. Peacocke told the story (83–85).

After questioning Mr Peacocke, there was no question in Dr Wortle's mind that the Peacockes were unfortunate victims of scoundrels and circumstance. Indeed, he goes so far as to tell Mr Peacocke, 'I would have clung to her, let the law say what it might – and I think that I could have reconciled it to my God. But I might have been wrong, I might have been wrong. I only say what I should have done' (88). Dr Wortle assures Mr Peacocke of his friendship, but asks for time to consider what he should do, since it is unclear whether the Peacockes can remain at Bowick.

Mr Peacocke assumes that they must leave in telling Mrs Peacocke of his interview. He says they must leave since 'a man cannot isolate the morals, the manners, the ways of his life from the morals of others. Men, if they live together must live together by certain laws' (90). But Dr Wortle is no ordinary man, and though his 'first conscience' told him that he owed his primary duty to his parish, his second duty to his school, and his third duty to his wife and daughter; his 'other conscience' told him that Mr Peacocke was more sinned against than sinning 'that common humanity required him to stand by a man who had suffered so much, and had suffered so unworthily' (92). Moreover, he was reminded that this was a man pre-eminently fit for his duties and that, if he were to lose him, he could not hope to find a replacement his equal.[17]

Yet he did not make the decision without consultation. Mrs Wortle was certain that they should be turned out, fearing what Mrs Stantiloup and the Bishop would say. Dr Wortle was still not convinced, so he sought counsel from the Revd. Mr Puddicombe, 'a clergyman without a flaw who did his duty excellently in every station in life . . . one who would preach a sermon or take a whole service for a brother parson in distress, and never think of reckoning up that return sermons or return service were due to him' (54); but whom Dr Wortle did not quite like because he was a little too pious and given to asking troubling questions – *e.g.*, 'So Mr Peacocke isn't going to take the curacy?'(54).

Yet Dr Wortle knew that he could trust Mr Puddicombe, for though he was apparently an unsympathetic man he was not given to harshness. So with Mr Peacocke's permission Dr Wortle told Mr Puddicombe the story. The latter's response was that Mr Peacocke had harmed Dr Wortle by not telling him from the first all the facts and suggesting that they should have separated. As a result, Mr Puddicombe maintained that Dr Wortle had no choice but to send them away. As he left the house the Doctor thought the man 'a strait-laced, fanatical, hard-hearted bigot. But though he said so to himself, he hardly thought so; and was aware that the man's words had had effect upon him' (100).

Troubled as he was about what he should do, a plan began to unfold in the Doctor's mind. During his interview with Lefroy, Dr Wortle had got the impression that though the brother had not been dead when the marriage between the Peacockes took place, he might now be so. If that were the case then things might yet be put straight. So Dr Wortle suggested to Mr Peacocke that he should return to America with Lefroy to discover if in fact the brother was dead. The latter was willing to do so on the promise of a thousand dollars if he would help to document the truth of his brother's death. In the meantime Mrs Peacocke would continue to live at the school. The Doctor, of course, would have to bear all the expenses of the expedition, but he was determined to have the matter so resolved. Mr Peacocke naturally accepted and left immediately with Lefroy for America.

Of course this 'solution' was no solution as far as the Doctor's reputation was concerned. The story would surely be told and 'all the world' would know that he was protecting at his school a couple who lived together but were not man and wife. This was the case and Dr Wortle soon found himself admonished by the Bishop, who felt 'that the Doctor was the bigger man; and . . ., without active malignity, he would take advantage of any chance which might lower the Doctor a little, and bring him more within episcopal power. In some degree he begrudged the Doctor his manliness' (114). Nor did Dr Wortle receive support from Mr Puddicombe who sympathized with his 'generosity and kindness of heart' but not with 'his prudence'. He had even more difficulty with Mrs Wortle, though he finally convinced her that she should periodically visit Mrs Peacocke since she was otherwise completely isolated.

For my purpose I need not detail further the plot of the story. Any reader of Trollope knows that he wrote comedies and would expect all to be resolved happily. Mr Peacocke's trip to America proved to be a trying adventure, though in the process we come to see him as a man of considerable courage and resources – *e.g.* with an unloaded gun he coolly blocks the attempt of a drunken Lefroy to rob and kill him. He does discover that the other Lefroy did die in San Francisco of delirium tremens. Moreover, from the still living brother he learns that the husband had returned to St Louis and left again because it was a 'lark'.

Back in England, however, things were not going nearly so smoothly for Dr Wortle. As he had anticipated, the news of the Peacockes was all that Mrs Stantiloup needed to stir up a scandal about the school. Soon Dr Wortle began receiving cancellation notices from important families for the next term. Indeed, it began to look as if he might have to consider closing the school.

Even worse, the affair soon got into the local Broughton Gazette. Dr Wortle again sought the advice of Mr Puddicombe as to how he should respond but received no comfort, being told that everything the Gazette said was true as the Doctor had in fact fallen into a 'misfortune'. He added that Dr Wortle should have expected the adverse reaction since in fact he has 'countenanced immorality and deceit in a fellow clergyman in his diocese' (142). Though denying such a charge and affirming that he had never come 'across a better man than Mr Peacocke,' Dr Wortle nevertheless came to understand that he must hold his peace no matter how much he might be attacked.

This resolve was soon tested to the limit, however, as the London weekly, *Everybody's Business*, soon ran the story insinuating by a choice phrase that Dr Wortle's behaviour might be explained by his own attraction to the very handsome Mrs Peacocke. This again brought the Bishop into action, writing to Dr Wortle to suggest that he pay no more visits to Mrs Peacocke until the matter was settled. The Doctor responded by admonishing the Bishop for paying attention to allegations made in such a paper. So furious was he with the Bishop that he even began a law suit against the paper, which would mean dragging the Bishop into court to prove that Dr Wortle had been injured. The Doctor knew that the Bishop had made a terrible mistake in writing to him and alluding to the article which he could use to 'crush' the Bishop. He was at first inclined to do so since his lawyer assured him that he would certainly win a settlement.

Yet 'in the cool of the evening' our good Doctor, 'combative but yet soft of heart', changed his mind. As he thought to himself, such a paper 'is beneath my notice. What is it to me what such a publication, or even the readers of it, may think of me? As for damages, I would rather starve than soil my hands with their money. Though it should succeed in ruining me, I could not accept redress in that shape' (168). Therefore, he refused even the offer of the editor of *Everybody's Business* to print an apology, knowing that he was letting the Bishop escape by so doing.

So the Doctor was left with the possibility of losing everything, yet realizing that he could do nothing else. In the meantime Mrs Peacocke had finally told her story to Mrs Wortle, entirely winning her sympathy. Mrs Wortle confesses to her husband that she now did not see how Mr Peacocke could have acted other than he did in remaining with Mrs Peacocke. To which Dr Wortle responded.

> It would have been very hard to go away if he had told her to do so. Where was she to go? What was she to do? They had been brought together by circumstances, in such a manner that it was, so to say, impossible that they should part. It is not often that one comes across events like these, so altogether out of the ordinary course that the common rules of life seem to be insufficient for guidance. To most of us it never happens; and it is better for us that it should not happen. But when it does, one is forced to go beyond the common rules. It is that feeling which has made me give them my protection. It has been a great misfortune; but placed as I was I could not help myself. I could not turn them out. It was clearly his duty to go, and almost as clearly mine to give her shelter till he should come back (213).

Then word came by mail of Mr Peacocke's success and it was arranged for Mrs Peacocke to meet Mr Peacocke as soon as he returned and for Dr Wortle to marry them. In the meantime, however, Dr Wortle thought that something must be done to make those who had been his enemies understand how the matter now stood – *i.e.*, as he felt unjustly treated. He therefore drafted a letter to be sent after the wedding explaining that matters were now put right and that he had no hesitation in re-employing the Peacockes.

Before sending the letter, however, he thought to show it to Mr Puddicombe. He did not intend to send him the letter since he had not interfered in the school and had on the whole acted as a friend. Moreover, he hoped that he might finally gain some praise from Mr Puddicombe, but was disappointed that Mr Puddicombe did not like the letter because 'It does not tell the truth'. For the truth is that Dr Wortle condoned the Peacockes living together when they were not man and wife. Mr Puddicombe said, 'I am not condemning you. You condoned it, and now you defend yourself in this letter. But in your defence you do not really touch the offence as to which you are, according to your own showing, accused. In telling the whole story, you should say: "They did live together though they were not married; – and, under all circumstances, I did not think that they were on that account unfit to be left in charge of my boys"' (257).[18]

So Mr Puddicombe recommended the Doctor to say 'Nothing, not a word. Live it down in silence. There will be those, like myself, who, though they could not dare to say that in morals you were strictly correct, will love you the better for what you did.' The Doctor turned his face toward the dry, hard-looking man and showed that there was a tear in each of his eyes' (258). Noting that 'a man should never defend himself' Dr Puddicombe then offered, if it would suit Dr Wortle's plans, to go to London with him to assist at the marriage. Dr Wortle agreed, went home, and burned the letters. Soon his school again enjoyed the support of the noble families in England, and Dr Wortle was once again honoured as a man of courage and learning.

IV *Why Barth Needs a Puddicombe*

I am sure that Dr Wortle would never have been tempted to read Barth, and that if he had he would probably have found him unintelligible. I suspect that Trollope, however, would have been much more sympathetic, and that Barth might well have liked *Dr Wortle's School*. At least, I hope that Barth has read it by now, for what good is heaven if it does not give us the time to read all of Trollope's novels? In terms of the subject of this essay, however, it is interesting that many of Barth's suggestions about the nature of honour are confirmed in Trollope's novel.

Barth and Trollope alike see honour finally more as a quality of person, of character, than of social recognition. Honour denotes a sense of self that is willing to risk social standing rather than abandon what is seen to be our duty. That is why Dr Wortle cannot abandon Mr Peacocke. It is a matter of honour since honourable people support one another, for without such support the risk is loss of honour. Therefore Dr Wortle, as he tells Mrs Wortle, must do what he thinks he must, not only because he cannot do otherwise but also because it is his duty – that is, it is what he owes himself, society, and God. He acts honourably, combining humility with pride, just as Barth suggests is required of a person of honour.

Moreover, Barth and Trollope are acutely aware that most of the time we are not and should not be called to act in an extraordinary way to preserve our honour. Yet there is a sense that they both know that our ordinary lives, in order to be sustained as ordinary, require people who are capable of acting in an extraordinary way when they find it necessary. No doubt the recognition of such 'necessity' depends greatly on the development of relationships and friendships based on respect such as that between Dr Wortle and Mr Peacocke.[19] For Trollope leaves no doubt that Dr Wortle acted as he did because of his genuine admiration for Mr Peacocke.

Trollope's *Dr Wortle's School* also illumines Barth's contention that acting honourably may sometimes require us to appear to act against societal standards. Even though being honourable depends greatly on embodying the highest ideals of our society as well as having them mirrored in our friends, it is still the case, as we saw with Dr Wortle, that we may have to act in a way that seems to be against the best wisdom of our society and friends. To do so is but to remind us, as Barth argues, that it is finally the honour of God that matters.[20] That such is the case does nothing to lessen the terror and loneliness occasioned by acting against the stream. Yet such loneliness can be confident, at least if we believe people like Dr Wortle who says that he thinks Mr Peacocke's support of Mrs Peacocke, as well as his support of them, can be reconciled with God.

Barth and Trollope even seem to agree about how honour is to be defended. For the temptation is to try to relieve our loneliness by attacking those we believe are slandering us. Barth and Trollope obviously give little weight to the world of print, thinking that those whose judgements are formed there lack the means to be honourable, for they are not their own people. The only matters that matter are those determined by honourable people. That is why Dr Wortle is so concerned with the Bishop whose occupancy of that office means that he must be a gentleman. Dr Wortle thinks that the Bishop should support him as he has supported the Peacockes, since that is the way gentlemen should act toward one another. Yet even Dr Wortle comes to see that, finally, the only defence is to live confident that God will honour our actions if they deserve such honour.

So it seems that, rather than using Trollope as a foil to Barth, I have only succeeded in supporting Barth's account of honour. While I have no reason to be unhappy with that result, I think it is not the whole story. For while it is no doubt true that at one level Trollope's novel confirms Barth's analysis of honour, I think that in another way Trollope offers the kind of concrete account of honour that Barth's method seems to prevent. For example, ask yourself the question, 'If you had to choose between recommending Barth or *Dr Wortle's School* to a young person beginning to think about honour, which would you recommend?' I think that most of us would recommend Trollope for the very good reason that Trollope's people are real.

Put more directly, Barth simply fails to provide an account of where Wortles, Peacockes, and most important, Puddicombes come from. Missing from Barth's account of honour is the kind of societal ethos, the concrete community, that is capable of producing a Wortle. For example, we have no idea on the basis of Barth's account of how Wortle's natural aggressiveness, ambition, and passion results in a person capable of such loyalty and passion. Trollope makes no attempt to hide Wortle's high estimation of his own abilities and importance exactly because Wortle finally does not hide them from himself. Wortle is honourable, not in spite of, but because he would like to defend himself. Wortle is honourable because he is a man capable of recognizing that in many ways Mr Peacocke is his superior, and yet wise enough to use those talents for service to himself and his school. What Barth fails to help us see is where such honesty comes and how it is sustained. And note that this is not a 'psychological or biographical' question, but rather a question of how Christian ethics is done.

Werpehowski is no doubt right to remind us that Barth was engaged in a project of conceptual description through which 'honour' – as well as other moral qualities such as humility, justice, prudence – are theologically disciplined by the imagination. In his discussion of honour, Barth certainly denotes the sense of constancy necessary to have a character capable of being honourable. Yet he seems to negate his own insight by insisting that God can and does command us to act 'out of character,' ensuring that our lives never exhibit God's honour. Barth is right to insist that an honourable person may be called by God to act against his or her society's sense of honour, but he uses that to suggest that he or she in so acting may act against any and all human sense of honour. That just seems to me to be an unintelligible claim.

Another way to put my criticism is to note that what is missing in Barth is Puddicombe. Puddicombe is the embodiment of Trollope's contention that honour is only possible in a society in which secrets are abhorrent. For only if we are able to live our lives openly can we avoid the manipulative and intrusive existence of *Everybody's Business*. By confessing that he hated secrets, Dr Wortle, of course, was not suggesting that anyone had a right to know how often he and Mrs Wortle had sex. Rather, he was suggesting that the health of a society depends on people who are unashamed of the way they live.[21] Modern moral philosophy tries to underwrite such a commitment by its insistence that moral actions can only be justified when reasons can be given that are anyone's. But that ironically results in the creation of the kind of moral anonymity that destroys a society capable of sustaining Puddicombes. For impersonal principles, or even commands of God, are not sufficient to replace the flesh and blood of Puddicombes.

But flesh and blood Puddicombes are possible only because they draw on the flesh and blood of the church. The church is surely made up of sinners, which is why we know that we need Wortles, Peacockes, and Puddicombes to help us through our muddles. Barth simply fails to provide any conceptual or empirical account of how honour requires the existence of such a community. As a result, his account of honour is susceptible of an individualistic interpretation that his theological programme is meant to counter.

Why Barth overlooked or failed to emphasize the importance of the kind of community that makes honour possible, I do not know. I do find it odd, however, given Barth's struggle against totalitarianism. For no breeding ground is more rich for the development of totalitarians than that prepared by a society that encourages individuals to live lives of secrecy. Of course, it can be suggested that Barth was simply acknowledging the fact that we no longer live in societies in which honour is valued. But if that is the case, then I can only wonder why Barth failed in his discussion of honour to indicate the challenge confronting Christians, and even more the church, to be people of honour in such societies and such times.

9

Barth, War and the State

ROWAN WILLIAMS

During the later 1950s, German-speaking theology made its first sustained attempt to engage with the problems posed for the Church by the development of atomic armaments. 1957 and 1958 in particular saw a flurry of ecclesiastical activity and theological discussion, in which perhaps the most significant episode was the presentation to the German Evangelical Church (EKD) Synod in April 1958 of ten theses on the question of atomic warfare and the possession of atomic weapons.[1] The theses had been adopted by a number of the 'Church brotherhoods' in West Germany, study-circles whose origins lay in the theological fellowship groups of the Church struggle days of the 1930s, and which established a formal network in 1957. The document presented to the Synod aroused spirited controversy, not least by its suggestion[2] that the atomic issue should be recognized as one on which the Church should adopt a *status confessionis*; the brotherhoods insisted[3] that they were simply drawing out the implications of the fifth article of the Barmen Declaration (on the function of the state), and, in October 1958, at a convention of the brotherhood groups in Frankfurt, a further declaration[4] was adopted by over 200 delegates, a declaration modelled on that of Barmen, and explicitly appealing not only to Barmen but to the post-war statements of Stuttgart (1945), on the need for repentance and acknowledgment of guilt in the German churches, and Darmstadt (1947), on the need to forswear ideological commitment to German reunification and anti-Communist militancy.[5] The Frankfurt declaration was in part a response to the Synod's reception of the ten theses. No official acknowledgement had been made, but a statement had been issued,[6] calling for agreed restraints on military research and the deployment of warheads; although the Synod supported the 1957 condemnation of total war issued by the WCC, it also acknowledged the wide difference of opinion that existed within the EKD on the question of whether *all* use (including defensive use) of atomic weapons was absolutely ruled out. The brotherhoods, understandably, were not prepared to let the matter rest with this splendidly synodical evasion, and the Frankfurt declaration was a challenge to the opposition to put forward a case equally grounded in the Christian gospel, rather than in any considerations of expediency.[7] A would-be neutral stance, leaving the question open as the Synod had sought to do, was 'incompatible with the confession of Jesus Christ'. 'Any attempt at a theological justification of any such employment [of atomic weaponry] or any such neutrality becomes false doctrine, seduces people from the truth and sets the will of the triune God aside as of no worth.'[8]

It may be useful, at this point, to reproduce the ten theses of spring, 1958 (they do not seem ever to have been seriously discussed in the English-speaking world). They form the third part of the *Anfrage* addressed by the brotherhoods to the Synod: the first section notes the theological unsatisfactoriness of preceding discussions of the question and outlines the considerations that make traditional categories for the theological justification of armed conflict useless in the new context of the atomic age. The second insists that, if the Synod declines to adopt the theses, it should reply with a defence of its refusal from Scripture, confession and reason. The third puts the question directly:

> Therefore we ask the Synod whether they are able to join with us in pronouncing the following ten propositions for the informing of consciences, as a response to the question of how the Christian should behave in respect of atomic weaponry:
> 1. *War* is the ultimate means of political confrontation between peoples and states, a means that is in all its forms questionable and ambiguous.
> 2. *Churches* of all lands and ages up to the present day have

maintained that preparation for and employment of this means, for particular good or less good reasons, are not inadmissible.

3. The prospect of a future war waged with the use of modern means of annihilation has created a new situation, in the face of which the Church *cannot remain neutral*.

4. War in the form of *atomic* war means the mutual annihilation of the peoples involved as well as of innocent people of other nations not involved in the conflict between the two parties.

5. War in the form of atomic war is therefore manifestly *useless as a means of political confrontation*, because it destroys the preconditions for such engagement.

6. The Church and the individual Christian can therefore only say *No* in advance to any war waged as an atomic war.

7. Even the preparation for such a war is in all circumstances *a sin against God and neighbour*, and no Church, no Christian can share in the guilt of this.

8. Thus we demand, in the name of the gospel, *that there be an immediate end* to all preparations for such warfare in our country and state, with no regard for any other considerations.

9. We call on all those who are serious in their wish to be Christians to *refuse* to co-operate in preparation for atomic warfare, unconditionally and in all circumstances.

10. An opposite viewpoint or a neutral stance on this question is *indefensible in Christian terms*. Both would mean the denial of all three articles of Christian faith.

Barth had been invited to speak at the convention of October 1958, but was obliged to withdraw because of ill-health and fatigue.[9] Since there had already been rumours that he disagreed with the ten theses, he was urged by Helmut Simon, one of the two moderators of the brotherhood network, to make a clear statement of his support for the *Anfrage* of March; and in an open letter, written in September 1958, Barth told Simon to proclaim loud and clear 'to each and all, that I fully concur with these theses . . . as if I had written them myself.'[10]

That is, of course, exactly what he *had* done, as Busch's biography reveals,[11], and as his correspondence of January 1958 makes clear![12] Why anyone should have thought him likely *not* to approve of the theses is a puzzle: he had already, in 1957, made clear public statements[13] in condemnation of the arms race and the already rapid burgeoning of military research. His views were sufficiently well-known for representatives of the brotherhoods to approach him for help at the beginning of 1958; and the consistency of his opposition to atomic armaments up to the time of his death is easily documented from his letters. Yet as late as 1963 his name was still being invoked by supporters of the nuclear deterrent – on the basis, it seems, of his discussion of the ethics of war in *CD* III/4.[14] He admitted more than once that this discussion (dating from 1951) was flawed by its failure to give serious consideration to the new problems raised in the era after Hiroshima; but unfortunately he was never able to present the kind of extended discussion that would be needed to do justice to these problems. What I shall propose in this essay is that it is possible to see the lines along which such a discussion would proceed if we trace the evolution of Barth's doctrine of the *state*, and not only what he has to say about war; and if we read the ten theses against this background, it is easier to see why Barth believed the nuclear issue to be a 'confessional' matter. At the same time, I believe, we must recognize the shifting and unfinished character of his reflections on the state, the need to develop some of his arguments more thoroughly and consistently, and some of the weaknesses still evident in his thinking in this area. But to recognize this is not at all to question the accuracy – and present pertinence – of his perceptions as they took shape in the later 1950s. As usual with Barth, the powerful underlying consistency of his thought can best be seen as the consistency of a lifelong process of reworking and purifying what was last said, and it is no tribute to him to exploit only one 'moment' of his exploration. Since it is manifestly important that we think far more deeply than before about the theology of the state in an age when concepts of state sovereignty and security bring forth monsters on all sides, it should be an enterprise worth pursuing to follow through one of the most integrally *theological* discussions of the question in this century, in the hope that we be enabled in some degree to continue the process of 'reworking and purifying'.[15]

II

The second *Römerbrief* (*R* II)[16] lays the foundations for a great deal of what is to follow in its discussion of Romans 13: here already are the main themes of Barth's view of the state – the emphasis upon its *soteriological* (and thus Christological and eschatological) foundation, the notion that the state is primarily to be seen as *limit* by the believer, and the consequent refusal to make Rm. 13 (or any other NT passage) the basis for a positive theology of 'citizenship' or a doctrine of the 'essence' of the state (*R* II:477). Commenting on Romans 12, Barth has been considering the significance of the 'negative possibilities' opened to faith, the varieties of not-doing that bear witness to the presence of transforming judgement (*R* II:461); and the culmination of this line of thought is that obedience to the state is described as 'the Great Negative Possibility' (*R* II:477). If Rm. 13.1–7 is meant to be a gloss on 12.21 ('Be not overcome of evil . . .'), then Paul's commendation of obedience to 'the powers' is an exhortation to the resignation of our supposed 'right' to overthrow the evil of worldly order. That it *is* an evil should not be in doubt: all *de facto* order rests more or less remotely upon violence and deceit, and we must not suppose that there exists any natural right whereby one human being rules another – even in the most seductive form of a democratically-represented majority. The more a state can point to its own legitimacy and justice, the more it embodies 'the supreme wrong-doing': *summum jus, summa injuria*. The claim is implicitly made to establish final peace and resolution in a self-consciously 'just' society; and that claim is blasphemous (*R* II:478–80).

But what makes each and every system of state authority evil is exactly what makes revolutionary *resistance* to the state equally evil; one form of legitimist idolatry is simply replaced by another (*R* II:480–84). This is not designed to give comfort to the conservative, for the Christian's refusal of worldly revolution has nothing to do with a 'principled' support of the existing order; and Barth very plainly says (*R* II:486) that if an existing order collapses, there is little justification for counter-revolution as for revolution ('there is also a conservative insubordination!'). Both conservative and revolutionary must be stripped of 'pathos' and romanticism, of the illusion of occupying a 'high place', a *locus standi* from which the radically (sinlessly) new can be devised and initiated, or the status quo sacralized (*R* II:483, 485). Worldly order in its full ambiguity must remain, seen for what it is, so that God's order remains visible in and as the world's negation. The only authentic revolution is that of God in Jesus Christ; no other *act* in judgement of the world's order is possible. *We* can utter that judgement only in our non-action, dying in the place where we were born, in Barth's phrase (*R* II:481). The present order is under God and answerable to God and works for God in the sense that its evil, and the 'terror' involved in it for the rebel, bring human action as such under judgement – human action as self-assertion and self-justification. The state condemns us as agents, as architects of our own salvation; but it has no terror for the good, since 'the good work is the "not-doing" by which all action is related to its Prime Origin' (*R* II:487). In a wholly ironic sense, the believer becomes a good citizen because he is 'invisible' to the powers, not an agent over against the organized agency of the state (which is in fact organized disorder, evil).

The extraordinary *prima facie* quietism of this analysis is a little qualified by Barth's observation (*R* II:488) that the demands of the state have a certain 'parabolic' significance for the believer. The state is a limit to the *eros* of the individual and represents the claims of fellowship and peace, and so it has a remote likeness to God's claim on our obedience, the offering of our bodies. Social efforts towards greater harmony or justice are not therefore worthless, and it is possible to imagine a 'political career' for the believer – but only if it is regarded as a 'game', as something which renounces absolutist commitment and trust in human possibilities (*R* II:489).

The good, the absolute good of God's righteousness, is the enemy of the (socially or politically) 'better', insofar as, and only insofar as, the latter is confused with the true end and work of human beings, as if action were what we are made for. Absolute good, righteousness, remains invisible and atemporal: our laying-hold of it in faith, in the non-action of obedience to the Word, is beyond time, *i.e.* it does not compete for a place in time with the multitudinous succession of our acts, it is not an *episode* in a biography. However, at another level, it is *as* temporal beings that we are aware of having no place to stand, no right to act; and so it is that our knowledge of our importance also appears to us as a kind of temporal future, as hope – 'the hope of the Coming World where Revolution and Order are one' (*R* II:491). From this point, Barth can go on, commenting on Rm. 13.8–14, to describe the 'Great Positive Possibility' of love: when we abandon our rights, negating the negations of worldly order, we are at once involved in love – the 'active' subversion (in a very paradoxical sense of 'active', the act worked by God in our emptiness) of the existing order (*R* II:493), and the miraculous presence of God's eternal freedom in time, the eschaton anticipated (*R* II:498–502). Love lies in the full appropriation of my own limitedness and mortality as this appears in encounter with the human other who is a mystery, a challenge and a summons to me, through whom I discover myself as a self eternally already called and loved of God, and lost and meaningless outside that relation (*R* II:494–95). 'It is the fact of the existence of our fellow men – the ethical problem – by which we are brought face to face with the great disturbance' (*R* II:505).

Active love in community is thus central for faith, and constitutive of what it concretely is; but we can only know what this means when we have first grasped that this love is essentially *non*-action. Here Barth most radically corrects the perspective of the first *Römerbrief* (*R* I),[17] with its far more explicit and 'undialectical' summons to political engagement (*eg. R* I:367,390) – and its direct confrontation with Leninism

(*R* I:354–392); the second commentary sweeps all this away with its eschatological critique of human organization as such, and establishes once and for all the impropriety in Barth's eyes of a theological legitimation of any specific social order *in itself* – i.e. as anything other than a reality dialectically caught up in the saving work of God. Here too, then, is the foundation of Barth's consistent repudiation of any variety of 'Two Kingdoms' doctrine: the state is answerable to and bound to the gospel in a direct if still preliminary way (as bringing us under judgement); and so it can equally obstruct the gospel, when its organization claims absolute legitimacy and justice, *summa jus*. The price paid for this in the second *Römerbrief*, however, is high: Dannemann, in his lucid and sympathetic account of Barth as political theologian remarks[18] on the *Statik und Geschichtslosigkeit* that overshadows what the work has to say about political action and observes that 'since there is in *R* II no real teleology and history for the reconciling and redeeming action of God, no corresponding teleology and history for human action in the world can appear.' This is a perceptive judgement. And the 'timelessness' of encounter with the Word is dramatically reflected in what is said in the second *Römerbrief* about Jesus: 'The particularity of the years A.D. 1–30 is dissolved by this divine definition, because it makes every epoch a potential field of revelation and disclosure' (*R* II:29); '[Jesus] sacrifices to the incomparably Greater . . . every claim to genius and every human heroic or aesthetic or psychic possibility, because there is no conceivable human possibility of which He did not rid Himself' (*R* II:97). Jesus is the paradigm, in fact, of timeless non-action; but the nature of his *continuity* with the world of human agents (and of human limit) becomes dangerously obscure.

It is not surprising, then, that Barth's reconstruction of a theological perspective on the state should advance in step with the maturation of his Christology and of his understanding of *time* as a category of God's action. He himself rapidly realized that 'abstract eschatological waiting',[19] an eschatology that failed to work transformingly on the painful realities of an increasingly nightmarish present, was a betrayal of the Church's call to 'political service'. In and after the period of the Church struggle, he attempted to make better sense of the state's inclusion in the *saving* work of God – at a time when it was of first importance to give no ground to another and more poisonous abstraction, that of an *Ordnungstheologie* abstracted from the decisive 'limit' of Christ.

III

The classical statement from the 1930s of Barth's rethinking of 'political theology' is the 1938 lecture, 'Rechtfertigung und Recht' (*RR*).[20] There are clear indications here of his unease with the positions outlined in *Römerbrief*, an awareness of the risk that these positions could weaken the Church's 'discernment of spirits' (*RR*:31–2), and justify a purely abstract or general critique of political reality. The Barth of this lecture is perceptibly post-Barmen: the insistence of Barmen that the state exists by God's dispensation for the sake of peace and justice is the kernel around which the argument is built up. But the decisively new element is the location of political power, as now constituted, in the period between resurrection and parousia: the state as it now is exists *after* the manifestation of Christ's victory, and so, along with all the other potentially ambiguous 'powers' in the cosmos, it is led captive, it does not belong to itself. There can be no ultimate and successful rebellion by the powers. The state cannot help manifesting Christ's glory at the end of time, and so, in time, it cannot help participating in the salvation of sinners, in God's *Rechtfertigung* (*RR*:27–9). Rm. 13 must be read in this Christological light: the state is to be obeyed because it is an (admittedly secondary) sphere of the work of justification. Its *Recht* allows the freedom necessary for the proclaiming and hearing of the gospel (*RR*:32–4, 50–1), and so is evidently something that shares in that divine authority which is *wholly* directed to our salvation. If the Church prays and gives thanks for the state as guarantor of its peace, this does not imply a longing for bourgeois ease: peace and liberty are given for preaching, not – in this aeon – as ends in themselves (*RR*:50–1).

Barth boldly claims that the 'demonization' of the state has nothing to do with its autonomy or secularity; on the contrary (and here the essential question of the 1930s appears), the problem is that the state is unwilling to be faithful to its proper *independence* – *i.e.* its *distinct* reality, over against the Church. The state as such 'knows nothing of the Spirit, nothing of love, nothing of forgiveness' (*RR*:29–30), nor is it gathered together by free decision; it exists in and only in coercion, and as such is essentially other than the Church (*RR*:54–5) – a kind of reverse image. If the Church comes to be seen as an uncomfortable, disturbing or alien presence in the state, this means that the state is failing to be itself, regarding the Church as a *rival* – because it (the state) is implicitly or explicitly laying claim to do what only the church can do – to pronounce a word of ultimate release and promise, to bestow meaning. And if the state then attempts to limit what is permitted to the Church, the time has come for resistance, non-cooperation, the refusal of participation (*e.g.* by conscientious objection). The Church cannot challenge the legal authority of the state as such, it cannot adopt an anarchist critique; it must and will become a victim of the state apparatus, bearing the punishment for its disobedience. In such active but not strictly revolutionary disobedience, it performs its proper service to the state by reminding the state of its *difference* from the Church and so recalling it to the foundation of its claim to obedience in the first place (*RR*:67–9). *Only* this kind of critical activity offers the state what it needs, the assurance of legitimacy: 'Apart from the Church, there is nowhere any fundamental knowledge of the reasons which make the State legitimate and necessary' (*RR*:70). The Church critique announces to the state that its order and its *Recht* exist on the firmest base possible – God's eternal will for *Rechtfertigung*; beyond this, the state has no reality, no coherence, no legitimate claim, no *Recht* in any sense. When the state seeks to do God's work as that work is committed to the Church, it subverts its own foundation (*RR*:85–86).

The advance from *Römerbrief* is remarkable. No longer is the state seen as evil; the rather tortuous exegesis connecting Rm. 13.1–7 with 'be not overcome of evil' has yielded to a related but more nuanced antithesis between the community of freedom and the community in which the *possibility* of freedom is secured by coercion. Participation in the work of the state is far more positively enjoined (*RR*:78–9), because that work is related to the justification of the sinner – not in the highly paradoxical way sketched in *Römerbrief*, but comparatively directly, as what enables concrete proclamation.

But this can only be affirmed because of the gradual shift towards commitment to the essential *temporality* of God's work. To quote Richard Roberts,[21] 'The dialectic of antithesis in *The Epistle to the Romans* has given way to a dialectic informed by a new conjunction of transcendence and immanence, that is a creative "inclusion" of time by eternity.' Already in *CD* I/1 (*e.g.* pp. 116,426) the notion of the 'time of revelation' is sketched out, and in *CD* I/2 it forms the subject of a lengthy discussion (§14): God's revelation cannot but be spoken of historically, temporally, though this does not and cannot mean that history is a category prior to revelation and intelligible apart from it for the theologian. The result is the Christology of *CD* I, in which, although history is the 'predicate of revelation (*CD* I/2:58), the specific temporal relations, the particularity of the history of Jesus can still *become* revelatory only according to the divine decision. History cannot be given a self-subsistent significance. The fleshliness of incarnation is necessarily both veiling and unveiling at once. It is clear that this relates on the whole quite neatly to 'Rechtfertigung und Recht', insofar as historical-political reality, the concrete 'time' of the state, is indeed caught up in the history of God's work from resurrection to parousia and works, willy-nilly, the righteousness of God, yet remains in itself something fundamentally opposite to the community of faith, without autonomous meaning, knowing nothing of love, a reverse image. As in the incarnation itself, God works in what he is not. In short, although the timelessness of *Römerbrief* has been set aside, the essentially *negative* character of the state's relation to the gospel is still insisted on. However, this is not a covert 'Two Kingdoms' theology; the relentlessly antithetical presentation of the 'communities' of state and Church preserves some echo of Lutheran dualism, but it is a dualism brilliantly and triumphantly deployed against the extraordinary muddles of Lutheran political theology in the 1930s.

Furthermore, at the time of the composition of 'Rechtfertigung und Recht', Barth was already considering the questions that were to dominate *CD* II, and these concerns seem to cast some shadow before them. The notion of a time *given* to the Church, between resurrection and parousia, for promise, hope, proclamation, already requires – on Barth's presuppositions – a theology of God's eternal choice to give this time (because he always *is* what he *shows* himself to be): we are on the frontier of the great discussion of election that pervades all of *CD* II. God's being is free act, self-determination, and that act is the life, death and resurrection of Christ: before all ages, God elects to be Christ for us, and so elects and ordains the consequence in our world of the event of Christ – including the time given us for proclamation (*CD* II/1:411ff.). It is clear, in this light, how, in *CD* II/2, Barth can move from the theology of election to his first major essay in ethics; and when we turn to the account of the state offered in *CD* II/2, (§38.3, 721–6), brief as it is, we can see something of the effect of this newly dominant theme of election. A very small step further is taken towards qualifying the negativity of the political order.

For the most part, *CD* II/2 recapitulates the conclusion of 'Rechtfertigung und Recht'; but, turning once again to Rm. 13, Barth links it in a new way with the passage that precedes the injunctions to obedience. Rm. 12 speaks of the imperatives of non-resistance, of a reconciliation that arises directly from our reconciliation with God: what the state then assures is that reconciliation does not lead to chaos. (*CD* II/2:721). Human life together is held in security by the powers that be. The shift from the 1938 lecture is in the idea that the state not only preserves social peace for the sake of the preaching of the gospel, but safeguards the possibility of active and creative reconciliation within ordered bounds. The severity of the state, its expression of God's 'wrath', is seen (in the light of Rm. 1.24–28) as the limiting of human powers of self-destruction: God defers the natural consequences of our competitive, mutually cannibalistic social behaviour to make time for faith – in the work of Church and state alike (*CD* II/2:721–2). Thus the state's unavoidable violence and 'gracelessness' is understood as a function of its eschatological orientation, the 'not yet' because of which it exists. It cannot be in itself the order of grace. But that order is already real in God and in faith; and the presence in the state of the Christian community reveals the grace that is actually within the superficially 'graceless order' of political life (*CD* II/2:722–3). As in 'Rechtfertigung und Recht', only the Church can manifest the true rationale of the state; but here it is the Christian's willing share in the preservation of order precisely *as* a believer that uncovers grace. Coercion is shown, by the believer's engagement, to be the indefinite postponement of disaster and mutual slaughter and social dissolution, for the sake of the universalizing of a reconciliation already secretly present. And the believer is free for political commitment because he knows that everything except reconciliation in community is provisional (*CD* II/2:723–4); such a person has the detachment which makes proper and truthful political action possible. The member of the Church, after all, knows that the Church itself as such is *provisional* – as Barth says in 'Rechtfertigung' (*RR*:40–1), the final goal of God's redeeming work is a *polis*, a *basileia*, not an *ekklēsia* – so that the experience of being in the Church generates an unavoidable solidarity with the provisional experience of the state. The one illuminates and uncovers the other (*CD* II/2:724).

The negative or antithetical note is still present, but significantly qualified both by the eschatological orientation of the state's coercive power, and by the recognition of the active presence of the other, reconciled, mode of existence within the historical and political order. Time is transformed as well as judged – or transformed *in* being judged; there is, *solely* by the gracious act of God, of course, positive achievement in the political world, and some hint of a positive or creative vocation within the political order. This is stated still more strongly in the post-war (1946) essay, 'Christengemeinde und Bürgergemeinde' (*CB*).[22] Here we find the notion of *Recht* as a provisional image of *Rechtfertigung* (*CB*:19–20), *Recht* as the gift of God, its gift-character brought out by the Church's witness (*CB:* 22), the Church's active responsibility for political freedom (*CB*:36–8), and, very significantly for our present enquiry, a firm denunciation of the positivist view of sovereignty: the Church, in committing itself to support for the *Rechtstaat*, commits itself to supporting political *potestas*, not *potentia*, power defined in terms of the purposive capacity to serve and effect law so as to realize harmony, as opposed to pure might, defining its own ends (*CB*:40). This is a necessary clarification of the earlier stress on the state as essentially coercive: the means and the limits of political coercion are, for the first time, brought within the horizon of this discussion. Also significant is the idea of the Church as actively resisting 'all abstract local, regional and national interests', and treating all *de facto* sovereign boundaries as relative and provisional (*CB*:40–1) – a working-out, it seems, of the emphasis in *CD* II/2 (pp. 719–20) upon the unlimited character of the Church's fellowship (also noted in 'Rechtfertigung'), its witness to God's decision to be *for* all his creation. The whole of this essay is, in fact, a further gloss on the theology of the election of Jesus Christ: 'the eternal history, encounter and decision between God and man', the primordial self-determination of God as saviour, is 'the presupposition of all the movement of creaturely life' (*CD* II/2:184). If this were not so, God's decision would be supplemented or superseded by other events, and could not be eternal. But in fact all things move in accordance with God's will to fellowship with his creatures; Israel and the new Israel manifest the core of authentic history (the story of God's salvation) within what the world thinks of as its own 'neutral' duration (*CD* II/2, §34). And in this light, it becomes harder to draw an absolutely clear line between the pre-evangelical 'time' of politics and the true time of the Church – not least because (as we have seen) the Church itself is in one aspect still pre-evangelical. The 1946 essay shows just how fluid the boundary can be; yet this fluidity can only be spoken of from the vantage-point of the Church. There can be no setting side by side of Church and state as empirically comparable types of community, no absorption of Church into state, no reduction of the gospel to a social programme – not least because no social goal has meaning without the gospel.

IV

The period from Barmen to 1946 represents Barth's most sustained and creative exploration of political theology; and I have suggested that it is no accident that this corresponds broadly to the period in which the still residually ahistorical Christology of *CD* I/1 is slowly remoulded in the direction of the magnificent synthesis of *CD* IV/1, where the highest possible evaluation is given to the historical specificity of Jesus Christ. *Römerbrief* could be taken as giving far too much ground to positivist politics because of its reiterated stress on the timelessness of the saving encounter; but by 1946, the commitment to a doctrine of God's election of historical predicates has produced a very thorough repudiation of positivism. The state remains other than the Church, and essentially involved in coercion (it is not *chosen* as a context by its members), but the means as well as the goals of its coercion are increasingly brought under the gospel's discernment, and it is held to have some responsibility in *creating* equity and harmony, not only sustaining security. When Barth returns to ethics in *CD* III/4, these insights are applied directly to the state's means of self-defence.

The political theology of *CD* III/4 is pursued under the general rubric of 'The Protection of Life'. (§55). Barth gives what at first seems a startling amount of ground to the Tolstoyan and Gandhian prescription of non-violence in all circumstances, insists that no human being has authority over another's life, denies any 'natural' right of self-defence, and generally demolishes any notion that the state's coerciveness is grounded in some order of unredeemed nature (*CD* III/4:430–4). If there is ever an imperative (not a right) to self-defence, it can only be seen in the light of our fundamental defencelessness before God, and is to be obeyed as part of *God's* assault, not ours, upon disorder (*CD* III/4:434–5). Thus the state has no natural right to inflict capital punishment, and usurps the place of God if it thinks otherwise (*CD* III/4:445); only in extreme circumstances where the very *esse* of the state is in question, may the possibility be raised, because the state's *esse* is willed by God (*CD* III/4:446–7).

The same principle applies to defensive war. The exercise of force is *not*, says Barth, part of the *opus proprium* of the state, and there can be no general legitimation of the right to wage war in such terms (*CD* III/4:456ff). The *opus proprium* is the nurture of life and the fashioning of peace (*CD* III/4:458–9). What makes war inevitable is an inadequate peace in the political order: 'It is when the power of the state is insufficient to meet the inner needs of the country that it will seek an outer safety-valve for the consequent unrest and think it is found in war' (*ibid.*). And Barth is keenly aware too of the economic factors making for war, not only the energy generated by the quest for new material acquisitions but the manipulative influence of what we have learned to call the interests of the military-industrial complex. (*CD* III/4:450–1,459). There are or may be circumstances in which, once again, the state is commanded to defend itself, insofar as its continuance is necessary to the fostering of the standing of its people before God. The *responsibility* (not the right) of the state in such a situation is to undertake defensive action – 'independent of the success or failure of the enterprise'

(*CD* III/4:462–3) – and the responsibility of the Christian is to support this. But even then, the question of each individual's responsibility remains open, because the state is not an 'hypostasis' over the individual, making his or her decisions (*CD* III/4:464). Although *general* opposition to war is inadmissible, each individual in each particular case is obliged to decide for or against involvement – and this is one aspect the Church's service of the state, sustaining it by setting limits for it, and reserving the right to object, as a body, or through individual decision by believers, to any particular decision by the state (*CD* III/4:468).

This argument is the furthest Barth goes towards a positive evaluation of the active struggle for justice in the political order, and a radical qualification of an identification of the essence of the state with *Gewalt* and coercion. Despite the challenge to absolute pacifism – the one aspect of the discussion in III/4 seized upon in the 1950s and 60s by those arguing for every possible level of rearmament[23] – Barth is entirely clear that the means the state uses to secure its continuance, both in its internal and external relations, are open to Christian discernment and judgement. The possibility of self-defence cannot be turned into a self-evident legitimation for military policy – not least because, when defensive violence is undertaken, it may well be in circumstances that will in practice make the state *more* not less vulnerable. It is witness not success that is at issue in self-defence, witness to and obedience to the God who ordains the ministry of the state, but does not guarantee its invulnerability.

Barth notes in passing (III/4:453) that modern (atomic) warfare makes any residual romanticism or idealism about war unthinkable: it reveals the real face of war. Despite this, as he admitted in 1963,[24] he did not regard the events of 1945 as having made a permanent difference to what could be said about war. By the 1960s, however, it is quite clear that he had become convinced that a 'just war' in the atomic age was impossible: war can no longer have any meaning as the defence of a state. As the 1958 theses put it, atomic war is 'useless as a means of political confrontation'. In the light of our tracing of Barth's development as a political theologian, it should now be possible to see why this conclusion imposes itself, and why the issue becomes a confessional one. The final section of this essay will attempt briefly to set out the implicit argument here – and to suggest some further questions for theology in our time arising from all this.

v

The state exists, not as a thing in itself, but as a means of getting things done. A political unit can look for no metaphysical, trans-historical ground: it *happens* to be there, and certain people *happen* to be born into it; it may or may not coincide with a 'nation', and it does not in the least matter whether it does or not (Barth in *CD* III/4, §54.3 effectively and decisively dismisses the idea that the nation in itself has any positive significance in God's dispensation). Its 'vocation' or 'destiny' is simply to contribute to the new creation, the reconciled and reconciling humanity willed and chosen by God in his decision to be our God in Christ; and its fulfils this vocation by resisting disorder, restraining, by compulsion where necessary, the mutual destructiveness of sinful human beings, creating equity and harmony. Because it is a way of preserving the world of human intercourse – even to the extent of not slaughtering the evildoer – it is not simply a negative limit, but a positive sign of hope. In a shadowy but still quite discernible way, it echoes the Church's promise of 'time for amendment of life and the grace and comfort of the Holy Spirit'. It is enabled to be and to do all this because, in electing Jesus, God elects to make the time from resurrection to parousia a gift to us. To the state, the Church announces the good news that it has a right to exist because God is God, and is God as Jesus Christ, and that therefore it has a legitimate task to perform. The Church unites itself with the state in what Barth at the end of his career (*ChrL*, §78.1) called the 'revolt against disorder', against the self-destruction of sin; and its service to the state lies in this proclamation of a *determinate* task for it. No political unit has any finality (in both senses of the word) independently of this determination by God in Christ.

So the Church cannot allow that the state can have different goals from itself – the goal of all human action is set by the will of the *one* God, who is never other than saviour. The Church judges, resists and disobeys the state as and when the state, by refusing to accept (implicitly or explicitly) its determination by the gospel, forgets its provisional nature, the specific integrity of its task, its proper *functional* autonomy. When this happens, the state ceases to be properly a state, a means of doing certain specific things, and lays claim to being the form of human existence as such; so it turns itself into a 'lordless power' and becomes itself an agent of disorder (*ibid.* §78.2). The Church's response is to declare itself over against such a pseudo-state, to announce how precisely the gospel should judge and limit the specific infidelities and disorders of this pseudo-state; in short, to declare a *status confessionis* and prepare for costly struggle.

The nuclear state, by the mere possession of the means of mass annihilation, pronounces its belief that it must survive at all costs; it identifies its own *Recht* with eternal value and legitimacy, and regards itself as having *in principle* the authority to exterminate what threatens it – not to resist, control, or discipline, but to exterminate. This is the meaning of the crucial fifth of the 1958 theses: the nuclear state has ceased to be a *political* (a determinately functional) reality. And it sets itself up in opposition to the goal of human fellowship, by exalting local right to unconditional status. Further – extrapolating from Barth's most important insight in this area – such a 'state' rejects the notion of time as promise. By conducting its policy under the sign of an *ersatz* eschatological menace, it denies that it lives between resurrection and parousia, and so turns its back on Christ. In so doing (as thesis 10 of 1958 states) it rejects 'all three articles of Christian faith'. The

Church is summoned to confession, and to non-cooperation (Barth's open letter of 1959 to the European Disarmament Conference in London[25] goes some way towards recommending civil disobedience) – though not to revolutionary anarchy. The state never becomes *wholly* demonic,[26] utterly incapable of fulfilling its calling (even against its will), and so the Church cannot ever attack the idea of a state, by, for example, offering to do the state's job itself, or by preaching a utopian ideal of non-institutional forms of human community.

I do not propose to argue that this is in every respect a political theology we are bound to adopt today; but I believe it goes far towards setting an agenda for such a theology. Many issues are left disturbingly in mid-air: notoriously, Barth gives only limited guidance as to how the state's definition of its *specific* priorities is to be informed by the Church – how the Church as such can participate in the formation of policy. If the state is a mechanism for getting things done, Christians are bound to be involved in the laborious job of political persuasion, the tactics of mapping out acceptable shared social goals (what *needs* getting done?) with those who work with different concepts of legitimacy, different accounts of history – though it is clear enough, on Barth's presuppositions, that the Christian is bound to be closer to any political outlook that maintains some ideal of social creativity or teleology than to a 'neutral' or static account of social order as something whose content as well as form is basically a 'given'. And, at the same time, the creative or teleological outlook has the possibility of being the Church's major enemy. The Church cannot but look for allies in more or less radical ideologies (*i.e.* among those who believe that states are *for* something), yet must do so in the fully ironic awareness that it thus courts profound conflict. I suspect that Barth's response to theologies of liberation would be to ask if they had fully grasped the latter point: if only the Christian can operate a properly 'secular' (non-utopian, non-messianic) polity, the Christian is therefore *ex professo* committed to resist all utopianism insofar as it becomes embodied in the structure of a state. The cautious tolerance between Church and state in East Germany or Czechoslovakia will always be an uneasy truce, in Barth's terms – though it is one to be glad of while it lasts, a necessary and profoundly fragile alliance.

Thus questions of tactical priorities, and of the ultimately tragic and paradoxical implications of Barth's thinking, remain unexplored in Barth's own work. But we could do worse than begin from his axiom that it is essential to have a theology of the state in *functional* terms – or, to quote Ernst Wolf,[27] that we have a theology of 'political virtue' rather than a *Staatsmetaphysik*; and that, consequently, we have a theological critique of positivist views of sovereignty. This requires us to turn back to Christological fundamentals, to the question of God's will towards us as historically embodied in Jesus and historically proclaimed in the believing community. *Of course*, all this is the wrong way round: our political critique does not generate our Christology, but vice versa. Yet Barth's own evolution – if my presentation of it in this essay is correct – shows that the interaction of political exigency and Christological exploration is close and subtle. Without Christology simply becoming an ideological tool to legitimate political resistance, it is clear enough that certain centrally serious theological issues – for us as for the first Christians – emerge only in and through fundamental conflicts over the nature and future of humanity. We may yet look to the programmatic and comprehensive political conflicts of our time to teach us something of how to do our theology; and Barth, at the very least, leaves us with the question of how we shall find anything interesting or hopeful to say in the political realm without some commitment to the proposition that what is said of Jesus in his living, dying and rising is said of the unchanging nature-in-act of God.

PART V

EPILOGUE

10

The Christian in Society

W. A. WHITEHOUSE

A Sermon preached at Christ Church, Oxford, on 21 September, 1986, the Feast of St Matthew, in commemoration of the centenary of the birth of Karl Barth.

The texts were: Ecclesiastes 5.4–12 and Matthew 19.16–30.

We meet, on this festival of St Matthew, to remember with special thanksgiving the birth, one hundred years ago, of our century's outstanding expositor of church dogmatics (catholic and evangelical), Karl Barth, recognized by this university as Doctor of Divinity *honoris causa* in 1938 when political tension was mounting to a world crisis. I was here, to learn the rudiments of theology, at Mansfield College, and I spent five shillings on a second-hand book (discarded, perhaps, by some eminent reviewer who had no further use for it) containing eight occasional lectures by Barth.[1] They date from what he later called his 'fine youthful days' as pastor of the Swiss Reformed congregation in Safenwil – an agricultural and industrial parish east of Basel – and from his first years in academic harness in the new Chair of Reformed Theology at Göttingen. The 1916 essay on 'The Strange New World within the Bible' still shapes my way of attending to Scriptures selected to direct public worship. And from the last of those lectures, given in 1919 to the Tambach Conference on Religion and Social Relations, I have found direction for the *sermon* – which Barth would expect to find (instead of a 'memorial address') at the heart of this service. From that lecture I first learned about a 'far-seeing happy patience, in which all things transitory, even in their abnormal forms, are seen in the light of the eternal'[2] – by the grace of the kingdom of God to which the social wisdom of Ecclesiastes bears witness in its own way as do the Gospel parables and sayings in theirs. Barth's deep commitment to right thinking in theology was offered in support of that ministry of the Word of God which Christ sustains in his Church. And at a time when the cult of wealth on the one hand and fanatical resort to violence on the other disclose to us a world where we see the poor oppressed and justice and right violently denied in shameless and dispiriting ways, it is proper to recall Barth's concern for the bearing of theology on politics, articulated in that lecture on 'The Christian's Place in Society' and developed through five decades of public turbulence which has not yet abated.

To Christians, puzzled and distressed by the granite-hard actualities of human society and all that deforms it into disgrace, Barth spoke of *the Christ* who through faith dwells in our hearts in love – over us, behind us, beyond us, and yet in us. *He*, rather than the self-conscious Christian social theorist, is 'the Christian in Society'. To him we must look for diagnosis of need and hope of remedy when we see the poor oppressed and justice and right violently denied. From him we learn not to be surprised at what goes on. From him we learn obedient respect for the active command of God ('fear' of God is a misleading rendering). That command is within us and there creates its own analogy in the *hope* we entertain of a world where life for mankind in society may be *enjoyed* as a project created, redeemed and perfected through God and in God. 'The earth *is* the Lord's and the fullness thereof.' It has been from the beginning, still is, and in the end will so appear in full glory. Hence our freedom to move in and out of its structures and provisions, respecting them for what they are, but never revering them for their own sake. We are less bedevilled today, perhaps, with a cult of art for art's sake, work for its own sake, science for its own sake – though cult of the family for its own sake, sport for its own sake, financial affluence and profitability each for its own sake, are right-wing watchwords of our sorry times. But all such cults of man-made idols are endemic symptoms of disease in any and every real society in this world; symptoms liable at any time to be marshalled under the greater idolatry of political absolutism – nation or state for its own sake – wherever human beings seek their happiness under the cloud of what Barth called 'the deadly *isolation* of the human from the divine'.[3] In Christ we know that all which for us is truly divine is the creation, redemption and immanent perfecting of the world, through God and in God – the active sovereignty of the *kingdom* of God which encompasses all our environment and all our works and ways.

Each of us moves in society through the history of particular times; and wisdom requires from us a two-pronged thrust: one which combines grateful affirmation of goodness in things as they are with radical criticism which says No to the pretensions which distort them; a two-pronged thrust of *hope*, grounded in what is *proposed* in their inherent goodness and what is *sought* in the critical opposition provoked in lives subjected in faith to the kingdom of God.

An appearance of child-like naïvety is not out of place in the first movement of grateful approval. Christian thinkers have often sought to correct that appearance by producing tidy self-contained accounts of goodness built into the world as it is by 'orders of creation'. We do better to think in terms of that world being charged with 'parables' and 'promises'; and to learn from the social wisdom of Ecclesiastes how to receive and pass on such parables and promises with a lively awareness of inherent futility in all for which man labours under the sun. Let me emphasise the *liveliness* – far removed from dispiriting cynicism – which makes Ecclesiastes such fun to read. If the spectre of despair still lingers round that pre-Messianic wisdom, it is wholly dispelled when Jesus elicits from the world as it is the parables and promises germane to his preaching of the kingdom of God. The counter-movement of critical opposition to things as they are, prompted by deep awareness of the tragedy inherent in their being so, can also be compressed all too readily into tidy ideological forms of protest (or resignation) which induce a social life for human beings in which the hiddenness of God becomes for them his real absence. Again, we do better to deal with the concrete needs and the concrete scandals of the hour in which we are so prompted, and be ready always to distinguish between the facts of one case and those of another. Where what is offered by promise and parable is tragically frustrated or monstrously corrupted, there we must say No! – not as a last or highest truth but as a call from the future when every promise will be sealed with God's final Yes!

The youthful exuberance with which Karl Barth presented this account of the Christian in society in 1919 – and amplified by a wealth of allusion to the aspirations of social and cultural theory dear to the hearts of his hearers in their dedication to a new shape of politics for shattered Europe – that exuberance was tempered, no doubt, as he and they took the strain of subsequent events. His prime commitment for the rest of his life was to produce food for scholars; the faithful provision of well-founded clarification for what may and must be said to the world by pastors in their Christian pulpits and, on occasion, by Councils of Brethren or by some lone prophet, as in the 1934 Synod of Barmen and in his own contribution to Cold War debate between East and West. 'We cannot reach the clarifications, especially in the broad field of politics, which are necessary today – and to which theology . . . might and should have a word to say, without having previously reached those comprehensive clarifications in theology and about theology itself' for which he wrestled in the *Church Dogmatics*. So he wrote in the preface to the first half-volume of that massive work.[4] His definitive account of ethics, ecclesiastical and political, properly placed in the Doctrine of Reconciliation, was left unfinished. It might have provided critical re-appraisal of his own bold interventions, made against the stream when the floods were at their height, in the struggle for Church integrity in Hitlerite Germany and later in the Cold War between East and West. It would certainly have provided directives for the words and deeds required from us, his fellow-believers, in our struggle to deal, in disillusioned wisdom, with the cult of worldly wealth re-established as the core of shop-keeping politics.

'That far-seeing happy patience, in which all things transitory, even in their abnormal forms, are seen in the light of the eternal' is not easily acquired or sustained, in its authentic lively form. Blessed are those to whom it comes as God's free gift. Barth, notoriously, held that that free gift had been granted, quite unpredictably, to Mozart, who '*heard*, and caused those who have ears to hear, what we shall not *see* until the end of time.' He heard 'the whole world of creation enveloped by the light' which will irradiate its end, when 'the whole context of providence' is finally disclosed (*CD* III/3:298).

Born one hundred years ago, Karl Barth has been translated into the society of those whose time on earth has passed. His work remains to guide our steps into the fresh obedience required in days yet to come. Our prayer for him, and for all into whose company he has passed, is the prayer of cheerful and courageous hope:

> Requiem aeternam dona eis, Domine;
> et lux perpetua, et lux perpetua, luceat
> eis . . . luceat eis.

NOTES

Notes

Introduction

1. *Time*, April 20, 1962, p. 47.
2. In the English edition.
3. T. F. Torrance, *Karl Barth, An Introduction to His Early Theology, 1910–31* (London: SCM, 1962), p. 30.
4. Hans Urs von Balthasar, *The Theology of Karl Barth*, trans. John Drury (New York: Anchor, 1972), pp. 20–21.
5. *A New Dictionary of Christian Theology*, eds. Alan Richardson & John Bowden (London SCM, 1983). Unlike the first edition (1969), this one does not include biographical entries; individual figures are treated as members of schools of thought or through their contributions to a particular field. Discussion of Barth, therefore, is found chiefly under the entries on 'Crisis Theology,' 'Dialectical Theology', and 'Neo-Orthodoxy'. One would not expect the first two entries to include discussion of the Barth of *Church Dogmatics*; but one would expect it of the third. In vain.
6. *E.g.* John Macquarrie, *Twentieth Century Religious Thought*, rev. ed. (London: SCM, 1971), p. 321; and in Robert E. Hood, *Contemporary Political Orders and Christ: Karl Barth's Christology and Political Praxis* (Pittsburgh: Pickwick Press, 1985), p. ix.
7. See below, pp. 11ff.
8. In the event John Webster was unable to be present.
9. John Baillie, *The Sense of the Presence of God* (London, 1962), p. 254.

1

1. Rolf Joachim Erler and Reiner Marquard, eds., *A Karl Barth Reader* (Grand Rapids: Eerdmans, 1986), p. 112.
2. K. Barth, *Letters 1961–1968* (Grand Rapids: Eerdmans, 1981), p. 105.
3. *Ibid.*, pp. 5f.
4. K. Barth, *Final Testimonies* (Grand Rapids: Eerdmans, 1977), p. 56.
5. *Ibid.*, p. 37.
6. Barth, *Letters 1961–1968*, p. 255, cf. p. 113.
7. *Ibid.*, p. 354.
8. *Ibid.*, pp. 174ff. 348ff.
9. J. Ellul, *Ce que je crois* (Paris: Grasset, 1987), p. 44.
10. Barth, *Letters 1961–1968*, p. 112.
11. Ibid., pp. 312ff., 333ff., 357f.
12. K. Barth and E. Thurneysen, *Revolutionary Theology in the Making* (Richmond: John Knox, 1964), p. 185.
13. Barth, *Letters 1961–1968*, p. 153.
14. *Ibid.*, p. 102.

15. *Ibid.*, pp. 102, 147.
16. *CD* III/3: 151ff.
17. Barth, *Letters 1961–1968*, p. 243.
18. Ibid., p. 194.
19. K. Barth, *The Word of God and the Word of Man* (New York: Harpers, 1957), p. 22.
20. *CD* I/2: 620ff.
21. Barth, *Letters 1961–1968*, pp. 82, 103.
22. Ibid., pp. 25f.
23. Barth, *Final Testimonies*, pp. 43ff.
24. *CD* III/4: 415ff.

2

1. I am indebted here to Frank Kermode's seminal work *The Classic: Literary Images of Permanency and Change* (New York: Viking Press, 1975).
2. Konrad Stock, *Anthropologie der Verheißung: Karl Barths Lehre vom Menschen als dogmatisches Problem* (Munich: Kaiser, 1980), pp. 15–35.
3. Kjetil Hafstad, *Wort und Geschichte: Das Geschichtsverständnis Karl Barths* (Munich, Kaiser, 1985), pp. 39–121.
4. See, e.g., Alister McGrath, *The Making of Modern German Christology: From the Enlightenment to Pannenberg* (Oxford/New York: Blackwell, 1986), pp. 94–126.
5. Gerhard Sauter, 'Weichenstellungen im Denken Karl Barths', *Evangelische Theologie* 46 (1986), pp. 476–88.
6. For the concept, see Jacques de Senarclens, 'La concentration christologique', in *Antwort: Karl Barth zum 60. Geburtstag* (Zurich: Zollikon, 1956), pp. 190–207.
7. Ingrid Spieckerman, *Gotteserkenntnis: Ein Beitrag zu Grundfrage der neuen Theologie Karl Barths* (Munich: Kaiser, 1985), pp. 21–55.
8. Wilhelm Herrman, *The Communion of the Christian with God* (Philadelphia: Fortress, 1971), p. 354.
9. For this point, see McGrath, *The Making of Modern German Christology*, pp. 56–8.
10. Note the important essay of that year: Karl Barth, 'Der christliche Glaube und die Geschichte', *Zeitschrift für systematische Theologie* 29 (1912), pp. 1–18; 49–72.
11. Karl Barth, 'Evangelical Theology in the Nineteenth Century', in *The Humanity of God* (London: Collins, 1961), p. 14.
12. Barth's relation to Luther (particularly in relation to his doctrine of justification) has been the subject of scrutiny recently: see A. E. McGrath, 'Karl Barth and the articulus justificationis: The Significance of his Critique of Ernst Wolf within the Context of his Theological Method', *Theologische Zeischrift* 39 (1983), pp. 349–61; idem, 'Karl Barth als Aufklärer? Der Zusammenhang seiner Lehre vom Werke Christi mit der Erwählungslehre', *Kerygma und Dogma* 30 (1984), pp. 273–83; Gerhard Ebeling, *Lutherstudien III: Begriffsuntersuchungen – Textinterpretation – Wirkungsgeschichte* (Tübingen: Siebeck, 1985), pp. 428–573.
13. Spieckerman,, *Gotteserkenntnis*, pp. 56–82.
14. As pointed out by W. Härle, 'Der Aufruf der 93 Intellektuellen und Karl Barths Bruch mit der liberalen Theologie', *Zeitschrift für Theologie und Kirche* 72 (1975), pp. 207–24. The reference to Barth's disillusionment with 'Marburg and German culture' in a letter to Thurneysen of 4 September 1914 (*Karl Barth – Eduard Thurneysen Briefwechsel*, ed. E. Thurneysen, 2 vols., [Zurich: Theologischer Verlag, 1973–4], vol. 1, p. 10) concerns the journal *Christliche Welt*, not the 'Manifesto of the Intellectuals'.

15. The full analysis of the significance of the 'Unterricht in der christlichen Religion' has recently been brought out by Spieckermann, *Gotteserkenntis*, pp. 140–225.
16. It is interesting to note the parallels between Barth's position and the insights of Kierkegaard's 1847 essay 'On the Difference between a Genius and an Apostle', a devastating parody of the liberal Protestant portrait of Jesus. 'If the thing is well said, the man is a genius – and if it is *unusually* well said, then God said it'. And so Jesus comes to be put on the same level, as Kierkegaard has it, as 'all those who have no authority, on the same level as geniuses, poets and the thinkers'.
17. *E.g.*, see Anthony C. Thistleton, 'Academic Freedom, Religious Tradition and the Morality of Christian Scholarship', in *Their Lord and Ours: Approaches to Authority, Community and the Unity of the Church*, ed. M. Santer (London: SPCK, 1982), pp. 20–45.
18. See *The History of Christian Theology I: The Science of Theology*, ed. P. D. L. Avis (Basingstoke: Marshall Pickering/Grand Rapids: Eerdmans, 1986), pp. 206–29.
19. See the memorable essay 'Theology', in *God in Action: Theological Addresses* (Edinburgh: Clark, 1936), pp. 39–57. *Cf* S. W. Sykes, 'Barth on the Centre of Theology', in *Karl Barth: Studies of his Theological Method*, ed. S. W. Sykes (Oxford: Oxford University Press, 1979), pp. 17–54.
20. Cf. Alister E. McGrath, 'Geschichte, Überlieferung und Erzählung: Überlegungen zur Identität und Aufgabe christlicher Theologie', *Kerygma und Dogma* 32 (1986), pp. 234–53.
21. See, e.g., Colin Gunton, *Enlightenment and Alienation: An Essay towards a Trinitarian Theology* (Basingstoke: Marshall Pickering, 1985), pp. 1–70.
22. Eberhard Jüngel, *God as the Mystery of the World: On the Foundation of Theology of the Crucified One in the Dispute between Theism and Atheism* (Edinburgh: Clark, 1983), p. 13 (my translation).
23. In the *Church Dogmatics*, however, Barth tends to marginalize the cross on account of methodological considerations. For an attempt to recover this emphasis, see Alister McGrath, *The Enigma of the Cross* (London: Hodder & Stoughton, 1987).
24. Spieckerman,, *Anthropologie der Verheißung*, p. 15.
25. Barth, 'Theology', pp. 56–7.
26. The study of E. Lessing, 'Dogmatik als Aufgabe der systematischen Theologie', *Zeitschrift für Theologie und Kirche* 75 (1978), pp. 350–60 appears to be based upon a non-existent 'Barthian' quotation (p. 351). Note the convincing rebuttal by Spieckermann, *Gotteserkenntnis*, p. 140 n. 2.
27. Barth, 'Theology', p. 50.
28. Barth, 'Theology', pp. 43–4.
29. Barth, 'Theology', p. 45
30. See Eberhard Busch, *Karl Barth und die Pietisten: Die Pietismuskritik des jungen Karl Barth und ihre Erwiderung* (Munich: Kaiser, 1978), for an analysis of Barth's critique of Pietism at this point.
31. Most significantly, see Friedrich-Wilhelm Marquardt, *Theologie and Sozialismus: Das Beispiel Karl Barths* (Munich: Kaiser, 3rd edn, 1985).
32. For Bultmann, Christian obedience entailed no particular type of moral conduct which differed visibly from that of the unbeliever: Rudolf Bultmann, *Theology of the New Testament* (2 vols: New York: Scribners, 1951), vol. 1 p. 138. A similar view is expounded by H. D. Betz, *Galatians* (Philadelphia: Fortress, 1979), p. 292.
33. See Sauter, 'Weichenstellungen', pp. 477–80.
34. Ritschl's dismissal of the idea of the 'wrath of God' neatly illustrates this tendency.

35. Two recent studies casting much light on the German church struggle should be noted: *Theologie und Kirche im Wirken Hans von Sodens: Briefen und Dokumente aus der Zeit des Kirchenkampfes 1933–1945*, ed. Erich Dinkler and Erika Dinkler-von Schubert (Göttingen: Vandenhoeck u. Ruprecht, 1986); Hermann Klemm, *Im Dienst der Bekennende Kirche: Das Leben des sächsischen Pfarrers Karl Fischer 1896–1941* (Göttingen: Vandenhoeck u. Ruprecht, 1986).
36. For these 'orders', see Emil Brunner, *The Divine Imperative: A Study in Christian Ethics* (London: Lutterworth, 1937), pp. 291–568.
37. See the important study of Ernst Wolf, 'Zum protestantischen Rechtslehre', in *Peregrinatio II: Studien zur reformatorischen Theologie, zum Kirchenrecht und zur Sozialethik* (Munich: Kaiser, 1965), pp. 191–206.
38. The 1933 essay 'Das erste Gebot als theologische Axiom', *Zwischen den Zeiten* II (1933), pp. 297–314; reprinted in *Theologische Fragen und Antworten: Gesammelte Vorträge III* (Zurich: Theologische Verlag, 2nd edn, 1986), pp. 127–43, should be noted in this connection.
39. *Barmen Declaration*, art. 1, in *Reformed Confessions of the Sixteenth Century*, ed. Arthur Cochrane, (London: SCM, 1966), p. 334.
40. For an analysis, see George Lindbeck, *The Nature of Doctrine: Religion and Theology in a Postliberal Age* (London: SPCK, 1984), pp. 30–45. The study of William R. Hutchison, *The Modernist Impulse in American Protestantism* (Oxford: Oxford University Press, 1982), illustrates the frightening extent to which contemporary cultural axioms appear to have been appropriated uncritically within American Protestantism.
41. Tom F. Driver, *Patterns of Grace: Human Experience as Word of God* (San Francisco: Harper & Row, 1977), passim.
42. And what, we may reasonably ask, happens when Driver no longer has this quasi-erotic experience upon leaving his bath? God, presumably, is concluded to be dead, in that he is no longer to be experienced in the present. The entire 'death of God' theology of the 1960s often seems to rest upon the unjustified and unjustifiable equation of 'God' and 'experience'. The wisdom of Barth's insistence upon an external criterion in the word of God is being appreciated increasingly as we move towards a post-liberal theology.
43. Note the comments of Stanley Hauerwas, *A Community of Character: Towards a Constructive Christian Social Ethic* (Notre Dame: University of Notre Dame Press, 1981), e.g. p. 231.
44. Reinhold Niebuhr, *The Kingdom of God in America* (New York: Scribners, 1937).
45. Lesslie Newbigin, *Unfinished Agenda: An Autobiography* (Grand Rapids: Eerdmans, 1985), p. 254.
46. Claus Bussman, *Who do you say? Jesus Christ in Latin American Theology* (New York: Orbis Books, 1985), demonstrates how insights similar to Barth's underlie contemporary Latin American liberation theology. Of particular interest is his careful analysis of how the category of 'praxis' is central as an epistemological principle for understanding Jesus.
47. Cf. Lesslie Newbigin, *The Other Side of 1984: Questions for the Churches* (Geneva: WCC, 1983).

3

1. Stephen Sykes, *The Identity of Christianity* (London: SPEC, 1984).
2. A *locus classicus* for what I shall call 'Abrahamic' theology is the paragraph of divine soliloquy, Genesis 18: 17–19, where the Hebrew *ye da 'tiw* (variously translated 'chosen', 'known', 'taken care of') can carry the meaning, perfectly suited to the context, 'I have made him acquainted with me.' *Cf.* Gerhard von Rad, *Genesis. A Commentary* (London: SCM, 1961), p. 205.

3. Von Rad, *Genesis*, p. 73.
4. On pp. 241-42, Barth comments on the apprehensive attitude taken towards water in the first saga and its status as companion and friend of man in this one, a contrast to which Abrahamic migration from one territory to another at the beginning of covenant-history is perhaps germane.
5. H. A. L. Fisher, *A History of Europe*, 2 vols. (London: Eyre & Spottiswoode, 1935), volume 2: 'Renaissance, Reformation, Reason,' pp. 432-33.
6. Jose de Vinck, *The Works of Bonaventure*, vol. v: *Collationes on the Six days* (Paterson, N. J.: St. Anthony Guild Press, 1970), p. ix.
7. *Idem*.
8. See John Berger, 'Beauty Out of Cruel World,' in *The White Bird* (London: Chatto & Windus, 1985).
9. R. S. Franks, *The Metaphysical Justification of Religion* (London: University of London Press, 1929).

4

1. Daniel W. Hardy, 'The English Tradition of Interpretation and the Reception of Schleiermacher and Barth in England,' forthcoming.
2. Bernard Ramm, *After Fundamentalism. The Future of Evangelical Theology* (New York: Harper and Row, 1983), pp. 46f.
3. Richard Rorty, *Philosophy and the Mirror of Nature* (Oxford: Blackwell, 1980), esp. pp. 38ff.
4. Michael Polanyi, *Personal Knowledge. Towards a Post-Critical Philosophy* (London: Routledge and Kegan Paul, 2nd ed. 1962), pp. 139f.
5. Colin E. Gunton, *Enlightenment and Alienation. An Essay Towards a Trinitarian Theology* (Basingstoke: Marshall, Morgan and Scott, 1985), pp. 26ff.
6. Ronald F. Thiemann, *Revelation and Theology. The Gospel as Narrated Promise* (Notre Dame, Indiana: University of Notre Dame Press, 1985), chapter 2.
7. See especially Richard J. Bernstein, *Beyond Objectives and Realism. Science, Hermeneutics and Praxis* (Philadelphia: University of Pennsylvania Press, 1985) and R. W. Newell, *Objectivity, Empiricism and Truth* (London: Routledge and Kegan Paul, 1986).
8. Karl Barth, 'Schicksal und Idee in der Theologie', *Theologische Fragen und Antworten* (Evangelischer Verlag AG Zollikon, 1957), pp. 54-92.
9. 'Einstein used to say that nature says "no" to most of the questions it is asked, and occasionally "perhaps". The scientist does not do as he pleases, and he cannot force nature to say only what he wants to hear.' Ilya Prigogine and Isabelle Stengers, *Order out of Chaos. Man's New Dialogue with Nature* (London: Fontana, 1985), p. 43.
10. Thiemann, *Revelation and Theology*, p. 47.
11. *Ibid.*, p. 42.
12. Karl Barth, *The Humanity of God* (London: Fontana, 1967), p. 40.
13. Steven G. Smith, *The Argument to the Other. Reason Beyond Reason in the Thought of Karl Barth and Emmanuel Levinas*. (Chico, California: Scholars' Press, 1983), pp. 48, 49.
14. Thiemann, *Revelations and Theology*, p. 48.
15. Robert W. Jenson, *Alpha and Omega. A Study in the Theology of Karl Barth* (New York: Thomas Nelson and Sons, 1963), p. 168.
16. Karl Barth, *Protestant Theology in the Nineteenth Century. Its Background and History*, ET by Brian Cozens and John Bowden (London: SCM Press, 1972), p. 17.
17. Hardy, 'The English Tradition'.
18. John Howard Yoder, *The Priestly Kingdom. Social Ethics as Gospel* (Notre Dame, Indiana: University of Notre Dame Press, 1984), p. 11.

19. Thiemann, *Revelation and Theology*, pp. 71ff.
20. Karl Barth, *Anselm: Fides Quaerens Intellectum. Anselm's Proof of the Existence of God in the Context of his Theological Scheme*, ET of 2nd ed. by Ian W. Robertson (London: SCM Press, 1960), p. 27.
21. For a discussion of Barth's conception of transcendence, see Colin Gunton, 'Transcendence, Metaphor and the Knowability of God,' *Journal of Theological Studies* 31 (1980); 503–16.
22. Eberhard Jüngel, *Gottes sein ist im Werden* (Tübingen: J. C. B. Mohr, 2ᵉ 1967). ET: *The Doctrine of the Trinity: God's Being is in his Becoming*, trans. Horton Harries (Edinburgh & London: Scottish Academic Press, 1976).
23. I owe to John Macken, *The Autonomy Theme in Karl Barth's Church Dogmatics and in Current Barth Criticism*, (Dissertation submitted to the Catholic Faculty of the University of Tübingen, 1984), p. 116, a reference to IV/3: 141: 'we may now make the further point that the world created by God does not merely exist but also speaks to one at least of its creatures, *i.e.*, to man, giving itself to be perceived by him.'
24. For example, Wolfhart Pannenberg, 'Die Subjectivität Gottes und die Trinitätslehre. Ein Beitrag zur Beziehen zwischen Karl Barth und die Philosphie Hegels,' *Grundfragen Systematischer Theologie. Gesammelte Aufsätze 2* (Göttingen, 1980), pp. 96–111.
25. For a discussion of the weakness of Barth's trinitarian theology in this respect, see Thomas A. Smail, 'The Doctrine of the Holy Spirit', *Theology Beyond Christendom. Essays on the Centenary of the Birth of Karl Barth May 10, 1886*, edited by John Thompson (Allison Park, Pennsylvania: Pickwick Publications, 1986), pp. 87–110.
26. John D. Zizioulas, *Being as Communion* (London: Darton, Longman and Todd, 1985).
27. Barth, *Protestant Theology in the Nineteenth Century*, p. 446.

5

1. Paul Ricoeur, *The Conflict of Interpretations: Essays in Hermeneutics* (Evanston: Northwestern University Press, 1974), p. 11.
2. Martin Heidegger, *Being and Time*, trans. John Macquarrie and Edward Robinson (Oxford: Blackwell, 1973), p. 195.
3. Cf. Eberhard Busch, *Karl Barth: His Life from Letters and Autobiographical Texts*, trans. John Bowden (London: SCM, 1976); Eberhard Jüngel, 'Einführung in Leben und Werk Karl Barths', in his *Barth-Studien*, Ökumenische Theologie 9 (Zürich-Köln: Benziger, and Gütersloh: Gerd Mohn, 1982), 22–60; Gerhard Wehr, *Karl Barth: Theologe und Gottes fröhlicher Partisan* (Gütersloh: Gerd Mohn, 1979).
4. *Karl Barth Gesamtausgabe* published by Theologischer Verlag Zürich.
5. Cf. Jüngel, 'Einführung', p. 40.
6. 'The Strange New World Within The Bible', in Karl Barth, *The Word of God and the Word of Man*, trans. Douglas Horton (London: Hodder and Stoughton, 1928), pp. 28–50.
7. Karl Barth, *Der Römerbrief*, 1st ed. (Bern: Bäschlin, 1919); 2nd rev. ed. (München: Kaiser, 1922; now Zürich: Theologischer Verlag, 12th ed., 1978). ET: *The Epistle to the Romans*, trans. Edwyn C. Hoskyns (Oxford: Oxford University Press 1975).
8. Karl Barth, *Evangelical Theology: An Introduction*, trans. Grover Foley (London: Weidenfeld and Nicolson, 1963), p. 5.
9. *CD* I/1 and I/2.
10. Barth, *Romans*, pp. 1–26.

11. Karl Barth – Rudolf Bultmann, *Briefwechsel 1922–1966*, ed. Bernd Jaspert, Karl Barth Gesamtausgabe v Briefe, Vol. 1 (Zürich: Theologischer Verlag, 1971). ET: Karl Barth – Rudolf Bultmann, *Letters 1922–1966*, ed. Bernd Jaspert, trans. and ed. Geoffrey W. Bromiley (Edinburgh: T. & T. Clark, 1982). This translation does not include all the letters printed in the original German edition.
12. For Bultmann's development of hermeneutics cf. esp. Rudolf Bultmann, *Glauben und Verstehen: Gesammelte Aufsätze*, 4 volumes (Tübingen: J. C. B. Mohr [Paul Siebeck], 1933 ff.); 'New Testament and Mythology', in Hans-Werner Bartsch, ed., *Kerygma and Myth: A Theological Debate*, trans. Reginald H. Fuller (London: SPCK, 1953), 1–44; and *Jesus Christ and Mythology* (London: SCM 1960).
13. Cf. *Glauben und Verstehen III* (Tübingen: J. C. B. Mohr [Paul Siebeck], 3rd ed., 1965), p. 147.
14. Barth – Bultmann, *Letters 1922–1966*, pp. 89f.
15. Karl Barth, 'Rudolf Bultmann – An Attempt to Understand Him', in Hans-Werner Bartsch, ed., *Kerygma and Myth: A Theological Debate*, Vol. II (London: SPCK, 1962), pp. 83–132, here esp. 112 ff.
16. *Cf.* Peter Eicher, *Offenbarung: Prinzip neuzeitlicher Theologie* (München: Kösel, 1977), pp. 189ff.
17. Barth, *Der Römerbrief*, p. xxi. The term *Treueverhältnis* is lost in the English translation, cf. *Romans*, p. 18.
18. Barth, *Romans*, p. 19.
19. Barth, *Der Römerbrief*, p. xii. Here, the English translation is not precise enough. *Cf. Romans*, p. 8.
20. *Ibid.*, p. x.
21. *Ibid.*, p. xiii (my translation), cf. *Romans*, p. 10.
22. *Cf.* Rudolf Bultmann, 'New Testament and Mythology', pp. 3f.; and Bultmann's reply to Barth in *Letters 1922–1966*, pp. 87f.
23. *Cf.* Barth, *Evangelical Theology*.
24. *Kirchliche Dogmatik* I/2, 7th ed. (Zurich: Theologischer Verlag, 1983): 805 (my translation).
25. Barth, *Romans*, p. 8.
26. Eberhard Jüngel, 'Die theologischen Antänge. Beobachtungen', *Barth – Studien*, pp. 61–126. Here, p. 94 (my translation).
27. *Cf.* Paul Ricoeur, 'Preface to Bultmann', in *The Conflict of Interpretations*, pp. 381–401, here 393f.
28. *Ibid*, p. 390.
29. cf. Peter Eicher, *Offenbarung*, pp. 234–242.
30. *Cf.* S. W. Sykes, 'Barth on the Centre of Theology', in S. W. Sykes, ed., *Karl Barth: Studies of his Theological Method* (Oxford: Clarendon Press, 1979), pp. 17–54, here 53f.
31. *Cf.* R. D. Williams, 'Barth on the Triune God', in Sykes, ed., *Karl Barth: Studies of his Theological Method*, pp. 147–193. Williams examines some major problems of Barth's doctrine of the Spirit.
32. See Eberhard Jüngel's recent assessment of Barth's *Theanthropologie* and its implications, in his essay 'Theologische Existenz: Erinnerung an Karl Barth', in *Evangelische Kommentare* 19 (1986): 258–260.
33. Karl Barth, 'Rudolf Bultmann – An Attempt to Understand Him' (see note 16), and Rudolf Bultmann's reply in *Letters 1922–1966*, pp. 87–104.
34. Karl Barth, *Fides Quaerens Intellectum: Anselms Beweis der Existenz Gottes im Zusammenhang seines theologischen Programms*, ed. Eberhard Jüngel and Ingolf U. Dalferth, Karl Barth Gesamtausgabe II. Akademische Werke (Zürich: Theologischer Verlag, 1981).
35. The same question has to be addressed to some of Barth's disciples. See for

instance Georg Eicholz, *Tradition und Interpretation: Studien zum Neuen Testament* (München: Kösel, 1965), pp. 190–209: 'Der Ansatz Karl Barths in der Hermeneutik'.
36. Hans-Georg Gadamer, *Truth and Method*, (London: Sheed & Ward, 1975), and *Kleine Schriften*, 4 volumes (Tübingen: J. C. B. Mohr [Paul Siebeck], 1967 ff.). Paul Ricoeur's critique of Gadamer's hermeneutics can be seen most clearly expressed in his *Hermeneutics and the Human Sciences: Essays on Language, Action and Interpretation*, ed., trans. and introduced by John B. Thompson (Cambridge: Cambridge University Press, 1981), esp. pp. 43–128.
37. For the reasons outlined above I disagree with Lewis S. Mudge's assessment that 'If anything, Ricoeur's position is closer to Karl Barth's'. Lewis S. Mudge, 'Paul Ricoeur on Biblical Interpretation', in Paul Ricoeur, *Essays on Biblical Interpretation*, ed. with an Introduction by Lewis S. Mudge (Philadelphia: Fortress Press, 1980), pp. 1–40, here p. 8.
38. See Jürgen Habermas, 'Der Universalitätsanspruch der Hermeneutik', in *Hermeneutik und Ideologiekritik* (Frankfurt/M.: Suhrkamp, 1971), pp. 120–159.
39. *Cf.* my recent study *Text und Interpretation als Kategorien theologischen Denkens* (Tübingen: J. C. B. Mohr [Paul Siebeck], 1986), esp. pp. 14–72.
40. Gadamer, *Truth and Method*, p. 258.
41. *Ibid.*, p. 273.
42. *Cf. Text und Interpretation als Kategorien theologischen Denkens*, pp. 27 ff.
43. Hans-Georg Gadamer, 'Replik', in *Hermeneutik und Ideologiekritik*, pp. 283–317.
44. Gadamer, *Truth and Method*, pp. 157–173.
45. Karl Barth, *The Theology of Schleiermacher*, ed. Dietrich Ritschl, trans. Geoffrey W. Bromiley (Edinburgh: T. & T. Clark, 1982), pp. 178–183.
46. *Cf. ibid.*, p. 183.
47. Gadamer, *Truth and Method*. p. 173.
48. Paul Ricoeur, 'Schleiermacher's Hermeneutics', in *The Monist* 60 (1977), pp. 181–197.
49. Manfred Frank, *Das individuelle Allgemeine: Textstrukturierung und interpretation nach Schleiermacher* (Frankfurt/M.: Suhrkamp, 1977).
50. Werner G. Jeanrond, 'The Impact of Schleiermacher's Hermeneutics on Contemporary Interpretation Theory', in David Jasper, ed., *The Interpretation of Belief: Coleridge, Schleiermacher and Romanticism* (London: Macmillan, 1986), pp. 81–96.
51. *Cf.* Mudge, 'Paul Ricoeur on Biblical Interpretation', p. 13.
52. Paul Ricoeur, *Le Conflit des Interprétations: Essais d'Herméneutique* (Paris: Seuil, 1969), p. 23.
53. Barth – Bultmann, *Letters 1922–1966*, p. 87.
54. *Cf.* here esp. Rudolf Bultmann, *Existence and Faith: Shorter Writings of Rudolf Bultmann*, ed., transl. and introduced by Schubert M. Ogden (London/Glasgow: Collins – Fontana, 1973), pp. 200f.; Paul Ricoeur, *Interpretation Theory: Discourse and the Surplus of Meaning* (Fort Worth: Texas Christian University Press, 1976), pp. 89–95; Karl Barth, *CD* I/2: 782–796: 'Dogmatics as Ethics'; Hans-Georg Gadamer, *Vernunft im Zeitalter der Wissenschaft: Aufsätze* (Frankfurt/M.: Surhkamp, 1976), pp. 78–109: 'Hermeneutik als praktische Philosophie'.
55. Eberhard Jüngel, *Gottes Sein ist im Werden: Verantwortliche Rede vom Sein Gottes bei Karl Barth, Eine Paraphrase*, 3rd ed. (Tübingen: J. C. B. Mohr [Paul Siebeck], 3rd ed., 1976), p. 27.
56. Barth, *Romans*, pp. 8ff.

6

1. Karl Barth, Letter to W. Spoendlin, 4 January, 1915. Quoted by Eberhard Busch in *Karl Barth. His Life from Letters and Autobiographical Texts* (London: SCM, 1976), p. 81.

2. Karl Barth, 'Ruckblick', in *Das Wort sie sollen lassen stahn*, Festschrift fuer Albert Schaedelin, 1950, 1ff. Quoted by Busch in *ibid*.
3. Karl Barth, 'The Strange New World within the Bible', in Karl Barth. *The Word of God and the Word of Man*, trans. Douglas Horton (New York: Harper & Row, 1957), pp. 28–50.
4. For Aquinas, practical reason is afflicted with ignorance, partly because its grasp of singular or contingent particulars is imperfect (*Summa Theologica* [*ST*], IIaIIae, Q.52, art.1), and partly because sin has diminished its inclination to virtue (*ST*, IaIIae, Q.85, art.1) and has utterly destroyed its rule over the other, sensitive powers of the soul (*ibid.*, and Q.71, art.2). Therefore, practical reason stands in need of that aid and perfection which the Holy Spirit provides through its gift of counsel (*ST*, IIaIIae, Q..52, art.1).

According to Luther, the Christian prince must 'cling solely to God, and be at him constantly, praying for a right understanding' as he seeks to apply the law equitably in particular cases (*On Temporal Authority*, in *Luther's Works*, 55 vols., vol. 45: *The Christian In Society*, II, ed. Walther I. Brandt [Philadelphia: Fortress Press, 1962], p. 119. Cp. *Whether Soldiers, Too, Can Be Saved*, in *Luther's Works*, vol. 46: *The Christian in Society*, III ed. Robert C. Schultz [Philadelphia: Fortress Press, 1967], pp. 102–3).

Calvin reckons that reason is daily overwhelmed by deceptions, and is most prone to ignorance in the process of applying principles to cases. Therefore, it needs the grace of divine illumination at every moment (*Institutes*, II.2.25).

It is arguable that Luther and Calvin are more sceptical of the capability of unaided practical reason than Aquinas, who affirms that sin does not entirely destroy rationality in man (*ST*, IaIIae, Q.85. art.2). John T. McNeill has noted, however, that while this may be true in their discussions of soteriology, both Luther and Calvin become much more approving of the products of natural reason in matters of civil law, justice and political prudence ('Natural Law in the Teaching of the Reformers', *Journal of Religion*, XXVI [1946]: 168–82).

In contrast to that which the magisterial Reformers and Aquinas share in common, Thomas Muentzer, the revolutionary Anabaptist, asserted an absolute contradiction between reason and the politically charge revelation granted daily to the elect by the Holy Spirit ('Sermon before the Princes', in *Spiritual and Anabaptist Writers*, Library of Christian Classics, ed. George H. Williams and Angel M. Mergal [Philadelphia: Westminster Press, 1957], pp. 49–70).
5. *E.g.*, James M. Gustafson, *Protestant & Roman Catholic Ethics* (Chicago and London: University of Chicago Press, 1978), p. 32; Robin W. Lovin, *Christian Faith and Public Choices. The Social Ethics of Barth, Brunner and Bonhoeffer* (Philadelphia: Fortress Press, 1984), pp. 78, 41; Charles C. West, *Communism and the Theologians* (London: SCM, 1958), pp. 245–46.
6. *E.g.*, Robert E. Willis, *The Ethics of Karl Barth* (Leiden: E. J. Brill, 1971), pp. 183, 421; James M. Gustafson, *Can Ethics Be Christian*? (Chicago and London: University of Chicago Press, 1975), p. 160; Robin W. Lovin, *Christian Faith and Public Choices*, p. 40.
7. I have let pass here Barth's rhetorical description of interpretation as a necessarily technical operation, expressive of the sinful human will to absolute autonomy. Contemporary reflection upon hermeneutics offers an alternative dialectical concept of interpretation in which interpreter and text act reciprocally. As in the case of ethical reflection, so in the case of interpretation generally, I argue that Barth was really in the business of trying, not to abolish, but to qualify it.
8. Barth, *The Word of God and the Word of Man*, pp. 136–82.
9. *ChrL*, not *CD* IV/4.
10. Karl Barth, *Against the Stream* (London: SCM, 1954), pp. 228–29.

11. Hans Urs von Balthasar, *The Theology of Karl Barth*, trans. J. Drury (New York: Anchor, 1972), p. 157.
12. See Stephen Sykes, *The Identity of Christianity* (London: SPCK, 1984), pp. 188ff.
13. Among those who share this misconception with Barth are Bonhoeffer, Brunner and Thielicke. Bonhoeffer believes that casuistry intends to articulate 'the whole immense range of conceivable contents' of the good, and to say in advance what would be good in every conceivable case (*Ethics*, ed. Eberhard Bethge, trans. Neville Horton Smith [New York: Macmillan, 1965]), p. 86.

    Brunner judges that 'the error of casuistry . . . consists in deducing particular laws from a universal law in ever greater and more scrupulous detail . . . Casuistry tries to imprison life in a net of "cases" as though all could be arranged beforehand . . . ' (*The Divine Imperative*, trans. Olive Wyon [Philadelphia: Westminster Press, 1937]), p. 134. It seeks to deduce the 'case' from a general law 'in the minutest particular' (*ibid.*, p. 138), reckoning 'the law in its general character logically includes within itself all particular propositions' (*ibid.*, p. 137).

    Thielicke regards casuistry as 'predetermined by law', and as encouraging the flight from responsible freedom to 'the security of the functionary' (*Theological Ethics*, 2 vols., vol. 1: *Foundations*, ed. William H. Lazarus [Grand Rapids: Eerdmans, 1979]), p. 457.
14. Writing of the Roman Catholic tradition of casuistry, the major casuistical tradition in Christian ethics, James Gustafson has suggested that 'perhaps . . . only the writer of the poorest manuals, the least nuanced and historically sophisticated have claimed that the gap between general principles and particular choices and actions would be closed by logic alone' (*Protestant and Roman Catholic Ethics*, p. 47).
15. K. E. Kirk, *Conscience and Its Problems: an Introduction to Casuistry* (London: Longman, Green and Co., 1927), pp. 106–29.
16. Gene Outka and Paul Ramsey, eds., *Norm and Context in Christian Ethics* (New York: Scribners's, 1968), pp. 67–135.

7

1. *The Christian Life. Church Dogmatics IV/4. Lecture Fragments* (Edinburgh: T & T Clark, 1981); ET of *Das christliche Leben. Die kirkliche Dogmatik IV/4. Fragmente aus dem Nachlass. Vorlesungen 1959–61*, ed. E. Jüngel, H.-A. Drewes (Zürich: Theologischer Verlag, 1976). In the text, the abbreviation *ChrL* is used to denote references to the English translation.
2. *Church Dogmatics IV/4* (ET Edinburgh: T & T Clark, 1969).
3. I. Murdoch, 'On "God" and "Good"', in *The Sovereignty of Good* (London: Routledge and Kegan Paul, 1970), p. 53.
4. R. E. Willis, *The Ethics of Karl Barth* (Leiden: Brill, 1971), p. 433.
5. D. M. Mackinnon, *A Study in Ethical Theory* (London: Black, 1957), p. 270.
6. K. Barth, 'Gospel and Law', in *God, Grace and Gospel* (ET Edinburgh: Oliver and Boyd, 1959), p. 15.
7. H. Thielicke, *Theological Ethics I* (ET London: Black, 1968), pp. 98–117.
8. H. R. Niebuhr, *The Responsible Self* (New York: Harper and Row, 1963).
9. G. Wingren, *Creation and Law* (ET Edinburgh: Oliver and Boyd, 1961); 'Evangelium und Gesetz' in *Antwort, Karl Barth zum 70. Geburtstag* (Zürich: EVZ, 1956), pp. 310–22.
10. E. Jüngel, 'Gospel and Law. The Relationship of Dogmatics to Ethics', in *idem.*, *Karl Barth. A Theological Legacy* (ET Philadelphia: Westminster, 1986), p. 124.
11. T. F. Torrance, 'The One Baptism Common to Christ and his Church', in *Theology in Reconciliation* (London: Chapman, 1975), pp. 82–105.

12. *Ibid.*, p. 90.
13. *Ibid.*, p. 87.
14. *Ibid.*, p. 103.
15. *The Christian Life* (ET London: SCM, 1930), pp. 20f.
16. *CD* III/3: 265–88; III/4: 87–115.
17. J. Butler, *Fifteen Sermons* (ed. T. A. Roberts; London: SPCK, 1970).
18. *ChrL*, p. 178. I have altered the translation of the third sentence. The ET reads, 'Would this *not* [italics mine] be asking for something ethically attainable . . . ', which reverses the sense of the original: 'Sagte man ihnen damit etwas ethisch Belangvolles, d.h. etwas, was sie praktizieren können und werden?' (*Das christliche Leben*, p. 300).
19. *CD* IV/2: 403–83.
20. W. Walsh, *The Use of Imagination* (London: Chatto and Windus, 1964), p. 29.
21. A. Camus, *The Rebel* (ET Harmondsworth: Penguin, 1962), p. 19.
22. *Ibid.*
23. *Ibid.*, pp. 26f.
24. For another example, see a variety of writings by Donald Mackinnon: his essay 'Prayer, Worship and Life' in *idem.*, ed., *Christian Faith and Communist Faith* (London: Macmillan, 1953), pp. 242–56; the closing pages of *A Study in Ethical Theory*; the studies 'Lenin and Theology' and 'Law, Change and Revolution' in *Explorations in Theology 5* (London: SCM, 1979), pp. 11–29, 30–54, and his Martin Wright Memorial Lecture 'Power Politics and Religious Faith' in *Themes in Theology. The Three-Fold Cord*, (Edinburgh: T & T Clark, 1987) pp. 87–109.
25. A. Camus, *op. cit.*, p. 23
26. *Ibid.*
27. *Ibid.*, p. 28.
28. D. M. Mackinnon, 'Prayer, Worship and Life', p. 248.
29. See here E. Jüngel, '". . .keine Menschenlosigkeit Gottes . . . ". Zur Theologie Karl Barths zwischen Theismus und Atheismus' in *idem.*, *Barth-Studien* (Gütersloh: Mohn, 1982), pp. 332–47.
30. I hope in a forthcoming study of Barth's final writings to undertake a fuller analysis and appraisal of the texts.
31. C. T. Waldrop, *Karl Barth's Christology. Its Basic Alexandrian Character* (Berlin: Mouton, 1984).
32. P. H. Nowell-Smith, 'Morality: Religious and Secular', in I. T. Ramsey, ed., *Christian Ethics and Contemporary Philosophy*, (London: SCM, 1966) p. 95.
33. J. Gustafson, *Christ and the Moral Life* (New York: Harper and Row, 1968), p. 6.
34. *Ibid.*
35. H. Frei, 'An Afterword' in H.-M. Rumscheidt, ed., *Karl Barth in Re-View* (Pittsburgh, Pickwick, 1981), pp. 110f.
36. N. Smart, 'Gods, Bliss and Morality' in I. T. Ramsey, ed., *op. cit.*, pp. 15–30; S. Sutherland, 'Religion, ethics and action' in S. Sutherland, B. Hebblethwaite, ed., *The philosophical frontiers of Christian theology* (Cambridge: Cambridge University Press, 1982), pp. 153–67.
37. Cf G. Lindbeck, *The Nature of Doctrine* (London: SPCK, 1984).
38. G. Outka, *Agape. An Ethical Analysis* (London: Yale University Press, 1972), p. 151.

8

1. Gerhard Sauter, 'Shifts in Karl Barth's Thought: The Current Debate Between Right and Left Wing Barthians', Paper for Barth Symposium at State University of New York, 1986 (unpublished).

2. David Ford's, *Barth and God's Story* (Frankfurt am Main: Verlag Peter Lang, 1985) is certainly the best treatment of this aspect of Barth's work.
3. Hans Frei, 'An Afterword: Eberhard Busch's Biography of Karl Barth', in *Karl Barth in Re-View*, edited by Martin Rumscheidt (Pittsburgh: Pickwick Press, 1981), pp. 110–111.
4. For the development of this theme see Peter Berger, 'On the Obsolescence of the Concept of Honor', in *Revisions: Changing Perspectives in Moral Philosophy*, edited by Stanley Hauerwas and Alasdair MacIntyre (Notre Dame: University of Notre Dame Press, 1983), pp. 172–181; and my 'Truth and Honor: The University and Church in a Democratic Age', *Proceedings of the James Montgomery Hester Seminar* (Winston-Salem: Wake Forest University Press, 1976), pp. 38–53.
5. William Werpehowski, 'Command and History in the Ethics of Karl Barth', *Journal of Religious Ethics* 9, 2 (Fall, 1981), pp. 298–320. Werpehowski is responding to my treatment of Barth in my *Character and the Christian Life: A Study in Theological Ethics* (San Antonio: Trinity University Press, 1981). A new edition of that book has just been published with an Introduction that indicates where I now believe myself to have gone wrong in the earlier one.
6. Werpehowski, p. 300.
7. R. H. Roberts, 'Barth's Interpretation of Time: Its Nature and Implications', in *Karl Barth: Studies of his Theological Method*, edited by Stephen Sykes (Oxford: Clarendon Press, 1979), pp. 107–108.
8. Werpehowski, p. 305.
9. *Ibid.*, p. 305.
10. *Ibid.*, p. 316.
11. Berger, *On the Obsolescence of the Concept of Honor*, p. 173.
12. Barth does not explain how all are equally honoured by God without that kind of egalitarianism undermining the specific nature of the honour of this or that man. Of course, Barth has an easy response as he can say that God honours each person differently without in any way qualifying his honouring each person.
13. Barth does little to explain how something can at once be unmixed yet interrelated.
14. For an extended analysis of Trollope's 'ethics' see Shirley Robin Letwin's, *The Gentlemen in Trollope: Individual and Moral Conduct* (Cambridge: Harvard University Press, 1982).
15. Trollope tells us that Dr Wortle 'left his position at Eton because the headmaster had required from him some slight change of practice. There had been no quarrel on that occasion, but Mr Wortle had gone'. Anthony Trollope, *Dr Wortle's School*, edited with an introduction by John Halperin (Oxford: Oxford University Press, 1984), p. 3. All references to the novel appear in the text.
16. For the importance of repentance and forgiveness in Trollope, see my 'Constancy and Forgiveness: The Novel as a School for Virtue', *Notre Dame English Journal*, xv, 3 (Summer, 1983), pp. 23–54. Soon to be reprinted in *Christian Existence Today*.
17. Trollope makes clear throughout the novel that Dr Wortle was a man who was quite able to locate his interests.
18. It is interesting that Trollope does not try to say that what the Peacockes or Dr Wortle did was right, but only that it was understandable. He is acutely aware how good communities must be able to maintain standards while forgiving the sinner.
19. Barth fails to provide any extended treatment of friendship in his work. Certainly his discussion of honour could have provided the context for that, but like so many moderns, he tends to overlook the moral significance of friendship.
20. One cannot help but think that Barth is attending to his own isolation as a result

of his refusal to take the oath of obedience to Hitler and consequent loss of his university position. That isolation, of course, was limited as it would have surely been much harder if Barth had been German and not Swiss. The fact that he was Swiss does not detract from the courage he demonstrated in the 1930s, but rather reminds us how important it is to have a place to be other than that defined by our nationalities.
21. For defence of this claim, see my 'In Praise of Gossip: The Moral Casuistry of Life', *Books and Religion*, 13, 8 and 9 (Nov/Dec, 1985), pp. 5, 23.
22. For a critique of Barth's ecclesiology in relation to his social ethics, see my 'On Learning Simplicity in an Ambiguous Age: A Reponse to Hunsinger', *Katallagete* (forthcoming).

9

1. Text in Werner Schmauch and Ernst Wolf, *Königsherrschaft Christi*, Theologische Existenz Heute 64 (Munich, 1958), p. 70, and – with a very comprehensive selection of other documents relevant to this issue from the period – Ernst Wolf with Heinz Kloppenburg and Helmut Simon, *Christusbekenntnis in Atomzeitalter?*', Theologische Existenz Heute 70 (Munich, 1959), p. 70.
2. Schmauch and Wolf, *Königsherrschaft*, pp. 68–9; Wolf, Kloppenburg and Simon, *Christusbekenntnis*, pp. 102–3.
3. Wolf, Kloppenburg and Simon, *Christusbekenntnis*, pp. 104–5.
4. *Ibid.*, pp. 15–6.
5. *Ibid.*, pp. 26–9.
6. *Ibid.*, pp. 107–8.
7. *Ibid.*, p. 6.
8. *Ibid.*, p. 16.
9. See the note with information from Helmut Simon in Barth's *Gesamtausgabe*, vol. v: *Offene Briefe 1945–1968* (Zürich: Theologischer Verlag, 1984), p. 440–2.
10. *Ibid.*, p. 444.
11. Eberhard Busch, *Karl Barth. His Life from Letters and Autobiographical Texts* (London: SCM, 1976), p. 431.
12. Barth, *Gesamtausgabe*, v: 440–1.
13. *Ibid.*, nos. 56 and 57; for later statements, see nos. 59, 67 and 72.
14. Barth, *Fragments Grave and Gay* (London: Collins, 1971), pp. 81–3; transcribed from a taped discussion with members of the Württemburg Church Fraternity in 1963.
15. Barth's doctrine of the state is discussed especially in R. E. Willis, *The Ethics of Karl Barth*, (Leiden: E. J. Brill, 1971), pp. 391–427; F.-W. Marquardt, *Theologie und Sozialismus. Das Beispiel Karl Barths* (Munich: Chr. Keiser Verlag, 1972); Robert E. Hood, *Contemporary Political Orders and Christ. Karl Barth's Christology and Political Praxis* (Allison Park, Pennsylvania: Pickwick Press, 1984), esp. pp. 63–90 and 137–166; and Eberhard Jüngel, 'Zum Verhältnis von Kirche und Staat nach Karl Barth', *Zeitschrift für Theologie und Kirche*, Beiheft 6: *Zur Theologie Karl Barths* (1986), pp. 76–135 – a magisterial exposition, responding to Lutheran criticism of Barth (Ebeling's in particular) for 'ethicizing' the gospel.

A number of important essays on Barth's political thought are translated in George Hunsinger, ed., *Karl Barth and Radical Politics* (Philadelphia: Westminster, 1976); and an overview of earlier controversies in this area may be found in Markus Barth, 'Current Discussions on the Political Character of Karl Barth's Theology,' in H.-M. Rumscheidt, ed., *Footnotes to a Theology. The Karl Barth Colloquium of 1972* (Corporation for the Publication of Academic Studies of Religion in Canada, 1974), pp. 77–94. Barth's stance on the nuclear issue is

barely mentioned in any of these – nor even substantially in J. H. Yoder, *Karl Barth and the Problem of War* (Nashville: Abingdon, 1970); for a fleeting reference, see Jüngel, *Zeitschrift für Theologie und Kirche*, p. 117 n. 158.
16. References are to E. C. Hoskyns' English translation of the sixth edition, *The Epistle to the Romans* (Oxford: Oxford University Press, 1933).
17. References to the Zürich 1963 reprint of the 1919 edition. See U. Dannemann, *Theologie und Politik im Denken Karl Barths* (Munich: Chr. Kaiser Verlag, 1977), pp. 354–392, on the political themes and priorities of this work, and the shifts of emphasis in the second edition.
18. *Ibid.*, p. 118.
19. Busch, *Karl Barth*, p. 290.
20. *Rechtfertigung und Recht*, Theologische Studien hft. I (Zollikon: Verlag der Evangelischen Buchhandlung, 1938). References to the English translation, *Church and State* (London: SCM 1939). A fuller discussion would need to relate this to Barth's 1935 lecture, 'Evangelium und Gesetz'; see Jüngel, *Zeitschrift für Theologie und Kirche*, pp. 96–108, and the same author's 'Gospel and Law' in *Karl Barth. A Theological Legacy* (Philadelphia: Westminster, 1986), pp. 105–126.
21. Richard Roberts, 'Barth's Doctrine of Time: its Nature and Implications', S. W. Sykes, ed., *Karl Barth. Studies of his Theological Method* (Oxford: Oxford University Press, 1979), p. 109.
22. Munich and Stuttgart 1946. References to the English translation, 'The Christian Community and the Civil Community' in Barth, *Against the Stream. Shorter Post-War Writings 1946–1952*, ed. R. Gregor Smith, (London: SCM, 1954), pp. 13–50. Jüngel *(Zeitschrift für Theologie und Kirche*, p. 122) rightly stresses the controlling importance of the notion of *analogy* in this essay, and relates it to the growing significance of the theme in Barth's work overall. §§14 to 26 of this piece (*Against the Stream,* pp. 32–42) illustrate how this is worked out in specific instances to do with 'the external, relative and provisional problems of the civil community (p. 42). For the Church as the *provisional* image of what the true state must become eschatologically, see p. 29–30, 48, echoing and elaborating some of the most significant themes of 'Rechtfertigung und Recht'.
23. Barth, *Fragments Grave and Gay*, p. 82: ' . . .and if people actually get up in the German Bundestag with the *Dogmatics* in their hand and quote it to justify war, that is of course sheer wickedness . . . sheer dishonesty.'
24. *Ibid.*, p. 83: 'I should have realized and said that the appearance of atomic weapons had so changed the situation that one must say: This is enough.'
25. No. 67 in Barth, *Gesamtausgabe*, v.
26. Barth, 'The Christian Community in the Midst of Political Change', *Against the Stream*, p. 81. This Hungarian dossier, *Die Christliche Gemeinde im Wechsel der Staatsordnungen: Dokumente einer Ungarnreise* (Munich: Chr. Kaiser Verlag, 1948), contains some of Barth's seminal reflections on the Christian in Marxist society; and pp. 80–2 provide an excellent summary of his theology of the state.
27. Ernst Wolf, 'Die Königsherrschaft Christi und der Staat,' in Schmauch and Wolf, *Königsherrschaft*, pp. 53–4 – a fine statement of the Christological approach to theologizing about the state. For resistance to the idea that we need a 'metaphysic' of the state, *cf.* also 'The Christian Community and the Civil Community', *Against the Stream*, p. 25.

10

1. Karl Barth, *The Word of God and the Word of Man*, trans. by Douglas Horton (New York: Harper, 1957). Henceforth: WGWM.
2. Karl Barth, 'The Christian's Place in Society', in WGWM, p. 305.
3. *Ibid.*, p. 292.
4. *CD* I/1: xvi.

Bibliographical Data for *Church Dogmatics* and *The Christian Life*

Church Dogmatics 8 vols. Edited by G. W. Bromiley and T. F. Torrance. Edinburgh: T. & T. Clark, 1956–75
Volume I: *The Doctrine of the Word of God*, Part 1.
  First edition: translated by G. T. Thompson (1936).
  Second edition: translated by G. W. Bromiley (1975).
    Volume I, Part 2. Translated by G. T. Thompson and Harold Knight (1956).
    Volume II: *The Doctrine of God*, Part 1. Translated by T. H. L. Parker, W. B. Johnston, Harold Knight, J. L. M. Haire (1957).
    Volume II, Part 2. Translated by G. W. Bromiley, J. C. Campbell, Iain Wilson, J. Strathearn McNab, Harold Knight, R. A. Stewart (1957).
    Volume III: *The Doctrine of Creation*, Part 1. Translated by J. W. Edwards, O. Bussey, Harold Knight (1958).
    Volume III, Part 2. Translated by Harold Knight, G. W. Bromiley, J. K. S. Reid, R. H. Fuller (1960).
    Volume III, Part 3. Translated by G. W. Bromiley, R. J. Ehrlich (1961).
    Volume III, Part 4. Translated by A. T. Mackay, T. H. L. Parker, Harold Knight, Henry A. Kennedy, John Marks (1961).
    Volume IV: *The Doctrine of Reconciliation*, Part 1. Translated by G. W. Bromiley (1956).
    Volume IV, Part 2. Translated by G. W. Bromiley (1958).
    Volume IV, Part 3.1. Translated by G. W. Bromiley (1961).
    Volume IV, Part 3.2. Translated by G. W. Bromiley (1961).
    Volume IV, Part 4. Fragment. Translated by G. W. Bromiley (1969).
The Christian Life. *Church Dogmatics*, Volume IV, Part 4. Lecture fragments. Translated by G. W. Bromiley. Grand Rapids: Eerdmans, 1981.